# READING BETWEEN THE LINES

## An Introduction to Bar Code Technology

BY CRAIG K. HARMON
and
RUSS ADAMS

## HELMERS PUBLISHING, INC.

(formerly North American Technology, Inc.)
174 Concord St., Peterborough, NH 03458

Printed in the United States of America

ISBN 0-911261-00-1

Third Edition

Bar code on cover courtesy of Symbology, Inc., St. Paul, MN

# TABLE OF CONTENTS

# SECTION VII—Applications

# APPENDIXES

# FOREWORD

In 1949 N.J. Woodland, et al. filed a patent for a circular bar code. In the 35 years that have followed, we have witnessed "bars and spaces" popping up everywhere. Over 50 unique symbologies have been developed, and to face this new "Tower of Babel" various industry groups have begun a process of standardization to one or two of the choices available. The grocery and retail industries have established the Uniform Code Council (UCC), the automotive industry Automotive Industry Action Group (AIAG), and the health industry the Health Industry Bar Code (HIBC) Council. Government has standardized with the LOGMARS Report, and NATO countries appear to be following the U.S. Department of Defense lead. Standards have been developed for the French pharmaceutical manufacturers. Industry groups have wrestled with the establishment of nationwide and worldwide standards through the efforts of the Distribution Symbology Study Group and the American National Standards Institute. And finally, a focal point for the distribution of information on bar coding has been established by the Automatic Identification Manufacturers.

Since 1980 there has been a torrent of information on bar coding. This book is an attempt to organize that information. It will introduce you to bar code and its benefits. We express our appreciation to the Automatic Identification Manufacturers (AIM) for their help in developing this text. Thanks also go to Dr. David Allais, President of Intermec, for his assistance.

In this updated, third edition, we have added new information and removed names and addresses of groups that no longer exist. Of major import is the addition of two new appendices—Appendix E, which addresses solutions to the problem of skew, and Appendix F, which includes the specifications for Code 39. A new chapter, Chapter 18, is concerned with justifying and implementing a bar code system.

The reader should note that the superscripts throughout Section I of this book refer to the footnotes listed in Appendix G.

If this book helps you understand bar code and the advantages it offers, then we have accomplished our task.

Craig K. Harmon
Russ Adams

# SECTION I
# OVERVIEW

# CHAPTER I

# INTRODUCTION

Without fanfare, bar codes have become an important part of our lives. They have crept into businesses as diverse as automobile factories and corner grocery stores. Bar code is the unsung hero of many computer-based business systems. Bar codes and automatic identification systems are the most cost-effective management tools for the 1980s. Their use is quickly rewarded by improved asset management and resource allocation. In an age of steadily declining productivity, companies that have adopted bar code–based management systems have quickly seen a reversal of this trend.

A bar code is a self-contained message with information encoded in the widths of bars and spaces in a printed pattern. Since bar codes are used with computers, binary code is used. Essentially, the black bars and white spaces represent ones and zeros—the language computers understand.

In their simplest form, bar codes are read by sweeping a small spot of light across the printed bar code symbol. The sweep starts at the white space before the first bar, continues past the last bar and ends in the white space which follows the last bar. Because a bar code cannot be read if the sweep wanders outside the symbol area, bar heights are chosen to make it easy to keep the sweep within the bar code area. The longer the information to be coded, the longer the bar code. As the length increases, the height of the bars must be increased to allow for more wandering during reading.

There are many different ways to arrange black bars and white spaces to code information. Each method of arranging bar code patterns has properties which achieve specific objectives. The many bar code formats used today attempt to:

1. Read only if the entire symbol is scanned.
2. Be scannable in both directions.
3. Clearly define the difference between bars and spaces.
4. Be readable over a wide range of scanning speeds.

The most familiar bar code format is the Universal Product Code, or UPC. This code is used widely in retail food and general merchandise stores. A quick look at cereal boxes, record album jackets, and magazine covers will acquaint you with bar code symbols in the UPC format.

In many supermarket checkout lanes, store clerks pass each grocery item over a laser scanner which reads the UPC bar code on the item's packaging. Let's say the item is a box of Cheerios. When the box is passed over the scanner, the digits 16000 66510 are read from the UPC symbol on the box. The first five digits indicate that the manufacturer is General Mills, and the second five digits indicate the product and volume of the package. The product number is transmitted to the store's computer. The price and name are looked up in the computer's memory and transmitted back to the correct cash register. The electronic cash register prints the name and price at the time on the register tape. If Cheerios is on sale, the cash register rings up the sale price. In addition, the computer automatically deducts one box of Cheerios from the store's inventory. The store's computer may be connected to the wholesaler's computer and automatically place an order when inventory drops below a predetermined level.

Such a bar code system increases productivity in three ways:

*Speed*: Data is entered into the computer more rapidly.

*Accuracy*: Bar code systems are almost error-free. They do not rely on the accuracy of a human entering data on a keyboard.

*Reliability*: Bar code formats are designed with various forms of error checking built into the code.

There are forms other than bar code for automatic identification, but bar code was designed to be read by simply constructed readers. The only hardware required to read bar code is a source of light and a single photoreceptor. Almost everything else can be done by software. It is the low-cost, simple nature of bar code–based systems, along with the productivity benefits they offer, which has brought about the "bar code explosion" we see around us. This book will introduce you to the technology that makes bar code identification work and show you how bar code is being used to save money by increasing productivity.

# CHAPTER 2
# A HISTORY OF BAR CODE

The UPC patch found on almost every product symbolizes the major advancements made in the automation of product distribution over the past two decades. The vast variety of products available in today's supermarket is the result of automated systems in production, packaging, and handling. But these innovations did not occur overnight. They were the result of the steady application of automation techniques throughout the food retailing industry.

The modern supermarket began with the concept of the self-service food store. In 1916, this concept was introduced by Clarence Sanders in his Piggly Wiggly stores. By the 1930s, the trend to the self-service supermarket was well under way with individually priced items and mechanized checkout counters. From 1934 to 1974, these improvements reduced the cost of distribution from 24 percent to 20.9 percent of gross sales.

In 1932, an ambitious project was begun by a small group of students at the Harvard University Graduate School of Business Administration. It was to foreshadow the automated checkout counter. The project proposed that the customer select the desired merchandise from an order catalog. Punch cards indicating the desired merchandise were to be removed by the customer and handed to the checker. The punch cards were placed into a punch card reader which entered the codes for the selected merchandise into the system. The system then provided belt delivery of the merchandise from a storeroom to the checkout counter. A complete customer bill was produced and inventory records were generated.

The students offered the plan to food chains around the country, but the plan was rejected by them all. Labor in 1930 was only 30 or 40 cents an hour. With such cheap labor costs, the capital investment to implement the students' system was not justified. The idea did not die, however. As labor costs advanced, the potential savings in the use of an automated checkout counter made the idea attractive. Manual price marking, manual cash register tallying, manual inventory control, and fuzzy information about store operations challenged innovative minds in the food store industry to develop better systems. In the late 1940s, the National Association of Food Chains (NAFC) began to study inventions which could improve the speed and reduce the cost of food checkout.

One invention examined by the Association was a system which used metal tags attached to every product in the supermarket. The price of each product was indicated by the tag's thickness. The merchandise was placed in a mesh bag, the bag was placed in a cabinet at the checkout counter, and an electric current sensed the total thickness of all of the tags in the bag. The sensed thickness value was used to calculate the total bill for the merchandise. However, the cost of the tags and attaching them to the merchandise in the store exceeded the total cost of the manual checkout system. And a customer who purchased products packed in metal cans ended up with an inflated bill.

By the 1950s the transistor had been invented and electronics was making explosive progress. It was time to look again at the possibility of automating food store checkout. In 1955, at the annual meeting of the U. S. Chamber of Commerce, a program titled "People, Products and Progress—1975" was presented. It offered predictions about what the world would be like in 20 years. The section of the program about food distribution featured an automated checkout stand with an overhead electronic scanner attached to a cash register. "When the shopping is over," the commentator said, "there will be no lengthy waiting at the checkout counter. The improvement here will be an automatic computer that will price all items as they pass under an electronic eye." Quite prophetic.

In the mid 1960s, the electronic checkout was still an idea for the future, but it was an idea that was beginning to look like it would save money and improve productivity. The Safeway chain, for example, had 400,000 checkout counters, over $60 billion per year in sales, over 450 million staff hours, and a payroll that exceeded $1 billion. At the 1966 NAFC Management Clinic on Physical Research, equipment manufacturers were asked to aid in the development of systems to improve supermarket operating efficiency. John L. Strubbe, vice president of The Kroger Company, characterized the benefits of automated systems in this way:

> Our stores are really the conduits for concentrated, high volume operations involving essentially repetitive processing movements. They represent the classic environment for success of production equipment and electronic controls. Store labor is expensive and scarce . . . I am not overstating the case when I say that the security of our employees depends upon our ability to increase our productivity, with the help of mechanical and electronic equipment and systems which do not exist today.

In the late 1960s, a number of companies and individuals began to seriously develop practical automated supermarket systems. Generally, the electronics equipment manufacturer worked with a food chain and kept the development work secret. In 1967, a pilot system was installed in a Kroger store in Cincinnati.

But all the systems under development had some common problems to solve. The entire food industry had to agree on a uniform coding system for product identification. It had to be accurately read by a variety of scanning systems. It had to be readable from any direction. And it had to be printable on a wide variety of package sizes and paper stocks. Even more important, the coding system had to be available free to all who needed to use it. The advantages and disadvantages to the consumer, distributor, and manufacturer of each proposed system had to be evaluated objectively. These common problems could only be solved by establishing a group representing all segments of the food industry. This group would have to set policy, keep records, and approve basic rules.

In 1969, the Board of Directors of the NAFC contracted with Logicon, Inc. to develop a proposal for a universal coding system. This resulted in Parts 1 and 2 of the "Universal Grocery Products Identification Code" (UGPIC) in the summer of 1970. The proposal served as an outline for the dimensions of such an automated coding system and provided specific recommendations. The proposal challenged the food industry and got action.

Based on the recommendations of the Logicon report, the U. S. Supermarket Ad Hoc Committee on Universal Product Coding was formed. Three years later, the Committee recommended the adoption of the UPC symbol set. By June 1974, one of the first scanners capable of reading the Universal Product Code was installed at Marsh's supermarket in Troy, Ohio. The scanning system was added to the store's existing computer-driven cash register. By 1980 it was estimated that better than 90 percent of all grocery items carried a UPC code. By December 1985, according to SCAN Newsletter, more than 12,000 grocery stores were equipped with scanner checkout systems.

While the American food industry was developing its bar code–based automatic product identification system, another industry was experimenting with a different automatic identification system. The North American railroad industry began to study the concept of automatic car identification in the late 1950s. By 1962, the Association of American Railroads formed a department to study and develop standards for such a system. The Association adopted an optical bar code system in 1967. The decision was surrounded by controversy from the beginning. The original specification had stipulated that no maintenance would be required for the vehicle label. As the car identification project progressed and optical systems were considered, this requirement was modified. It was evident to the project participants that label maintenance, including washing, would be required.

Car labeling and scanner installation began on October 10, 1967. The task was immense. Labels had to be applied to more than two million freight cars scattered over millions of miles of railroad. As a result, it took seven years before 95 percent of the fleet was labeled. While the labeling continued, railroads around the country began to develop improved management information systems. The systems were designed to improve how well the freight cars were used and to help raise the level of service provided to customers.

These management information systems relied on accurate data about car location. Since 70 percent of rail shipments used tracks owned by two or more companies, success depended on industry-wide labeling and proper label maintenance. Since so many railroad operating companies were involved, it was difficult for any prediction to be made about how well the proposed automatic car identification system would perform.

Because no prediction could be made, many railroad operation companies took a wait-and-see attitude. They did not install all of the scanners called for in the original plan. Since few railroads were using scanners, labels were not maintained as called for in the original plan. By 1975, 20 percent of the labels were unreadable. Several studies were undertaken to determine how to solve the problems and make the system work. Many of the findings were controversial. The most controversial finding suggested that some operating companies did not want the system to succeed because of railroad tariff rules. The end result was the virtual abandonment of bar code for freight car identification.

# SECTION II

# THE WORLD OF BAR CODES

# CHAPTER 3
# SYMBOLOGY

Symbology is defined as the art of expression by symbols or the study or interpretations of symbols. A symbol is defined as something that stands for or suggests something else by reason of relationship, association, or convention. A bar code symbol is an array of rectangular bars and spaces that are arranged in a specific way to represent elements of data. A bar code character represents, for example, a letter, a number, or some other graphic symbol in a machine-readable form.

But what advantage is there to a symbol which can be read by a machine? And why can't machines read the same letters, numbers, and graphic symbols that humans read? Machine-readable symbols help input information more quickly. Information so collected is more accurate and costs less than if manually entered using keys. For many years computers have automated the number crunching tasks associated with business management. Data collection, however, has been quite a different matter. The data "crunched" by computers have continued to be entered manually. Traditionally, data are collected by writing them down on paper. The paper is given to a supervisor who checks their accuracy. If the paper is readable, it's given to a key-entry operator who types the information into a computer. Managers then use the entered data to make decisions. How much time has elapsed? What is the reliability of the information that finally was entered? How much did it cost to get that information to managers?

Under the best conditions, a minimum of three days is required between collection of the information until the data are in a form usable by management. Often the time is closer to two or three weeks. These delays are bound to affect the accuracy of decisions made by management.

Traditional manual data collection lacks high reliability. Translation errors occur when the information is written down and when it is key entered. The number of translation errors is directly proportional to the number of characters written down during data collection. The longer the string of characters, the higher the probability that it contains an error when it is written down. When a key-entry operator reads the transcribed data, often the operator must interpret what was written. Is that an S or a 5, an O or a 0, a B or an 8, an H or a K, an F or a T? Transposition errors can also occur, such as recording 1234 as 1243. But translation and transposition errors are not the only errors inherent in manual data collection. Additional errors are introduced in the key-entry process. It is common for a key-entry operator to make one character error in every 300 characters entered.

In analyzing the benefits of automatic data entry, you must consider the personnel cost to write the information down, check the forms, and key enter the information into the computer system. There are the costs of the errors and the costs of correcting the errors. Finally, there are very substantial costs associated with management not having current information when decisions are made.

Machine-read information can be sent to the computer as the data is captured. The reliability of the data is at least 50 times better and can be more than a billion times better than manual systems. Costs are reduced so much that frequently machine-readable systems produce a positive change in a firm's cash flow within a matter of months. Industry is accustomed to amortizing equipment over several years before realizing a payback. It's no wonder there is a rush to install machine-readable systems.

Why can't machines read the same letters, numbers, and graphic symbols that humans read? Of course, they can. But with what reliability and with what speed of entry? There are numerous vision systems available that have the capability of recognizing human-readable characters. One such system is the OCR reader. OCR stands for optical character recognition. OCR uses special fonts that can be read by both human and machine. OCR is a more reliable method of data entry than the key-entry process, but it is invariably less reliable than bar code. Someone using an OCR reader frequently has to make multiple passes over the human-readable information to read it. The reading difficulty of OCR is the result of the technology employed in OCR. The OCR reader must be within a very precise orientation to the symbol being read, much more precise than that required by bar code. Most OCR characters in use today are between 0.10 inch and 0.15 inch in height. When long strings of information are read, it is difficult to maintain correct placement of the wand over the entire string. OCR is far more sensitive to the motion of the operator's hand during scanning than bar code. Finally, vision systems cannot easily read information printed on moving objects. To do so requires, for example, a strobe light synchronized with the object's movement. While OCR is significantly better than key entry, bar code is better in data integrity and speed of data acquisition. Table 3-1 shows comparisons between key entry, OCR, and bar coding.

**Table 3-1**
**Data entry comparisons**

| Characteristic/<br>Method | Key-entry | OCR | Bar Code |
|---|---|---|---|
| Speed* | 6 seconds | 4 seconds | .3 seconds to<br>2 seconds |
| Substitution<br>error rate | 1 character<br>error in 300<br>characters<br>entered | 1 character<br>error in<br>10,000<br>characters<br>entered | 1 character<br>error in<br>15,000 to<br>36 trillion<br>characters<br>entered |
| Size* | 1 inch to<br>1.2 inches | 1 inch to<br>1.2 inches | .7 inch to[†]<br>7 inches |
| Encoding costs | High | Moderate | Low |
| Reading costs | Low | Moderate | Low |
| Advantages | Human | Human-readable | Low error rate<br>Low cost<br>High speed<br>Can be read at<br>a distance |
| Disadvantages | Human<br>High cost<br>High error<br>rate<br>Low speed | Low speed<br>Moderate error<br>rate<br>Cannot read<br>moving objects<br>without special<br>equipment | Requires<br>Education of<br>the User<br>Community |

*Note—Comparisons for speed and size assume the encodation of a 12-character field.
[†]Note—The lower limit of size is a function of the symbology specification. Future scanning systems may permit 12 characters to be encoded in 0.2 inch.

One of the basic advantages of bar code over OCR is that bar code reads information by measurement of width. Further, the bar width is repeated vertically (vertical redundancy). Vertical redundancy permits the bar/space pattern to be read with less precise orientation of the reader as well as providing improved tolerance for localized printing defects. Unlike OCR, bar codes also have a repeating pattern that exists in every character, e.g., Code 39 has nine elements and three are wide and Interleaved 2 of 5 has five elements and 2 are wide. OCR must be read by identifying features of the characters. OCR must identify the horizontal and vertical strokes, curves, and endings of the characters. Bar code systems often use a progression of checking characteristics to improve the reliability of reading. Bar codes can be checked at both the character level and the message level, in much the same way that data communication systems check reliability, by examining each character to establish the presence of a certain pattern of bars and spaces, wide elements and narrow elements, or a defined parity pattern. Message level checking systems add a character or combination of characters at the end of a message. This check character is derived from a mathematical computation based on the characters in the message. Message level checking can be used with key entry, OCR, or bar code systems.

## The Structure of Bar Codes

A bar code consists of a number of printed bars and intervening spaces. The widths of the bars and spaces, as well as the number of each, is determined by a specific convention, referred to as a specification for that symbology. The specification sets the minimum nominal width of the narrowest elements (bars and spaces), the ratio of the wide elements to the narrow ones, the printing tolerances (the change in width because of the printing process), the structure of unique bar and space combinations to represent various characters, the bar/space patterns that signify the beginning and the end of the bar code message, and the clear area, or quiet zone, required in front of and at the end of the symbol.

The basic element of a bar code is the width of the narrow element. This width is called the X dimension. Frequently, the widths of the wider elements are measured in multiples of X (see Figure 3-1). In some codes, however, the width of each element is precisely defined. Some symbologies have only two widths, one for the narrow elements and one for the wide elements. Still other symbologies have four widths or more. Beyond simply varying the widths of

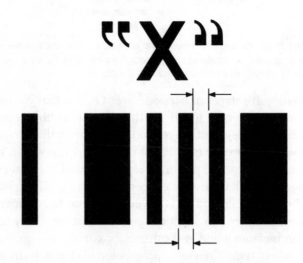

**Figure 3-1. Elements of a bar code character**

the elements, individual characters can be coded by using differing numbers of bar code elements. Different bar code symbologies use five, seven, eight, and nine elements to code a single character. Some symbologies can represent letters, numbers and other graphic symbols. Most bar code symbologies, however, encode strictly numeric data and a few special characters. Most codes have a unique start/stop character combination, although a few permit multiple start/stop codes with varying purposes.

Bar codes are said to be either discrete or continuous. Simply stated, discrete bar codes start with a bar, end with a bar, and have a space between characters, referred to as an intercharacter gap. By contrast, continuous codes start with a bar, end with a space, and have no intercharacter gap. Bar code symbologies can achieve differing densities (numbers of characters per inch of code). The density of a bar code is determined by the minimum X dimension, the wide-to-narrow element ratio, the number of elements required to represent a character of information, and the overhead characters needed by the symbology, such as start and stop codes and check characters.

There are two measures of a bar code symbology's "friendliness." The first is its "human friendliness," often referred to as its first and second pass read rate. The first pass read rate (FRR) is the ratio of the number of times in which a good read occurs on the first try, divided by the number of attempts. The second pass read rate (SRR) is the ratio of the number of times in which a good scan occurs in two or fewer tries, divided by the number of attempts. Bar code systems should achieve at least an 85 percent FRR and at least a 99 percent SRR. Low read rates ultimately lead to user dissatisfaction and a bar code system which will not be used. While low read rates indicate a high level of no scans, user dissatisfaction is the main concern.

Far more difficult to measure is the symbology's "system friendliness" or substitution error rate (SER). A substitution error exists when the data encoded in the printed symbol does not agree with the data read by the bar code reader. The SER measure is the number of substitution errors which occur over all symbols read. Some bar code symbologies have a proven SER of better than one character in one million scanned. A no scan can be detected by the operator or bar code reading system. But a bad scan, or substitution error, is not detected until after the data has been stored in the data processing system. Even then, the error may not be caught. There is a direct relationship between a symbology's FRR and its SER, since the bar code reading system vigorously attempts to decode the scanned message. Generally stated, the first read rate of a bar code system is a reflection on the printed symbol. Substitution errors, on the other hand, are more attributable to the bar code reader. The more times required to scan a symbol, the higher the probability that a substitution error will occur. However, bar code substitution error rates are much lower than the rate of one substitution error for every 300 characters entered experienced in manual key entry. Even the weakest symbologies are substantially better.

# Code 39 (Also known as Code 3 of 9 and 3 of 9 Code)

Code 39 was developed in 1975 by Dr. David Allais and Ray Stevens of Interface Mechanisms (now Intermec). It is rapidly becoming "The Code" for industrial and commercial applications. Code 39 was selected as the official Department of Defense (DoD) symbology in 1981, with the publication of the "Final Report of the Joint Steering Group for Logistics Applications of Automated Marking and Reading Symbols" (acronym LOGMARS). It was established as the official government standard with the issuance of MIL-STD-1189 (now MIL-STD-1189A) in early 1982. Within the federal government, the General Services Administration (GSA) also uses MIL-STD-1189A markings on all material coming into GSA supply depots. The Department of Defense now requires its contractors to mark all items with a Code 39 bar code, identifying the product by National Stock Number (NSN) and the government contract number. Code 39 was recommended in 1981 by the Distribution Symbology Study Group (DSSG) for the labeling of corrugated shipping containers with alphanumeric information. The Automotive Industry Action Group (AIAG) bar code standard recommends Code 39 symbology, and Code 39 enjoys similar status in the health care industry's Health Industry Bar Code (HIBC) standard issued in 1984. In mid-1983, the French pharmaceutical industry adopted Code 39 as a national standard for pharmaceutical product marking. Code 39 is also one of the three symbologies identified in the American National Standards Institute (ANSI) standard MH 10.8M-1983. Code 39 is further recommended by the aluminum industry, the EMBARC standard, and standards promulgated by the International Air Transport Association (IATA).

The name Code 39 is both a descriptor of its original character set of 39 characters (currently, Code 39 has 43 characters) and the structure of the code, namely that three of the nine elements per character are wide, with the remaining six being narrow. Each character in Code 39 is represented by a group of five bars and four spaces. The complete character set includes a start/stop character (conventionally decoded as an asterisk) and 43 data characters consisting of the 10 digits, the 26 letters of the alphabet, space, and the six symbols -, ., $, /, + , and %.

The strong self-checking property of Code 39 provides a high level of data security. With properly designed scanning equipment and excellent quality symbol printing, you can expect only one substitution error out of 70 million characters scanned. Bar code printed by a well-maintained, better quality dot-matrix printer typically will provide less than one substitution error in 3 million characters scanned. The U.S. Department of Defense, in its LOGMARS testing, reported four substitution errors out of 563,243 bar code labels. These labels were separately reported to average 24 characters in length. Thus, in this practical test, 3,379,458 bar code characters were scanned for each substitution error. Bar code symbols in the LOGMARS test were printed by various means, including printing presses, formed font impact printers, and dot-matrix printers. For those applications that require exceptional data security, an optional check character is often used. The Health Industry Bar Code (HIBC) includes such a check character implementation, due to the high level of data integrity required in patient care.

Code 39 is one of two bar code symbologies (as of January 1, 1986) that have independently developed empirical test results regarding data security. The other symbology is Codabar. The testing done by the Distribution Symbology Study Group was to establish whether bar codes could be printed directly on corrugated shipping containers. Several symbologies were tested; Interleaved 2 of 5 and Code 39 were found acceptable.

Code 39 is a variable length code whose maximum length depends upon the reading equipment used. Code 39 is self-checking and does not require a check character in normal commercial and industrial applications. Code 39 characters are discrete with a range of intercharacter gaps permitted. Code 39 is bidirectional, meaning it can be scanned from left to right or right to left. The size of Code 39 is variable over a wide range, lending itself to light pen, hand-held laser, and fixed mounted scanner reading. High density Code 39 is 9.4 characters per inch, but densities as low as 1.4 characters per inch are included in the recommended practices of corrugated containers. A unique character, conventionally interpreted as an asterisk (*), is used exclusively for both a start

**Figure 3-2. Code 39 character structure**

and stop character. A Code 39 symbol consists of a leading quiet zone, a start character, appropriate data characters, a stop character, and a trailing quiet zone. In Code 39, wide elements are considered multiples of the narrow elements. The minimum nominal wide-to-narrow ratio is 2.0:1 and the maximum is 3.0:1.[1] The best first pass read rates and substitution error rates can be expected when the wide-to-narrow ratio is at its maximum of 3.0:1.

To achieve the standard density of 9.4 characters per inch, the nominal width of the narrow elements must be 7.5 mils and the wide-to-narrow ratio must be 2.25:1. When printed at a 3.0:1 ratio, the Code 39 character density with a 7.5-mil nominal narrow element width is 8.3 characters per inch. Figure 3-2 illustrates the character structure of a Code 39 character. Figure 3-3 shows the Code 39 character set, with its bar/space configurations. Figure 3-4 shows a sample HIBC Primary Symbol, encoded in Code 39. Table 3-2 lists various printing tolerances for the Code 39 symbology (see Appendix F, Code 39 Specifications, for more details).

| CHAR. | PATTERN | BARS | SPACES | CHAR. | PATTERN | BARS | SPACES |
|-------|---------|------|--------|-------|---------|------|--------|
| 1 | | 10001 | 0100 | M | | 11000 | 0001 |
| 2 | | 01001 | 0100 | N | | 00101 | 0001 |
| 3 | | 11000 | 0100 | O | | 10100 | 0001 |
| 4 | | 00101 | 0100 | P | | 01100 | 0001 |
| 5 | | 10100 | 0100 | Q | | 00011 | 0001 |
| 6 | | 01100 | 0100 | R | | 10010 | 0001 |
| 7 | | 00011 | 0100 | S | | 01010 | 0001 |
| 8 | | 10010 | 0100 | T | | 00110 | 0001 |
| 9 | | 01010 | 0100 | U | | 10001 | 1000 |
| 0 | | 00110 | 0100 | V | | 01001 | 1000 |
| A | | 10001 | 0010 | W | | 11000 | 1000 |
| B | | 01001 | 0010 | X | | 00101 | 1000 |
| C | | 11000 | 0010 | Y | | 10100 | 1000 |
| D | | 00101 | 0010 | Z | | 01100 | 1000 |
| E | | 10100 | 0010 | - | | 00011 | 1000 |
| F | | 01100 | 0010 | • | | 10010 | 1000 |
| G | | 00011 | 0010 | SPACE | | 01010 | 1000 |
| H | | 10010 | 0010 | * | | 00110 | 1000 |
| I | | 01010 | 0010 | $ | | 00000 | 1110 |
| J | | 00110 | 0010 | / | | 00000 | 1101 |
| K | | 10001 | 0001 | + | | 00000 | 1011 |
| L | | 01001 | 0001 | % | | 00000 | 0111 |

The ∗ symbol denotes a unique start/stop character which must be the first and last character of every bar code symbol.

**Figure 3-3. Code 39 character set**

* +A123B4C5D6E711 *

**Figure 3-4. HIBC Primary Symbol**

**Table 3-2**
**Open System Code 39 Printing tolerances**

| W Nominal width of narrow bars and spaces | | N Nominal width of wide bars and spaces | | N Nominal ratio of wide to narrow elements | T Bar and Space width tolerance | | CPI Character Density per inch |
|---|---|---|---|---|---|---|---|
| Inches | Milli-meters | Inches | Milli-meters | | Inches | Milli-meters | |
| 0.0075 | 0.19 | 0.0169 | 0.43 | 2.25 | ±0.0017 | ±0.04 | 9.40 |
| 0.0075 | 0.19 | 0.0225 | 0.57 | 3.00 | ±0.0024 | ±0.06 | 8.30 |
| 0.0115 | 0.29 | 0.0345 | 0.88 | 3.00 | ±0.0040 | ±0.10 | 5.40 |
| 0.0200 | 0.51 | 0.0600 | 1.52 | 3.00 | ±0.0069 | ±0.18 | 3.00 |
| 0.0320 | 0.81 | 0.0800 | 2.03 | 2.50 | ±0.0088 | ±0.22 | 2.04 |
| 0.0360 | 0.91 | 0.0900 | 2.29 | 2.50 | ±0.0099 | ±0.25 | 1.87 |
| 0.0400 | 1.02 | 0.1000 | 2.54 | 2.50 | ±0.0110 | ±0.28 | 1.70 |
| 0.0400 | 1.02 | 0.1200 | 3.05 | 3.00 | ±0.0140 | ±0.36 | 1.50 |
| 0.0440 | 1.12 | 0.1100 | 2.79 | 2.50 | ±0.0121 | ±0.31 | 1.55 |
| 0.0480 | 1.22 | 0.1200 | 3.05 | 2.50 | ±0.0132 | ±0.34 | 1.42 |
| 0.0800 | 2.03 | 0.2000 | 5.08 | 2.50 | ±0.0220 | ±0.56 | 0.85 |
| 0.0800 | 2.03 | 0.2400 | 6.10 | 3.00 | ±0.0276 | ±0.70 | 0.75 |

# Universal Product Code (UPC) and European Article Numbering (EAN)

In 1970, a grocery industry ad hoc committee was formed under the chairmanship of R. Bert Gookin for the purpose of selecting a standard code and symbol for that industry. This ad hoc committee established guidelines and a subcommittee to select an industry standard symbol. Proposals were solicited from interested manufacturers of computers and point-of-sale (POS) equipment. Seven equipment manufacturers responded with proposed symbols.

A massive symbol evaluation was undertaken, including laboratory tests by Battelle Memorial Institute, tests of printing tolerances assisted by the Graphic Arts Technical Foundation, printability tests by participating grocery manufacturers, and store tests of complete working systems. This effort concluded with the selection of the UPC symbol as an industry standard on April 3, 1973. The final symbol closely resembles the IBM® proposal. Structural principles for bar code symbols of this type were described in an earlier IBM position paper by McEnroe and Jones dated October 1971, and a U.S. Patent dated June 28, 1971.

Subsequent to the adoption of the UPC symbol, several additions and enhancements were incorporated into the standard. In August 1976, a supplemental code for use with the UPC symbol on periodicals and paperback books was established.[1] This supplemental code, developed by George Wright, is used to encode the issue dates of periodicals. Foreign interest in UPC led to the adoption of the EAN Code in December 1976. Both EAN—also known as the World Product Code (WPC) and as International Article Numbering (IAN)—and UPC share a common symbology.[1] The primary difference between UPC and EAN is that, in the UPC format of 12 characters, the first character is a number system character, such as 0 for grocery items and 3 for drug and health related items, while the 13-character EAN symbol uses the first two characters as a country code. UPC is a subset of the more general EAN Code and readers equipped to decode EAN can also decode UPC. The converse, however, is not true. Readers with capability of decoding UPC cannot necessarily decode EAN, since such readers focus on the subset (UPC) and not the entire symbology structure (EAN). In April 1978, Version D of the UPC symbol was specified for potential use in nonfood retail and other applications which require more than 12 data digits. As of January 1, 1986, the only major user of Version D has been VISA. At this time, few scanner manufacturers support UPC Version D.

UPC was established for the benefit of the supermarket industry to facilitate automatic scanning of item numbers with associated price look-up at the point of sale. By December 1985, there were approximately 12,000 supermarkets using UPC symbol-based point-of-sale systems. Return issues of magazines and paperback books with the UPC symbol and supplemental code on their covers are being processed at over 100 scanning centers. UPC symbols are now found on recorded music, liquor, and many nonfood items sold in supermarkets. At this writing, UPC and EAN are being adopted by other types of retail establishments. Mass merchandisers such as K-Mart and Wal-Mart and convenience stores are planning to use UPC-based point-of-sale systems. In 1986, the National Retail Merchants Association acknowledged changes in industry conditions, requirements, and technological direction in its endorsement of UPC as the preferred voluntary standard for the general merchandise industry. A transition period was endorsed by NRMA for vendors who had been using OCR-A/UVM as recommended in the NRMA 1975 *Voluntary Retail Identification Standard Specifications OCR-A.*

The structure of the UPC symbol and the reasons for selecting such a structure are best explained by reviewing some of the explicit and implicit criteria leading to its selection. A primary criterion was to enable packaging companies to print the UPC symbol directly on grocery packages along with text and promotional materials without increasing the printing cost. Grocery packages are printed by a variety of printing processes, including offset lithography, flexography, letterpress, gravure, and silkscreening. Some of these processes are inherently more precise and controllable than others. A further objective was to choose a symbol that could be scanned in an omnidirectional fashion at the point of sale. Omnidirectional scanning allows any package orientation, provided the symbol faces the scanner. Other objectives included the ability for the symbol to be scanned by a light pen and the ability for the symbol to be printed by specialized in-store equipment. Additional guidelines included the capability of a 99 percent first read rate with a slot scanner and a substitution error rate at the scanner not to exceed one in 10,000 symbols scanned.

Printing presses are subject to ink spread, such that the width of printed lines generally exceeds the corresponding line width on the printing plate. The amount of ink spread depends upon press conditions, amounts and viscosity of ink, and other factors which are difficult to control precisely. IBM proposed a technique called delta distance, whereby a bar code symbol is made insensitive to uniform ink spread. This property, as embodied in the UPC symbol, is illustrated in Figure 3-5. Dimension T1 is taken from the leading edge of the first bar to the leading edge of the second bar, while dimension T2 is from the trailing edge of the first bar to the trailing edge of the second bar. Dimension C is the distance from the leading edge of the character to the leading edge of the adjacent character. Such measurements are unaffected by uniform ink spread. If ink spread is excessive, however, some spaces become too small for the scanner to resolve, and the symbol will be unreadable.

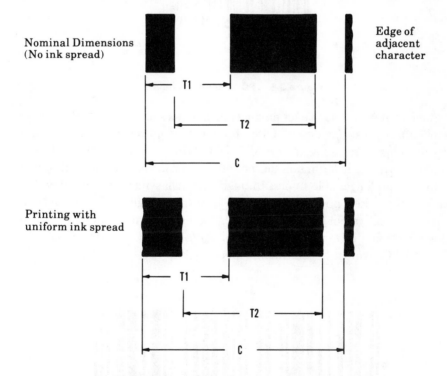

**Figure 3-5. Delta distance decoding technique of UPC**

A complete Version A UPC symbol is shown in Figure 3-6. The longer bars at the center (center guard bars) divide the symbol into a left half and a right half. Slot scanners are constructed with orthogonal beams (the simplest format being two beams that cross at a 90-degree angle), such that at least one beam will pass through each half-symbol, regardless of orientation. The bars in each half-symbol are sufficiently taller (referred to as being over-square) than the half-symbol width so that the omnidirectional scanning feature can operate reliably while the symbol moves rapidly over the scanner.[1]

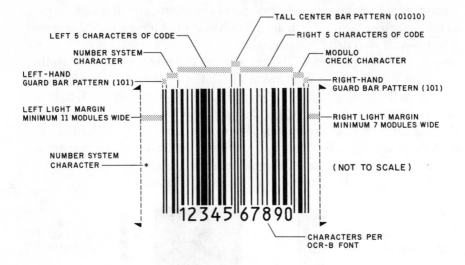

**Figure 3-6. UPC Version A symbol**

Some manufacturers market products such that a standard size UPC symbol would affect packaging design. Often these manufacturers solve the problem by truncating, or reducing, the overall height of the symbol. The effect of truncation is that the half-symbols are no longer over-square and the orthogonal beams are no longer able to pass through each half-symbol, except when the package is precisely positioned over the slot scanner. Figure 3-7 shows a truncated symbol. Symbol truncation reduces the first pass read rate of the scanning system and is *strongly recommended against* in UPC Location Guideline #3 and UPC Symbol Specification, Appendix F-1.

**Figure 3-7. Truncated UPC symbol**

Individual UPC/EAN characters are constructed from combinations of two bars and two spaces. They occupy a total of seven modules, as illustrated in Figure 3-8. Dark modules are associated with binary one and light modules with binary zero, so that the sum of these bits equals the number of dark modules in the character. Odd characters have either three or five dark modules, while even characters have two or four dark modules. Twenty possible left-hand and 20 possible right-hand characters can be constructed using these rules. With UPC/EAN, only numbers can be represented, but each character contains an additional bit of information (a parity bit), depending on whether it contains an odd or even number of dark modules. UPC Version A is constructed from left-hand odd characters and right-hand even characters. Each half-symbol contains a total of six digits, with the last digit in the right half being a check digit (modulus 10) computed from the preceding 11 information digits. UPC Version A symbols have two levels of checking. The first is a parity check of individual characters within the half-symbol. The second is a symbol check digit. The scan direction of UPC/EAN is determined from character parity rather than from start/stop characters.

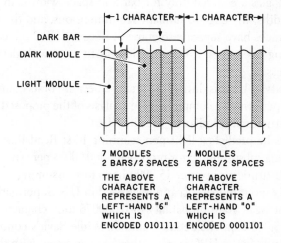

**Figure 3-8 UPC/EAN character construction**

A shorter UPC Version E symbol is only six digits long and uses only left-hand characters. It uses both odd and even parities. The basic EAN symbol encodes 12 data digits plus a check digit with the same geometry as a UPC symbol. This is accomplished by allowing both odd and even parity for the left-hand characters and arranging them such that three of the six characters have even parity. The 13th digit representation is thus encrypted in the parity sequence of the left half-symbol. In UPC Version D, all four parity types of characters are utilized to create a family of compatible omnidirectional symbols of various lengths up to 29 data characters.

The bars and spaces of UPC characters can be either one, two, three or four modules wide. This relationship is nominally exact for the digits 0, 3, 4, 5, 6, and 9. For digits 1, 2, 7, and 8, however, the nominal bar and space width dimensions are altered so that they are no longer exact multiples of a module. For the characters 1 and 2, the bars are narrower by 1/13 module width and for the characters 7 and 8, the bars are widened by 1/13th module. The reason for this shaving, or distortion, of nominal bar width is that the edge-to-similar-edge measurements (T1 and T2 distances) are identical for the characters 1 and 7 and for the characters 2 and 8. In these cases, it is appropriate for the scanner to measure bar widths in order to separate ones from sevens and twos from eights. All other decoding in UPC can be done using only edge-to-similar-edge measurements that are inherently immune to ink spread. Altering the dimensions of characters 1, 2, 7, and 8 provides improved margins for the scanner in those cases where it is appropriate to measure bar width.

The structure of UPC/EAN is quite different from the industrial symbologies, such as Code 39, Interleaved 2 of 5, and Codabar. Printing tolerances for the industrial symbologies are stated only for bar and space widths. In UPC, the bar and space widths, the edge-to-similar-edge dimensions, and the character-to-character distances have separate tolerances. Because UPC is a continuous code with exacting tolerances, it is more difficult to print with devices other than printing presses.

The data security of UPC is difficult to analyze because of its complex structure. David Savir performed a comprehensive analysis of the proposed IBM symbol which was structurally similar to the final UPC.

In that analysis he predicts a light pen scanning First Read Rate of 95.7% and a corresponding substitution error probability of 0.00073 per symbol scanned (equal to one substitution error per 15,000 characters, assuming 11 character symbols). For a fix mounted laser scanner, as used in U.S. Supermarkets, Savir establishes a First Read Rate probability of 0.000076 (one character substitution error per 145,000 data characters scanned). While Savir's conclusions do not necessarily apply to the UPC symbol, they are consistent with the original UPC guidelines. The actual substitution error probability for source printed UPC is unknown and may differ widely depending on the design and manufacture of specific scanners and the degree to which scanned symbols conform to specification.

When UPC is scanned at the supermarket point of sale, an important third level of checking is available. This third-level checking is accomplished by a file look-up operation in which 11 or 12 digits read from the UPC symbol by the scanner are matched with UPC numbers in the store file. If a substitution occurs during scanning, the misread number will probably not be in the store file. With 10,000 items on file, the chances that a misread number would match a number on file are about one chance in 100 million items scanned. A different situation prevails for random weight items, such as fresh meat or cheese, which are sold by weight and for which the item price is contained in the UPC symbol. For these random weight UPC symbols, a second check digit, covering the price field, is strongly recommended. Experience has shown that it is prudent to utilize this second check digit for standard and random weight items.

UPC/EAN is an excellent choice for supermarket point-of-sale systems and other retail stores. In retail stores, items can be identified with numbers having a fixed number of digits. Item identification must be inexpensive, because of the high volume of item turnover. Finally, retail store identification systems must have a high level of data checking (file matching) for the majority of the scanned symbols. Because most other bar code applications have different requirements and conditions, the UPC symbol is seldom recommended and rarely used outside of retail stores.[1]

## 2 of 5 Code and Interleaved 2 of 5 Code

The 2 of 5 Code was developed by Gerry Woolf of Identicon Corporation in 1968. It is principally used for warehouse inventory handling, identification of photofinishing envelopes, airline ticketing, and baggage and cargo handling. The 2 of 5 Code is simple and straightforward. All information is contained in the widths of the bars, with the spaces serving only to separate the individual bars. Bars can be either wide or narrow, and the wide bars are conventionally three times the widths of the narrow bars. Spaces may be any reasonable width but are typically equal to the narrow bars. Narrow bars are identified as zero bits and wide bars as one bits. A sample of a completed symbol is given in Figure 3-9.

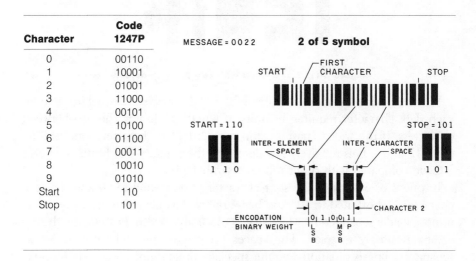

| Character | Code 1247P |
|-----------|------------|
| 0 | 00110 |
| 1 | 10001 |
| 2 | 01001 |
| 3 | 11000 |
| 4 | 00101 |
| 5 | 10100 |
| 6 | 01100 |
| 7 | 00011 |
| 8 | 10010 |
| 9 | 01010 |
| Start | 110 |
| Stop | 101 |

MESSAGE = 0 0 2 2    **2 of 5 symbol**

START   FIRST CHARACTER   STOP

START = 110    STOP = 101

INTER-ELEMENT SPACE   INTER-CHARACTER SPACE

1 1 0    1 0 1

CHARACTER 2

ENCODATION   0 1 0 0 1
BINARY WEIGHT   LSB   MSB

**Figure 3-9. 2 of 5 coding conventions**

25

The code structure is easily remembered by associating the bar positions from left to right with weighting factors 1, 2, 4, 7, and parity. Exceptions to this rule are zero, start, and stop.

The 2 of 5 Code is a discrete code, since the white spaces between the characters are not part of the code. Because the white spaces carry no information, their dimensions are not critical. Discrete codes are easily printed by formed font printing devices, such as letterpress numbering heads. Formed font printers can be very accurate within a single character but are less accurate in the space between adjacent characters.

The 2 of 5 Code is self-checking. The example in Figure 3-10 shows the character 6 with a printing void in one of the wide bars. A scan line passing through this void would see a character composed of four narrow bars and one wide bar. Since all valid characters require two wide bars out of the total of five bars (the source of the name 2 of 5 Code), a nonread would occur. Two independent printing defects occurring along the same scan line within the same character, as shown in Figure 3-11, could produce a character substitution error. Such an error would result only if a void in the wide bar is aligned with a spot on a narrow bar within the same character.

**Figure 3-10. 2 of 5 Code with one printing defect**

**Figure 3-11. 2 of 5 Code with two printing defects**

When the wide-to-narrow bar ratio is 3:1 and the spaces are equal to one unit, each data character requires 14 units of length, including the gap between characters. If the wide-to-narrow ratio were 2:1, each character would still require 12 units. This relatively low density is the primary disadvantage of 2 of 5 Code compared with other numeric symbologies.

In one 2 of 5 variant, the start character is shortened to 00 and the stop character is shortened to 10. Another variation has been the use of narrowly printed marks separated by white spaces of variable width. In this case, the encoding is simply reversed. The spaces carry meaning and the bars act as separators. These variations require specially programmed bar code readers.[1]

In October 1972, Intermec proposed certain bar code printing equipment to Computer Identics. In this context a problem arose over the low density of 2 of 5 Code, coupled with a limitation on bar height imposed by the printing equipment. The use of 2 of 5 Code would have resulted in a long, slender bar code symbol, which was deemed unsuitable for laser scanning in a warehouse. As a solution to this problem, Dr. David Allais of Intermec proposed the Interleaved 2 of 5 symbology.

Interleaved 2 of 5 has been widely accepted as a numeric bar code symbol in warehouse and heavy industrial applications. Its use has been particularly prevalent in the automobile industry. Interleaved 2 of 5 was recommended by the Distribution Symbology Study Group (DSSG) in 1981 as a standard for numeric labeling of corrugated shipping containers. In November 1981, it was adopted by the Uniform Product Code Council (UPCC), now known as the Uniform Code Council (UCC), as the standard symbology for use on outer containers in the grocery industry.

The encoding technique in Interleaved 2 of 5 is the same as for 2 of 5 code with one exception—bars and spaces both carry information. The odd number position digits are represented in the bars, while the even number position digits are represented in the spaces. The start character to the left of the symbol consists of the following sequence: narrow bar, narrow space, narrow bar, narrow space. The stop character to the right of the symbol consists of a wide bar, narrow space, narrow bar. A four-digit Interleaved 2 of 5 symbol is shown in Figure 3-12.

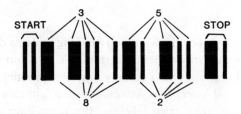

**Figure 3-12. Interleaved 2 of 5 encoding four digits**

Current specifications require Interleaved 2 of 5 symbols to contain an even number of digits. For data made up of an odd number of digits, a leading zero may be added to the data before encoding. Some early uses of Interleaved 2 of 5 allowed the last characters (represented by the last five spaces before the stop code) to be a null character. The null character was encoded using five narrow spaces. Use of the null character is now strongly discouraged, since it has been found to reduce the security of the symbol. It also restricts the design of decoding algorithms used in Interleaved 2 of 5 readers.

Interleaved 2 of 5 is self-checking but is continuous rather than discrete. Specifications allow the nominal width of wide elements to range between two times and three times the nominal width of the narrow elements. However, if the narrow elements are less than 20 mils, the ratio must exceed 2.2:1. The UPC Shipping Container Symbol specifies a 2.5:1 ratio.

Interleaved 2 of 5 is most commonly used with a check digit and with scanners that anticipate the exact number of digits in each symbol. If scanners were programmed to read variable length Interleaved 2 of 5 messages and no check digit were used, it would be possible for a partial scan to be interpreted as a valid, shorter message.[1] The probability of short reads containing embedded strips of shorter information was calculated in August 1983 by Malcolm Beers of Eastman Kodak. Beers found Interleaved 2 of 5 symbols having four characters had a 20 percent chance of being read as embedded strips if the scanner left the symbol before reaching the stop code. These short reads are a type of substitution error. The probability of short reads expands proportionately with the number of characters contained in the symbol, such as 6 characters/40 percent, 8 characters/80 percent, and 10 or more characters/nearly 100 percent.

The addition of a check digit within the symbol improves the probability of a proper read, but only by a factor of 10, as 10 represents the possible characters that could randomly appear as the last position in the "Short Read." Multiple check digits can substantially reduce the probability of substitution errors, but the most secure method is to fix the length of the symbol and include a check digit. No substantiated data existed prior to January 1, 1986 regarding Interleaved 2 of 5's first pass read rate or substitution error rate, though such data will be established in 1986 through both independent testing and testing by scanning manufacturers' trade associations.

## Codabar

Codabar was developed by the Monarch Marking Systems division of Pitney Bowes for use in retail price–labeling systems. A variation of Codabar was among the original proposals for a grocery universal product symbol. Following the National Retail Merchants Association standardization on OCR-A in 1975 for department store price labeling, the promotion of Codabar was redirected toward diversified nonretail applications. However, some department stores continue to use the Codabar symbology.

Federal Express employs an 11-digit Codabar symbol on each of their airbills and processes over 450,000 packages each night, using the Codabar symbol. Codabar has been widely accepted by libraries and the medical industry. It has also been extensively used on photofinishing envelopes. In 1977, Codabar was adopted as a standard for blood bag labeling by the American Blood Commission's (ABC) Committee for Commonality in Blood Banking Automation (CCBBA).

Codabar is a discrete, self-checking code with each character represented by a standalone group of four bars and three intervening spaces. A sample Codabar label is shown in Figure 3-13. The 12 principal characters (0 through 9, –, and $) have one wide bar and one wide space. Four additional characters ( : , / , . , and +) have three wide bars and no wide spaces. Four different start/stop characters are defined and designated a, b, c, and d. These stop/start characters are constructed using one wide bar and two wide spaces. A complete Codabar symbol begins with one of the start/stop characters followed by some number of data characters and ending with one of the start/stop characters. Since any of the start/stop characters may be used on either end of the symbol, it is possible to use the 16 unique start/stop combinations to identify label type or other information.

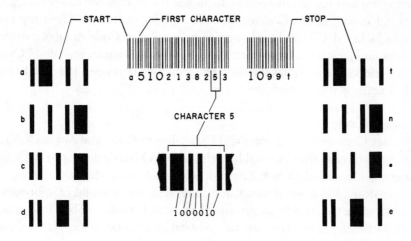

Figure 3-13. Sample Codabar symbol

Since Codabar is variable length, discrete, and self-checking, it is a versatile symbology. The width of space between characters is not critical and may vary significantly within the same symbol. The character set consists of 0 through 9, −, $, :, /, ., and +. The specified dimensions for bars and spaces in Codabar were originally chosen to optimize performance of certain early printing and reading equipment. Unfortunately, these bar and space dimensions are not even multiples of units.[1] Numerous attempts have been made to rationalize the coding structure of Codabar from 18 element widths down to 2 (wide bar/wide space and narrow bar/narrow space). Most notably these efforts have given rise to names like Ames Code, 2 of 7 Code, and Rationalized Codabar. Comprehensive works, such as those by Stephen Stewart of Interface Solutions,[2] have lent considerable credibility to the superficial nature of the 18 different printing widths, suggesting that two-element widths (wide and narrow), would have equal or better performance than the Codabar specifications currently in existence.

Codabar has 18 different dimensions for bar and space widths. So many different dimensions often result in labels which are printed out of specification and causes Codabar printing equipment to be more expensive.

Work done by the CCBBA task force suggests a first pass read rate of 99 percent and a substitution error rate of better than 1 in 1 million characters without a check digit and 1 in 1 billion characters with a check digit. In 1981 Dr. Eric Brodheim, et al., published "An Evaluation of the CODABAR Symbol in Blood Banking Automation" reporting their evaluation of Codabar's substitution error rate as experienced by the New York Blood Center. This eight-month test showed an empirically established error rate of 1 in 9.1 million digits read, excluding one atypical ten-day period. Including the atypical ten-day period, their tests yielded an SER for Codabar of 1 in 1.5 million digits read. These test conditions included 432,000 blood samples with a 7-digit Codabar label (without a check digit), each read three times and 10% of the samples repeated.[3] Other than Code 39, Codabar has the only independently developed test data to support a defined substitution error rate.

## Plessey Code

Plessey Code and its variants (MSI Code, Telxon Code, and Anker Code) all find their origins in the pulse width modulated (PWM) code developed by Plessey Company Limited of Dorset, England. It is widely used for shelf markings in grocery stores. Pulse width modulated codes represent each bit of information by a bar/space pair. A zero bit consists of a narrow bar followed by a wide space, while a one bit consists of a wide bar followed by a narrow space. This is shown in Figure 3-14.

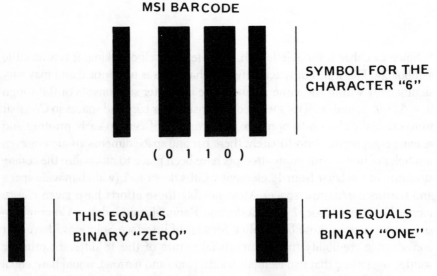

Figure 3-14. Pulse width modulated code (MSI) encoding the digit 6

**Table 3-3**
**Pulse width modulated code character structure**

| Digit | Bits | | |
|-------|------|---|---|
| 0 | 0000 | Alphabetic or other symbols may be assigned | |
| 1 | 1000 | to the remaining 6 possible four bit | |
| 2 | 0100 | combinations, e.g., | |
| 3 | 1100 | | |
| 4 | 0010 | A | 0101 |
| 5 | 1010 | B | 1101 |
| 6 | 0110 | C | 0011 |
| 7 | 1110 | D | 1011 |
| 8 | 0001 | E | 0111 |
| 9 | 1001 | F | 1111 |

4 1 5 8 9 6 3 6 4 1

**Plessey Code**

Each decimal digit is represented by a binary code decimal (BCD) number consisting of four bits according to Table 3-3.

PWM codes are not self-checking and employ a variety of check characters. The MSI Code employs a Modulus 10 Check, Plessey Code employs a polynomial–based Cyclic Redundancy Check (CRC), and Anker employs an inverted CRC. For start and stop characters, Plessey and Anker employ a 1101 (B) and previously used a 0101 (A). MSI employs a single bit pair of 1 as a start symbol and a single bit pair of 0 as a stop symbol. Telxon employs a right and left bar pattern (start and stop code) of 010. MSI and Telxon reverse the 1-2-4-8 BCD pattern for bit pair weighting to 8-4-2-1. PWM codes for individual digits range in length from 12 times the width of the narrow nominal element width for MSI and Telxon to 20 times the nominal width for Plessey and Anker.

## Other Data Storage Codes

Table 3-4 lists other data storage codes. The symbologies described in the foregoing discussions represent those "popular" codes in use today. Following Table 3-4, we will discuss four other symbologies which are having an impact on industrial and commercial applications, namely, Code 11, Code 93, Code 128, and Telepen.

**Table 3-4**
**Data storage codes**

| Name of symbology | Alternate names |
| --- | --- |
| 2 of 7 Code | Codabar |
| 3 of 9 code | Code 39, USD-3 |
| ACI* | |
| AGES | |
| Ames | A variant of Codabar |
| Anker | A variant of PWM |
| AS-6 | |
| AS-10 | |
| Bar/Half Bar* | |
| Bi-Level Code* | |
| Binary Code* | |
| Binary Coded Decimal | |
| Bullseye Code* | |
| Codabar | USD-4, 2 of 7 code |
| Code 11 | USD-8 |
| Code 39 | USD-3, 3 of 9 Code |
| Code 93 | USD-7 |
| Code 128 | USD-6 |
| Code B | |
| Color Bar* | |
| Delta Distance A | |
| Delta Distance B | A variant of Delta Distance A |
| Delta Distance C | A variant of Delta Distance A |
| Digital Code* | |
| Distribution Symbol | |
| Double Track Symbol Code* | |
| EAN—European Article Numbering | WPC and IAN |
| F2F | Norand |
| Frequency Code | |
| Fujitsu | |
| IER | |
| IAN—International Article Numbering | WPC and EAN |
| Interleaved 2 of 5 | I 2 of 5, USD-1 |
| Matrix Two of Five | Two of Five Matrix |
| Modified BCD | |
| MSI Bar Code | A variant of PWM |
| Nixdorf | |
| Norand | F2F |
| Octal Coded Decimal | |
| Periodic Binary | |
| Plessey Code | A variant of PWM |
| Presence/Absence Code* | USD-5 |
| PWM | Pulse Width Modulated |
| RTC | |
| Scope Code | |
| Siemens Code* | |
| Sunburst Code* | Wagon Wheel Code |
| Telepen | |
| Ten Segment Decimal Code* | |
| Toshiba | |

## Table 3-4
## Data storage codes

| Name of symbology | Alternate names |
|---|---|
| Two of Five | |
| Two of Five Matrix | Matrix Two of Five |
| UPC | Universal Product Code |
| USD-1 | Interleaved 2 of 5 |
| USD-2 | A Subset of Code 39 |
| USD-3 | Code 39, 3 of 9 Code |
| USD-4 | Codabar |
| USD-5 | Presence/Absence Code |
| USD-6 | Code 128 |
| USD-7 | Code 93 |
| USD-8 | Code 11 |
| Wagon Wheel Code* | Sunburst Code |
| WPC—World Product Code | EAN and IAN |
| Zellweger Code | |

*Note: These symbologies require specialized equipment other than a simple line of light.*

# Code 11

Code 11 was developed by Intermec in early 1977 to satisfy specialized requirements for a very high density, discrete numeric bar code. The most extensive application of Code 11 has been the labeling of telecommunications components and equipment by AT&T. The name Code 11 is derived from the fact that 11 different data characters can be represented, in addition to a start/stop character. The character set includes the 10 digits and the dash symbol.

Each character is represented by a standalone group of three bars and two intervening spaces. Although Code 11 is discrete, it is not self-checking. A single printing defect can transpose one character into another valid character. Data security is obtained by using one, or preferably two, check digits.[1]

The specifications for Code 11 suggest that this code should have a narrow element width of 7.5 mils. This results in an information density of 15 characters per inch. The wide-to-narrow element ratio is 2.24:1 for characters with two wide elements and 3.5:1 for characters with one wide element. This unusual structure leads to a constant character length of 56 mils, not including the intercharacter space. The constant character length facilitates printing with certain high density bar code printers.[4]

# Code 93

Among the industrial bar codes, Code 39 is the preeminent symbology. The main technical limitation of Code 39 is that each character consumes 13 to 16 units of width. Such coding density can cause problems in some applications. The introduction of Code 93 by Intermec in April 1982 provided a higher density alphanumeric symbology designed to supplement Code 39. The set of data characters in Code 93 is identical to that of Code 39.

Each character consists of nine modules arranged into three bars and three spaces. Forty-eight of the 56 possible combinations are used in Code 93. One of these characters, represented by ⧠, is reserved for a start/stop character, four are used for control characters, and the remaining 43 data characters coincide with the Code 39 character set. A single module termination bar is added after the stop character to close off the final space.

Code 93 is a variable length, continuous code that is not self-checking. Bar and space widths may be one, two, three, or four modules wide. Its structure uses edge-to-similar-edge decoding. This makes the symbol immune to uniform ink spread, which allows liberal bar width tolerances.

Code 93 uses two check characters and is claimed by its supporters to be the highest density alphanumeric bar code. The dual check digit scheme provides for high data integrity. All substitution errors in a single character are detected for any message length. All two character substitution errors are detected in messages as long as 50 characters. 99.5% of all substitution errors involving more than two characters are claimed by the developer to be detectable for message lengths of one through 50 characters.[1] No independently developed statistics are available for Code 93 with regard to first pass read rate or substitution error rates.

## Code 128

Code 128 was introduced in the fall of 1981 by Computer Identics in response to the need for a compact alphanumeric bar code symbol that could be used to encode complex product identification. The fundamental requirement called for a symbology capable of being printed by existing data processing printers (primarily dot-matrix printers) which produce daily work-in-progress, job, and product traceability documents. The ability to print identification messages between 10 and 32 characters long on existing forms and labels was deemed an important requirement.

Code 128 uniquely addresses this need with the claim as the most compact, complete, alphanumeric symbology available. In addition, Code 128 was designed with geometric features to improve scanner read performance, to be self-checking, and to provide data message management function codes.

Code 128 encodes the complete set of 128 ASCII characters without adding extra symbol elements. Code 128 is designed to be a variable length symbology and has the ability to link one message to another for composite message transmission. In symbols representing fields of numeric data, Code 128 can code pairs of numeric digits (00 through 99) in place of alphanumeric characters. This cuts the required space in half. Where four or more digits of adjacent numeric data exist in a message, coding can be done in numeric pairs to double the density. Code 128 is decoded and checked at two levels. First, it is checked at the individual character level using character self-checking parity. Second, it is checked as a complete message using the calculated end-of-message check character.

Code 128 follows the general bar code format rules of quiet zone, start code, data, check digit, stop code, and quiet zone. The X dimension can be selected to suit either the capability of the printer used or the optical requirements of the scanner.[5] However, an absolute minimum bar or space dimension of nine mils must be maintained (0.010 inch minimum nominal ±0.001 inch tolerance). Characters in Code 128 consist of three bars and three spaces such that the total character width is 11 modules. Bars and spaces may be one, two, three, or four modules wide. There are 103 different characters in the Code 128 character set, including three different start characters and a stop character. The choice of start code selects one of three possible character sets, so that 128 different ASCII characters can be represented. In one of these character sets, each character represents two decimal digits, thus doubling the code density for numeric-only data. Various control, function, and shift characters are defined, allowing switching between character sets within a symbol.

The correct method of decoding Code 128 begins with the preferred edge-to-similar-edge measurements to decode each character. To detect all single "X" module code errors within a character, a second algorithm must be employed which compares the measured sum of the bars and spaces with the predicted sums required by the decoded character. Every character containing one "X" error, which results in the wrong character being decoded by edge-to-edge measurements, will not only have the wrong internal parity (odd parity for the bar sum and even parity for the space sum), but will differ from the bar sums and space sums defined for the erroneously decoded character by 3 "X." This difference is easily detected even with large amounts of ink spread or bar dimension shrinkage. Thus, all 1 "X" errors in Code 128 characters are detectable, and Code 128 is character self-checking.

The second algorithm is possible exclusively with Code 128 because of its character internal parity scheme and cannot be applied to other edge-to-edge decodable symbols (UPC, EAN, or Code 93) because of their geometric construction.[6]

No independently developed data is available regarding the first pass read rate or substitution error rate of Code 128.

## Code 93 vs. Code 128

Within the two preceding discussions, both Code 93 and Code 128 were said to have the highest density of current alphanumeric bar codes. Can both be true? The answer is yes, depending. Depending upon the content of the symbol, strictly numeric or mixed alphabetic and numeric data and the "X" dimension size, either Code 128 or Code 93 could be the highest density alphanumeric bar code. Code 128 can be higher density when long strings of numeric data are contained within the symbol, permitting Code 128 to shift to double density numeric. Where the symbol structure is mixed randomly with alphabetic and numeric data, Code 93 would have the highest density. It is not possible to make an apples-to-apples comparison without knowing the application code structure. It is further important to realize that the minimum open system nominal element size (which does impact character density) for Code 39 is 7.5 mils, for Code 93 it is 8.0 mils, and for Code 128 the minimum nominal element size is 10.0 mils.

**Table 3-5**
**Symbol size calculations for codes 39, 93, and 128**

|   | Bar code symbology | Data character "X" elements | Code overhead "X" elements |
|---|---|---|---|
| A | Code 39 | 16X | 31X |
| B | Code 128 (numeric only) | 5.5X | 35X |
| C | Code 128 (alphanumeric) | 11X | 35X |
| D | Code 93 | 9X | 37X |

Referring to Table 3-5; to determine the overall length of a given bar code symbol in terms of "X", multiply (the "X" dimension) times (the data character element "Xs") times (the number of characters) and add (the "X" dimension) times (the code overhead).

Assume 16 characters. Now at the minimum element size

$$A = (7.5 \text{ mils} \times 16 \times 16) + (7.5 \text{ mils} \times 31) = 2.153''$$
$$B = (10.0 \text{ mils} \times 5.5 \times 16) + (10.0 \text{ mils} \times 35) = 1.230''$$
$$C = (10.0 \text{ mils} \times 11 \times 16) + (10.0 \text{ mils} \times 35) = 2.110''$$
$$D = (8.0 \text{ mils} \times 9 \times 16) + (8.0 \text{ mils} \times 37) = 1.448''$$

Now let's specify a specific "X" dimension, e.g., 20 mils (that which many dot-matrix printers are currently printing.)

$$A = (20 \text{ mils} \times 16 \times 16) + (20 \text{ mils} \times 31) = 5.740''$$
$$B = (20 \text{ mils} \times 5.5 \times 16) + (20 \text{ mils} \times 35) = 2.460''$$
$$C = (20 \text{ mils} \times 11 \times 16) + (20 \text{ mils} \times 35) = 4.220''$$
$$D = (20 \text{ mils} \times 9 \times 16) + (20 \text{ mils} \times 37) = 3.620''$$

It can be seen in the above examples that Code 128 and Code 93 are shorter than Code 39. Code 128 (Numeric Only) is the shortest of all. However, when mixed alphanumeric data, such as A1B2C3D4E5F6G7H8, are computed for length, Code 93 is shorter than Code 128. It is also important to realize that Table 3.5's identification of data character and code overhead "X" elements were defined at a wide-to-narrow ratio of 3:1 for Code 39. Were the ratio at the Code 39 specified minimum of 2.25:1 and the minimum element size also defined at its open system minimum (i.e., 7.5 mils), Code 39 would have been shorter than Code 128. In the battle for the shortest code, the winner will be determined by the composition of the symbol that is to be encoded. Where four or more numeric characters appear adjacent to one another, Code 128 may be the winner, assuming a specified "X" dimension. Without knowing the composition of the symbol with regard to numeric and alphabetic content, and the printing methods to be employed, and the wide-to-narrow ratios to be used in a specific application, the relative lengths of the various symbologies cannot be determined.

## Telepen

Telepen was developed in 1973 by George Simms of S.B. Electronic Systems, Limited in Harpenden, Hertfordshire, England. The code was marketed only in Europe until 1981, when S.B. Electronics, through their U.S. distributor KPG, began actively promoting the use of Telepen to the U.S. automobile industry. It was this active promotion that gave rise to the introduction of Code 128 and Code 93.

Telepen code employs 16 modules (or units) per character, with black modules representing one bits and white modules representing zero bits. The wide-to-narrow element ratio in the Telepen symbology is defined at 3:1. Individual characters may contain four, five, six, seven, or eight bars. The character set includes 128 characters corresponding to the complete ASCII character set. The minimum X dimension specified for Telepen is 5 mils. Each block of characters (symbol) is comprised of a left-hand lead-in code (start code), the block of codes for the characters (data characters), the check character, and the right-hand lead-in code (stop code). The left-hand lead-in code is represented by an underline character (ASCII 95). The right-hand lead-in code is represented by a lowercase z (ASCII 122). In the full ASCII mode Telepen employs a Modulus 127 check character (BCC).

Through the programming of the bar code reading device or by encoding an ESC E control code combination in the data field, Telepen is able to encode double density numeric data. In the ESC E mode, the ASCII values of 26 through 126 are assigned the numeric values 00 through 99 respectively. In its double density mode, Telepen can utilize a Modulus 11 Check Digit at the end of the numeric string. Where space is critical, printing quality is high, and only an odd number of digits are to be encoded, it is possible to leave the Mod 127 BCC out of the code and rely instead on the Mod 11 check digit, saving some 24 elements of code length.[7]

Telepen is a variable length, continuous code that employs internal even character parity and a block check character (BCC). The parity check within each character meets the requirement of self-checking codes. A checking algorithm can be applied against each character such that a substitution error can occur only if an even number of printing defects appears within a single character. Telepen does not have a constant bar/space pattern as do other codes. Telepen, thus, does not have the substitution error safeguard of a bar/space pattern check.[8] No independently developed data is available regarding the first pass read rate or substitution error rate of Telepen.

## Symbology Comparisons

Table 3-6 shows a comparison of four popular bar code symbologies, (UPC/EAN, Code 39, Interleaved 2 of 5, and Codabar).

Table 3-7 shows the comparisons of Other Selected Bar Code Symbologies (Code 11, Code 93, Code 128, and Telepen).

Note that in both Table 3-6 and Table 3-7 most symbologies are listed with an "Unknown" *Substitution Error Rate*. Only Code 39 and Codabar have empirically developed data: Code 39 by LOGMARS and Codabar by CCBBA. It must be remembered that a symbology does not have a given SER. Systems that employ a specific symbology are evaluated when establishing an SER. A system includes the substrate, the printing, the ink, the reader, and the decoder which decodes the specific symbology. Even the LOGMARS and CCBBA studies evaluated Code 39 and Codabar, respectively, with specific equipment reading specific printed symbols. Technologies improve and one realistically must believe that errors will lessen.

Corporate and industry standards organizations must rely upon the best information available at a given point in time. If a symbology has not been field proven such organizations generally tend to shy away from them. The lack of hard, empirically derived data on various combinations of symbologies, symbols, and readers have caused four independent efforts to be undertaken. Two of these, Bell Laboratories (under the direction of Allan Gilligan) and Eastman-Kodak/Q.E.D. Systems (under the direction of Gary Ahlquist, Eastman Kodak and Craig K. Harmon of Q.E.D. Systems) are proprietary to the sponsoring organizations. The third, undertaken by Automatic Identification Manufacturers (AIM), should be available to the public in 1986. Also, by that time, AIM will have revised their Uniform Symbol Descriptions, expanding the Descriptions to more detailed Specifications while perfecting some of the material currently contained in the USDs.

**Table 3-6**
**Comparison of primary bar code symbologies**

| Characteristic | UPC/EAN | Code 39 | Interleaved 2 of 5 | Codabar |
|---|---|---|---|---|
| Character set | Numeric | Alphanumeric, plus – , $ / + % and space | Numeric | Numeric, plus $ – / . + |
| Number of characters encoded | 10 | 43 (with double character full ASCII capability) | 10 | 16 |
| Start and stop codes | Unique, both (101) | Unique, both (*) | Start NB/NS/NB/NS Stop WB/NS/NB | Combination of any four a/t, b/n, c/*, d/e |
| Number of module combinations used | 4 | 2 | 2 | 2 (though 18 widths specified) |
| Substitution error rate without check digit (CD) | Unknown CD required | 1 in 3,000,000 characters | Unknown | 1 in 1,500,000 to 1 in 9,100,000 characters |
| Substitution error rate with check digit (CD) | 1 in 15,000 characters (light pen) calculated 1 in 145,000 characters (laser) | 1 in 45 trillion characters calculated for 15 characters | Unknown | 1 in 10,000,000 to 1 in 100,000,000 characters calculated |
| Standard nominal X dimension | 13 mils | 7.5 mils | 7.5 mils | 6.5 mils |
| Recommended wide-to-narrow ratio | N/A | 3:1; though higher densities can be achieved within a range of 2.25:1 to 3:1 | 3:1, though higher densities can be achieved within a range of 2.25:1 to 3:1 | 3:1, though somewhat inapplicable with existing specifications having 18 print widths |

| | | 13.7 characters per inch at .80 magnification | 9.4 characters† per inch with 2.25:1 | 178 characters per inch at 2.25:1 | 10 characters per inch |
|---|---|---|---|---|---|
| Highest achievable density within open system standards | | 13.7 characters per inch at .80 magnification | 9.4 characters† per inch with 2.25:1 | 178 characters per inch at 2.25:1 | 10 characters per inch |
| Specified print tolerance at maximum open system density | Bar width | 0.0010 inch | 0.0017 inch (2.25:1) | 0.0018 inch | 0.0015 inch |
| | edge-edge | 0.0015 inch | N/A | N/A | N/A |
| | pitch | 0.0030 inch | N/A | N/A | N/A |
| Discrete/Continuous | | Continuous | Discrete | Continuous | Discrete |
| Variable length | | No, although in Version D 13–29 characters can be encoded | Yes | No, to achieve any appreciable data integrity, either a length check or multiple check digits must be used | Yes |
| Self-checking | | Yes | Yes | Yes | Yes |
| Date introduced | | 1973 | 1974 | 1972 | 1972 |
| Corporate sponsor | | N/A, although structure developed by IBM | Intermec | Computer Identics | Welch-Allyn |
| Codified in standards | | UCC/IAN | USD-3/ANSI/DoD/GSA AIAG/HIBC/DSSG | USD-1/ANSI/UCC/DSSG | USD-4/ANSI/CCBBA |
| Market Influence | | Retail | Industrial/health/commercial/government | Industrial/Retail | Blood industry/photo/libraries/Federal Express |

†Note—60 cpi with a 0.001 inch nominal narrow element.

**Table 3-7**
**Comparison of other selected bar code symbologies**

| Characteristic | Code 11 | Code 93 | Code 128 | Telepen |
|---|---|---|---|---|
| Character set | Numeric, plus (–) | Alphanumeric, plus – $/ + % and space and 4 control characters | Full ASCII | Full ASCII |
| Number characters encoded | 11 | 47, full ASCII of 128 can be encoded using two character combination | 103/128 | 128 |
| Start and stop codes | Unique, both (00110) | Unique, ( ▯ ) | Start code unique to code subset (3) Unique and common stop code | Start code underline (ASCII 95) Stop code lowercase z (ASCII 122) |
| Double density numeric | No | No | Yes | Yes |
| Number of module combinations | 3 | 4 | 4 | 4, 5, 6, 7 or 8 |
| Substitution error rate without check digit (CD) | CD required | CD required | CD required | CD required |
| Substitution error rate with check digit (CD) | Unknown | Unknown | Unknown | Unknown |
| Standard nominal X dimension | 0.0075 inch | 0.008 inch | 0.010 inch | 0.005 inch |

| | | Column 1 | Column 2 | Column 3 | Column 4 |
|---|---|---|---|---|---|
| Recommended wide-to-narrow ratio | | 2.24 for Medium elements. 3.48 for Wide elements | N/A | N/A | 3:1 |
| Highest achievable density | | 15 characters per inch | 13.9 characters per inch | From $(5.5 \times X \times$ number of characters $+ (35 \times X) + (11 \times X$ per shift) to $(11 \times X \times$ number of characters $+ (35 \times X) + (11 \times X$ per shift) | 12.5 characters per inch for alpha-numeric 25.0 characters per inch for double density |
| Specified print tolerance at maximum density | Bar width | 0.0017 inch | 0.0022 | 0.0010 | 20% of bar width |
| | edge-edge | N/A | 0.0013 | 0.0014 | N/A |
| | pitch | N/A | 0.0013 | 0.0029 | N/A |
| Discrete/continuous | | Discrete | Continuous | Continuous | Continuous |
| Variable length | | Yes | Yes | Yes | Yes |
| Self-checking | | Yes | Yes | Yes | Yes |
| Date introduced | | 1977 | 1982 | 1981 | 1973 |
| Corporate sponsor | | Intermec | Intermec | Computer Identics | S. B. Electronics, Ltd. KPG, Inc. (U.S.) |
| Codified in standards | | USD-8 | USD-7 | USD-6 | None |
| Market influence | | AT&T | Unknown | Unknown | Unknown |

# CHAPTER 4

# BAR CODE MEDIA

For a bar code symbol to be successfully read, the optical sensor in the reader must be able to discern the transitions between the bars and the spaces in the symbol. The sensor must also be presented with a bar code whose dimensions do not deviate significantly from the predetermined pattern of the symbology. To be successfully and reliably read, the printed symbol must have sufficient optical contrast between the bars and spaces. Ideally, the printed bar should be observed as perfectly black and the unprinted spaces should be perfectly white. In practice, however, this condition is seldom met. Bar codes are printed on a wide range of substrates in numerous colors, so as not to conflict with the existing artwork of the package.

Bar codes are commonly printed on adhesive labels, cards, and documents. Since the media is an optical storage device, optical characteristics should dominate the selection considerations. The most important optical specification to consider is the surface reflectivity of the media at a specific wavelength or range of wavelengths. Second in importance is the radiation pattern of the media. A third optical parameter to consider is the transparency or translucency of the media. In addition to the optical characteristics, it is important that the media selected be durable enough for the application or that the media and printed symbol be covered with a protective laminate.

Optimally, the labeling media should reflect at least 70 percent of the light. On some substrates, such as corrugated stock, 70 percent reflectivity may not be achievable. In such cases, it is necessary to rely upon the print contrast between media and ink. The optical pattern of light that leaves the media surface describes the reflected radiation pattern. A shiny or specular surface results in a narrow radiation pattern. A dull, or matte, surface provides a diffuse, or broad, pattern. A shiny surface may reflect so much light that at near-perpendicular angles the scanner may be overloaded, while the mirror-like reflection at large scan angles may send little light back to the scanner. This mirror-like effect is generally not desirable, although some manufacturers have made use of the effect by printing the spaces in white or red, while letting the shiny metallic, unprinted surface serve as the bars. Generally, however, such practice is discouraged. A dull, or matte, surface is recommended to ensure a radiation pattern that is acceptable to the scanner over the entire range of scan angles.

Another optical characteristic that is important to consider is the media's transparency or translucency. If the media is too transparent, the material underneath affects the reflectivity. If the underlying surface contains printed material or is dark in color, the media's reflectivity is adversely affected. Highly transparent paper such as vellum, lightweight paper, and low weight computer paper should be avoided. Where the application dictates the use of such media, a highly reflective white surface placed behind the media prior to scanning will help.

A second phenomenon, paper bleed, also occurs when a transparent or translucent media is used. This phenomenon is caused by the scattering of incidental light rays within the media or from the underlying surface. Some of the scattered light will be detected by the scanner, thereby adding to the light reflecting off the media's surface. However, as the scanner approaches the edge of a bar, some of this scattered light is absorbed in the ink before it can be reflected back to the detector. As a result, the reflectivity of the media begins to drop off before the bar edge is reached. This optical effect tends to make the bars appear larger and the spaces narrower than they were actually printed.

The systematic error introduced by paper bleed is relatively constant in magnitude for a specific media. Its effects are therefore more pronounced when narrow element bar codes are used, because the error will be a larger percentage of the module width. This is particularly true for certain photographic papers commonly used to print high density (small element width) symbols. In general, factors that influence paper bleed are the rag content, the type of binder used, the thickness of the media, and the media's transparency. Paper bleed can be minimized by using heavyweight stock with a high rag content.

The final consideration in the selection of the media is durability, or how many times the light pen can be moved across the surface without degrading the reflectivity of the media, smearing the bars, or abrading the symbol. When evaluating the media durability required by the application, the user should consider the number of times that a symbol will be scanned by contact scanning devices during its lifetime and the severity of the environment to which the symbol will be exposed. If the expected number of scans is less than 50 and the environment is clean and dry, heavyweight paper with a smooth surface texture is acceptable. In applications where the symbol will be exposed to adverse environments such as dirt, grease, temperature extremes, and weather, or the label will be scanned at least 50 times by contact devices, the symbol should be protected with a transparent coating.[4,1]

# CHAPTER 5
# PRINT CONTRAST

One optical characteristic of the symbol that must be evaluated is the inter-relationship between the reflectivity of the media (spaces) and the ink (bars). This relationship, commonly referred to as the print contrast signal (PCS), is defined by the following equation:

$$PCS = \frac{R_L - R_D}{R_L} \times 100\%$$

where:

$R_L$ = The reflectivity of the light areas, or media (spaces)
$R_D$ = The reflectivity of the dark areas, or ink (bars)[9]

The key to the evaluation of bar and space interrelationships is the difference in reflected light that is observed by the scanner. Different scanners have light sources which emit light at different wavelengths. Consequently, some symbols that are readable by one variety of scanner may not be readable by another. Helium-neon (He-Ne) lasers, the type used in grocery store checkout systems, emit light having a wavelength of 632.8 nanometers (nm). Helium-neon laser light sources are also used in many fix mounted industrial scanners as well as in many hand-held laser scanners. These scanners interpret a red bar as if it were a white space because of the red color of the emitted light. Many hand-held light pens also use a visible red light source which operates in a range of 630 to 700 nanometers. Recently, one manufacturer introduced a visible red laser diode having an output wavelength of 720 nanometers. Each of these scanning devices interprets yellow, orange, and red bars to be the same as white spaces. Other light pens operate in the infrared (IR) spectrum, around 900 nanometers. They experience difficulty reading symbols printed with dye-based or colored inks. IR scanners, however, operate exceptionally well when the bar codes are printed using ink that has a high carbon content. Unfortunately, most inks are not carbon based. In many printing applications it would be too costly to print the artwork in a dye-based ink and the bar code in a carbon-based ink. Furthermore, IR readers are incapable of reading many electrostatically and thermally printed labels. Readers using visible red light, on the other hand, can read carbon-based inks, many dye-based colored inks, and electrostatically/thermally printed labels.

Where the bar code system designer has complete control of the symbol printing and the type of scanner, print contrast is not usually a problem. But where the symbols are to be scanned and printed at various locations, under no central control, the printer should print labels which have adequate contrast in the visible red range, from 630 nm through 720 nm. This does not mean that carbon-based inks should not be used, since visible light scanners can read carbon-based inks. It is simply that carbon-based inks and IR scanning should not be required.

Good scannability of a bar code symbol is obtained when the print contrast is greater than 75 percent. To achieve a contrast of 75 percent, the guidelines in Table 5-1 have been developed:[9]

### Table 5-1.
### PCS guidelines

| Space reflectance $R_L$ (%) | Maximum bar reflectance $R_D$ (%) |
|:---:|:---:|
| 25 | 6.25 |
| 30 | 7.50 |
| 35 | 8.75 |
| 40 | 10.00 |
| 45 | 11.25 |
| 50 | 12.50 |
| 55 | 13.75 |
| 60 | 15.00 |
| 65 | 16.25 |
| 70 | 17.50 |
| 75 | 18.75 |
| 80 | 20.00 |
| 85 | 21.25 |
| 90 | 22.50 |
| 95 | 23.75 |
| 100 | 25.00 |

The preceding PCS Guidelines all have a minimum $R_L/R_D$ ratio of 4.0 The higher the ratio, the better the reflection value.

Although natural kraft linerboard looks relatively dark to the human eye, its reflectance values, when measured with a light source of 633 nanometers wavelength, are sufficiently high to be used as a substrate for bar codes when used with properly applied inks. Lighter color substrates, such as mottled and bleached linerboards (or white label stock) will provide even higher reflectance values, which may allow selection of a broader range of colors than those shown in Table 5-2.

**Table 5-2.**
**Ink color guidelines**

| Color (GPI)* | Typical ratio $R_L/R_D$ | Color (GPI)* | Typical ratio $R_L/R_D$ |
|---|---|---|---|
| 394 Blue | 4.80 | 20 Green | 5.00 |
| 33 Blue | 5.00 | 2008 Green | 5.00 |
| 32 Blue | 5.00 | 22 Green | 4.17 |
| 31 Blue | 5.50 | 2014 Green | 4.17 |
| 3086 Blue | 5.00 | 523 Brown | 4.50 |
| 387 Blue | 5.00 | 52 Brown | 4.17 |
| 38 Blue | 4.17 | 90 Black | 5.50 |
| 3213 Aqua | 5.60 | 39 Blue | 5.50 |
| 24 Green | 5.00 | 29 Green | 5.50 |
| 21 Green | 5.00 | 300 Blue | 4.50 |

Table 5-2 presents the Glass Packaging Institute's (GPI) (Edition VII natural) list of colors which provide acceptable contrast values, when printed on a variety of corrugated linerboards.[9] This does not mean that all the inks listed give acceptable values on all substrates. The light reflectance will depend upon the specific ink formulation and the reflectance of the substrate.

If X dimensions of 25 mils or less are specified, the minimum space reflectance should be 50% or greater.

# CHAPTER 6
# PRINT QUALITY

The print mechanism, the media (or substrate), and the ink together determine the quality of the printed symbol. Assuming the printer is capable of printing the density desired, the major factors influencing quality are:

- ink spread/shrinkage
- ink voids/specks
- ink smearing
- nonuniformity of ink
- bar/space width tolerances
- edge roughness

All of these factors are potential sources of both systematic and random errors. These errors must be closely controlled to ensure that the symbol will be easily scannable.

As shown in Table 6-1, the application of ink to the media is a potential source of many different errors. These errors are caused by a complex interaction of the print mechanism, the ink, and the media. Table 6-1 presents the predominant inking errors for impact printing mechanisms, listing their primary causes and the type of error that generally results.

Table 6-1.
Impact printing inking errors

| Error | Cause | Type |
|-------|-------|------|
| Ink spread | Absorptive paper<br>Over-inked ribbon<br>Too much hammer pressure | Systematic |
| Ink shrinkage | Worn-out ribbon<br>Too little hammer pressure | Systematic |
| Ink voids and specks | Dirty print head<br>Dirty paper<br>Defective ribbon<br>Defective print head | Random |
| Ink smearing | Ink not cured<br>Poor wetting of paper | Random |
| Non-uniform inking | Dirty print head<br>Mechamism not adjusted | Random |

The amount of ink spread or ink shrinkage that occurs is determined by the condition of the ribbon and the hammer pressure. Ink spread results in wider bars and narrower spaces, whereas ink shrinkage has the opposite effect. Both ink spread and ink shrinkage may cause degradation in the bar edge definition.

Ink voids and specks are characteristic of any printing process. If the ink void or speck is large enough, it is possible for the scanner to recognize the transition across the void/speck as a space or bar. This leads to the creation of an invalid character. If the decoding software is well designed, the invalid character will not be read. Since the problem is only a localized one, there is a good chance that the same void or speck will not be encountered on the second scan and that the correct character will be read. The effects of ink voids and specks will be minimal if they are small relative to the narrow element width. Figure 6-1 shows the effects of voids and specks on scanning.

Ink smearing and nonuniform inking may also lead to poor read rates. Ink smearing is a problem, because it may cause a narrow bar to appear wide or a wide space to appear narrow. Consequently, the scanner may misread the symbol. As with ink voids and specks, this error is usually localized and random. A good read can occur on a second or third scan. Nonuniform inking can lead to a similar difficulty if the inking across the bar is so poor that the scanner does not see a sufficient drop in reflectivity. In such a case, the scanner will not recognize the presence of a bar. Once again, a good read may result by scanning a different section of the symbol.

The various inking errors, combined with the characteristics of the print mechanism, determine the bar/space width tolerances that can be maintained when printing bar code symbols. These tolerances may be specified by the printer vendor. The printer's tolerance can also be determined by using a toolmaker's microscope on sample symbols or by using a diagnostic verifier. A larger percentage of errors occurs if the element width is near the largest available for the printer. This could lead to a more severe degradation in performance than if a smaller element size is used. It is important to overall system performance that the printing tolerances be maintained within the limits specified by the symbology. This is particularly true of the wide-to-narrow element ratio.

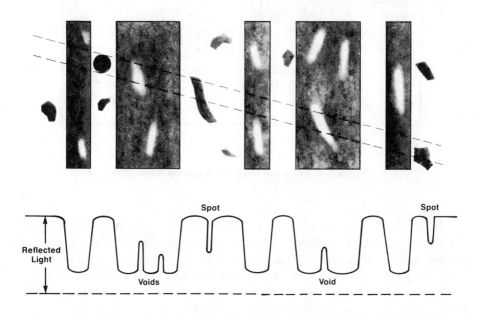

**Figure 6-1. Void/spot effects on scanning**

Edge roughness is caused by the combined effects of inking and the printing technique. Edge roughness can be considered as one of the factors determining bar/space width tolerances. In effect, the scanner senses a different bar width depending upon which part of the bar it passes over. Bar edge roughness is a common error in symbols printed with some dot-matrix printers.[4] For many dot-matrix printers the narrow element width is large enough to make this error small. Other dot-matrix printers have a sufficiently small dot size and dot overlap to cause virtually no degradation in the symbol's readability. A worst-case example of bar edge roughness is illustrated in Figure 6-2. See also Figure IV-3 for characteristic dot-matrix printing defects.

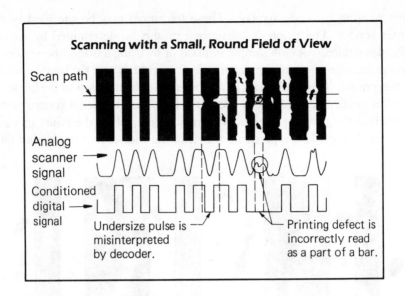

**Figure 6-2. Bar edge roughness effects on scanning**

Referring back to Chapter 3, and specifically Table 3-2 (Code 39 printing tolerances), one notes Column T (bar and space width tolerance). The tolerances listed are how far the bars and spaces may expand or contract and still be within specification, or *printing tolerances*. Each bar code symbology has an Absolute Tolerance which is nearly evenly allocated to printed symbol and scanner. When these *printing tolerances* are exceeded, part of the scanner's tolerances are consumed, increasing the possibility of a no-read or a bad read. It is therefore quite important that the quality of the bar code symbol be within the specifications for that specific symbology.

There are several schools of thought regarding quality control of the printed symbol. One assumes that if the symbol can be read by one bar code reader, it can be read by any other. This theory disregards the differences in bar code scanner aperture size and light source wavelength and is quite incorrect.

A second theory concludes that if the bar code reader's aperture size and light source are matched to the specifications of the printed symbol, another bar code reader of the same light source and aperture size could correctly read the bar code. In a vast majority of cases, this theory is correct. But it does assume that bar code reader manufacturers share commonly designed and well-designed circuitry and decoding software, a reasonable assumption to make.

A third school of thought contends that to be absolutely certain that the symbols being printed will be readable requires a routine sampling and analysis of print quality, or *verification* of the printed symbol. Verification involves the check-

ing of four elements of a bar code symbol:
- Data format
- Encodation
- Print contrast
- Bar and space dimensions

The data format is the order and placement of the data in the bar code. This can be checked visually by looking at the human-readable data printed beneath the bar code symbol. If it conforms with the data expected, the label passes the first test.

Verifying encodation ensures that the data read match the data intended to be represented by the symbol. The symbol is scanned, and the read data are compared with the human-readable data printed beneath the bar code. If they compare, the label passes the second test.

As explained in Chapter 5, print contrast is the ratio of the reflectivity of the bars and spaces in the symbol. The minimum contrast permitted is defined in the specification for the symbology or application. In bar code applications stipulating a visible red light source in the B633 band, poor contrast will result if the bars are printed with ink colors having red pigmentation. Bars printed in red, orange, reddish-purple or reddish-brown, for example, will not appear sufficiently different from the white spaces when viewed by a red light source, such as that in lasers and many light pen reading devices.

Another common contrast problem results when the symbol is to be read by a scanner having an infrared light source. A bar printed with an ink which has a low carbon content will be unseen by the scanner, though to the human eye this symbol may appear totally acceptable. If the symbol or application specification does not specify either the B633 or B900 and the symbol might be scanned by readers having either visible red or infrared light sources, the symbol's readability should be tested using both visible red and infrared light sources.

The bar/space dimensions of each symbol should be within the allowable tolerances of the specification. These limits vary with the scale of the printed symbol. Compare Column T in Table 3-2 with its scale of characters per inch (CPI). A symbol printed with bar/space dimensions outside the allowable limits for *printing tolerance* will be successfully read only if the total tolerance consumed by both symbol and reader does not exceed the Absolute Tolerance of the symbology.

Most generally bar/space dimensional variations from the specification are caused by the application of too much or too little ink or pressure in the printing of the symbol. Worn ribbons and too little pressure can cause bars to shrink and spaces to widen. Too much ink or too much pressure in applying the ink can cause the bars to widen while the spaces become more narrow. The growth or shrinkage of the various bar code elements is generally uniform across the bar code symbol. Samples can be taken and analysis made of the various elements (wide bars/wide spaces/narrow bars/narrow spaces) from two or more points in the printed symbol. And for an even greater degree of confidence that all of the elements are represented by the samples taken, one can employ automated verification equipment which will measure each bar and compare that measurement to the published standard and tolerances for that symbology. There are many ways in which the quality of a bar code symbol may be measured. Appendix F—Bar Code Specification for Code 39 includes those methods of measuring symbol quality that have been, or soon will be, adopted by the bar code printing industry. There are also many devices available to aid in this analysis. Table 6-2 summarizes the features of each of these devices. Sources for verification equipment can be found in the annual *Automatic Identification Manufacturers & Services Directory*, published by North American Technology, Inc. (See Appendix A under Periodicals).

**Table 6-2**
**Verification tools**

| Areas to be Verified | Printer's Gauge | Projection Optical Comparator | Measuring Microscope | Densi-tometer | Light Pens* | Laser Verifiers | Electro-Optical Verifiers |
|---|---|---|---|---|---|---|---|
| Encodation | □ | □ | □ | □ | ■ | ■ | ■ |
| Print Contrast | | | | | | | |
| At 633 nm | □ | □ | □ | ■ | ⊞ | ■ | ■ |
| At 900 nm | □ | □ | □ | ■ | ⊞ | □ | ■ |
| Bar/Space Dimensions | | | | | | | |
| To .001″ | ■ | □ | □ | □ | □ | ■ | ■ |
| To .0001″ | □ | ■ | ■ | □ | □ | □ | ■ |
| Features Capability of measuring all bars/spaces in one scan | □ | □ | □ | □ | □ | ■ | ■ |
| Data Averaging Capability | □ | □ | □ | □ | □ | ■ | ■ |
| Capability of verifying multiple codes | ■ | ■ | ■ | ■ | ⊞ | ■ | ■ |
| Cost < $2000 | ■ | □ | ⊞ | ⊞ | ■ | □ | □ |

Key
□ = None
⊞ = Some
■ = All

*See preceding discussion of utilizing a light pen as a verification tool.

# CHAPTER 7
# LABEL ADHESIVES

Probably the most frequently used bar codes in industrial and commercial environments are on pressure-sensitive labels. The typical pressure-sensitive label includes a paper face stock, an adhesive back, and a carrier, or release sheet. Pressure-sensitive labels come in all shapes and sizes, on many facing stocks (paper, vinyl, polyester, and mylar), in special die cuts and perforations, and with numerous adhesives. Asset tags may require a combination of stock and adhesive that makes the label permanent once it is applied, so that it is impossible to remove without destroying the label. The stock and adhesives may have to resist outside environments of varying temperatures, humidity, and other weather conditions.

The tire industry requires labels that can withstand the vulcanizing process. The primary metals industry requires a label that can be applied to an ingot or roll several hundred degrees in temperature, withstand various reheat processes, and resist weathering. Circuit boards are identified with bar coded labels that actually polymerize in the wave solder and cooling process to become a permanent part of the circuit board and then to resist various solvents and remain readable. The automobile industry needed an adhesive that could be applied and remain on an oily part. The blood industry required an adhesive for blood bags that would withstand freezing and thawing, as well as a label stock that was resistant to blood and urine.

Each environment has its own unique adhesive requirements. Most can be accommodated, once the environment in which the labels will be applied and used has been well defined. The environment in which the label must survive is an important consideration in the development of any bar code system that uses pressure-sensitive labels.

# CHAPTER 8
# LAMINATES

In applications that require the bar code symbol to be exposed to adverse environments, such as dirt, grease, temperature extremes, and weather, or if the symbol is going to be scanned at least 50 times, it should be protected with a transparent coating having a thickness of 10 mils or less. Suitable coating materials include clear plastic laminate, polypropylene film, matte acetate film, polyester film, and lacquer spray. A matte surface on the coating material is preferred to avoid the problems discussed in Chapter 4. If shiny coatings must be used, a degradation in symbol performance can be expected. One alternative to protective coatings is the use of vinyl or polyester media. Though more expensive than paper, these media offer very good durability plus a great tolerance to cleaning solutions.

A laminate is a thin, transparent film or mylar, polyester, vinyl, or other polymer substance, which is applied to label stock after the symbol is printed. Laminate stock generally comes in sheets or rolls and is typically 1 mil thick. The laminate is bonded to the printing surface by heat or pressure. Laminates can be applied to one side of a pressure-sensitive label or to both sides, as is the case for catalog order forms, identification badges, and menu cards.

Some preformed character impact printers and dot-matrix impact printers have laminating systems integrated within the printing device. Certain pressurized liquid lacquers have been used as label laminates with varying degrees of success. The application of a lacquer can distort the printed image. If the lacquer runs, the irregularities of the dried label can interfere with the symbol's scannability.

Protective laminates are often required in Department of Defense and GSA marking requirements. Laminates have also been found extremely useful in bar coded shelf tags for grocery, drug, and mass merchandise retailers. Preprinted labels, provided by a wide variety of commercial sources, are most generally laminated to increase the durability of the labels. In any application where durability is a factor, lamination of some sort deserves strong consideration.

## SECTION III

# BAR CODE PRINTING

The success of any bar code system requires close attention to the bar code reading equipment and the quality of the printed bar code. Bar codes can be printed in numerous ways. Each has its own unique benefits and limitations. The methods for printing bar codes can be broadly classified into three categories: commercial printing, methods for printing labels on-site and off-site, and demand printing.

As you consider the selection of a specific bar code printing technique, it is important to ensure a match between the reader and printed symbol. The nature of the bar code application and its relationship to the printing process should also be considered. Consideration should be given to whether the application requires numerous (hundreds to thousands) labels with the same information or whether only one or a few identical symbols are required. In defining the size of the bars and spaces within the symbol, you need to determine the number of characters to be encoded and where the bar code symbol will be applied. You need to consider the type of ink, whether the use of colored inks is anticipated, and the type and color of the stock onto which the bar code symbol will be printed. Finally, relative costs of the printing alternatives need to be carefully weighed. Keep these considerations in mind, as you read about the three alternatives for bar code printing.

# CHAPTER 9

# COMMERCIAL PRINTING

Commercial printing relates to various wet ink and other processes employed in creating numerous images of the same code. By reproducing the same symbol many times, economies of scale make this technique the least costly of any bar code printing method. Offsetting this economy, however, is the lack of flexibility if the mode must be changed. For a comparison of the various printing processes see Tables 10-1 and 11-2.

## Film Masters

The heart of many commercial printing techniques is the master image on the printing plate. This image must be extremely accurate. The plate production technique begins with a very precise film master of the bar code symbol. The accuracy of the film master must be controlled within a range of .2 mils to .5 mils. Depending upon the printing technique, the film master can be produced as either a film positive or negative and with the emulsion side up or down. The printed bars of the bar code can vary significantly from the bars on the film master. This variance is caused by any combination of factors, such as mold shrinkage, over- or under-etching of metal masters, amount of printing plate/substrate impression, and ink viscosity. Mold shrinkage and improper metal master etching can be controlled through a quality control program that checks the bar dimensions during plate production. Printing plate/substrate impression and ink viscosity are a result of the printing process. Dimensional variations can be controlled to provide fairly consistent printing. Normally the bars show a uniform increase in size with an associated uniform decrease in the size of the intervening spaces. The approximate increase in bar width size, or print gain, can be established for each printing press operation.

Since the print gain for a specific press can be established, the film master manufacturer can reduce the size of the bars on the film master to compensate for the bar gain during printing. This amount, called bar width reduction (BWR), should be determined for each printing press, with specific attention given to BWR when producing bar codes with an X dimension approaching the minimum for a particular printing process. The amount of BWR is a function of many variables, including printing technique, printing press, printing plate material, ink viscosity, substrate, printing impression, and press operation. It is impossible to recommend a standard Bar Width Reduction due to the number of influencing factors. A controlled bar code printing program is required to establish BWR for a given printing operation.[10]

## Flexography

Flexography is used most often for rotary tag and label presses. It is an inexpensive and simple printing process heavily used in decorative and packaging printing. Flexography employs a flexible rubber or photopolymer plate onto which the image has been etched in relief. These plates wrap around a cylinder and squeeze the paper against a rubber impression roller, as shown in Figure 9-1, to produce the printed image.

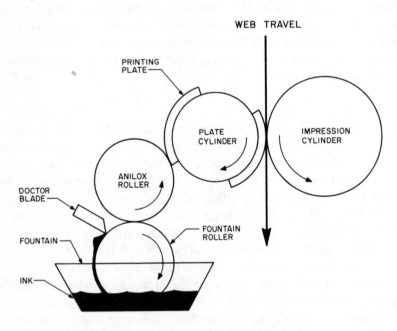

**Figure 9-1. Flexographic press operation**

With flexography (sometimes shortened to "flexo"), the tradeoff is between versatility of substrate selection and print quality. Since rubber plates distort and compress, it is necessary to employ special techniques to allow for stretch and shrinkage of the rubber during printing to assure a faithful reproduction. On the other hand, the flexographic process is very versatile and well established as a method of printing for business forms, labels, tags, folding cartons, and corrugated boxes, as well as foils and the various cellulosic and plastic films.

The flexographic press permits maximum widths to range between 6 inches and 16 inches. Each printing plate can vary in size and be mounted with a matching die-cutting cylinder. Such flexibility permits length, width, and shape of the labels to vary greatly.[11]

## Offset Lithography

Offset lithography, commonly called offset, has rapidly become the most important of the commercial printing processes. Offset's primary advantage is its ability to produce a clear image on a number of materials, no matter how rough or smooth the surface.

Offset is basically a chemically controlled printing process, where the image and non-image areas are etched on the surface of a thin metal plate. To do this requires a special plate preparation process, whereby the printing image is made oil receptive and water repellent, while the non-image areas are water receptive and oil repellent. Inks employed in offset lithography are oil based. The plate is wrapped around a pickup (or dampening) roller for wetting and cleaning. The ink is picked up by the image areas of the plate, and the image is printed on an intermediate image carrier (blanket cylinder). The paper, passing between the blanket cylinder and a pressure (or impression) cylinder, picks up the image, as illustrated in Figure 9-2.

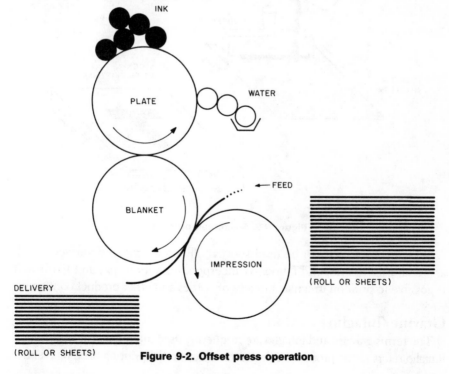

**Figure 9-2. Offset press operation**

The term "lithography" refers to the process of printing with the oil receptive/water repellent image; the term "offset" refers to the two-step printing process of plate-to-blanket and blanket-to-paper. Technically, the offset principle can be used with all commercial printing processes, but its near exclusive usage in combination with lithography has made the terms "offset" and "offset lithography" synonymous.

For bar code printing, the significance of offset is its widespread use on presses of all sizes, speeds, and configurations (sheet fed and rotary web), and its ability to produce fixed codes of the highest quality and density. It would be difficult to imagine a business form that could not be produced efficiently, in whole or in part, on some offset press somewhere.[11]

## Silkscreen Printing

The screenprinting process consists of forcing ink through a porous stenciled screen, usually consisting of mylar, dacron, or stainless steel. The screens are photographically reproduced, so that the image areas are porous and the nonimage areas are nonporous. In its simplest form, a paste-like ink is forced through the screen onto the substrate by a rubber squeegee, as illustrated in Figure 9-3.

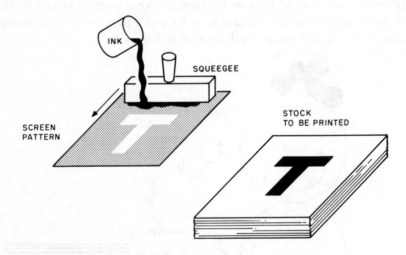

**Figure 9-3. Silkscreen printing**

Silkscreen printing can be used successfully on a variety of surfaces, such as wood, glass, plates, and fabric. By incorporating various jigs and fixtures, it is possible to print on irregular surfaces of bottles and other product containers.

## Gravure/Intaglio

The terms gravure and intaglio are frequently used interchangeably, although intaglio refers to the process, while gravure refers to the printing press or cylinder on which the image created by the intaglio resides. A gravure press can be either sheet fed or web (rotogravure). The rotogravure printing station consists of an ink fountain, an etched cylinder partially submerged in ink, a doctor blade for maintaining film thickness, and an impression cylinder for controlling impressions and supporting the substrate. An illustration of the gravure press operation is shown in Figure 9-4.

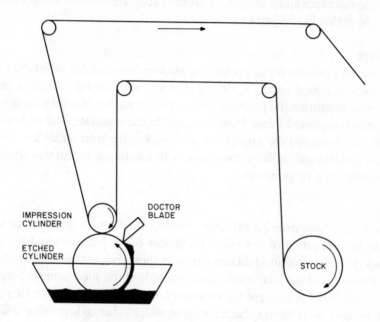

**Figure 9-4. Principle of the gravure press**

The printing plate or cylinder for gravure printing has the image to be printed etched below the surface, forming an array of microscopic cells. The ink used for this process is very fluid and flows into the cells when rolled over the plate. The surface of the plate, which is the nonprinting area, is wiped clean of ink by a doctor blade before the paper is brought into contact. When the paper comes into contact with the printing plate, the cells dump their contents, forming the printed image.

While intaglio/gravure is used in such diverse applications as the printing of packaging materials, as well as currency and stock and bond certificates, the process yields a bar code of lower quality than those produced using flexo and offset printing presses. The lower quality is due to the cell pattern, which creates fine toothlike edges on the bars.[12]

## Letterpress

Letterpress is the original method of printing with type. It is still used by commercial printers and business forms manufacturers. The process employs metal, rubber, and photopolymer plates with the image surfaces raised. The process differs from flexographic printing basically because paste inks are used, as opposed to the fast-drying liquid inks used in flexo. The letterpress printing station consists of inking rollers which transfer the ink to the printing plate, a plate cylinder for mounting the printing plate, and an impression cylinder for controlling impressions and supporting the substrate.[10] Letterpress is used in rotary numbering machines and is capable of printing accurate bar code images if care is taken to maintain the printing equipment.

## Letterset

The letterset process utilizes rubber or photopolymer plates with raised image surfaces. A typical letterset printing station consists of inking rollers, plate cylinders for mounting the printing plate, an offset rubber blanket cylinder for transferring the printed image from the plate to the substrate, and an impression cylinder to control the impression and support the substrate.[10] The printing stocks and inks are similar to those used with letterpress, except that stronger ink pigments may be required.

Each of the above printing processes involves the transfer of an image to a substrate by application of wet ink. Film master–based processes and set-type processes are well suited in situations requiring thousands of copies of the same image. Product package labeling is a good example of the success of such printing processes in the printing of bar code symbols. All of the above printing processes have another common characteristic as well; the bar code printing is done off-site, away from the location where the symbol is used or applied. But wet ink/film master systems share off-site printing with other technologies as well.

## Hot Stamping

Hot stamping uses a dry carbon ribbon with a predetermined ink thickness, thus eliminating certain wet ink problems. Closely akin to letterpress, a separate metal plate is required for every legend desired. As these plates are etched from photographic film masters, they are very accurate. Bar widths having an X dimension of 10 mils are possible with consistent quality. Print quality is superb and the scan rate is high. Hot stamping, however, is expensive relative to other printing methods. It is used mainly for high quality multicolor labels. The hot stamp technique is illustrated in Figure 9-5.

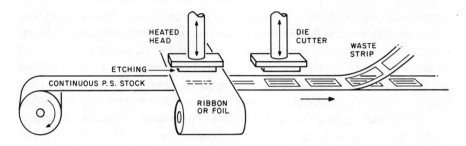

**HOT STAMP TECHNIQUE**

HEATED HEAD

DIE CUTTER

WASTE STRIP

ETCHING

CONTINUOUS P.S. STOCK

RIBBON OR FOIL

**Figure 9-5. Hot Stamp Technique**

## Rotary Numbering

Applications such as business forms often require sequential numbering. The printing of sequentially numbered business forms with the number represented in human-readable and bar code form was pioneered by Graphic Systems. Rotary numbering is also done by preprinted label manufacturers. Federal Express air-bills, for example, consist of multipart forms printed on a rotary web press. The press has a mechanical numbering tower that prints the number in bar code (Codabar) and human-readable form. Previous to the Federal Express system, numbering towers had been used only to print sequentially numbered human-readable characters.

The numbering wheels within the tower have the engraved images of the bar code/human-readable characters and are advanced in sequence to the next number after the entire symbol is printed. The actuating mechanism, or pawl, in the numbering machine is located between the character engravings. This arrangement requires a bar code symbology that is discrete. The mechanical numbering wheels also generate a check digit that changes and is printed with each 11-digit code. The airbill is a five-part form with interleaved patterned carbons. Each part is printed separately and collated at the end of the print run. With each part bar coded, extreme care is exercised to ensure that when the form is collated, all parts have been printed with the same bar code symbol. A rigorous quality control program by both the printer and the customer currently realizes an accuracy rate of 99.9999997 percent over the hundreds of millions of airbills produced. Federal's use of infrared scanners requires the use of ink with a high carbon content to achieve such an accuracy rate. And while the high-carbon inks provide excellent readability, their carbon content wears down the numbering wheels more quickly than if noncarbon inks are used, and consequently the wheels require periodic replacement. The artisan skill required in the engraving of the numbering wheels causes the replacement costs to be moderately high.

## Photocomposition Printing

Bar codes created by photocomposition come as labels and film masters that are produced on specialized phototypesetting equipment. Such equipment uses a photographic process that exposes characters on photographic film or paper. Character sets are stored electronically as digital, or bit, patterns. Composed images are drawn in raster fashion on a CRT. The image passes through a lens and is projected onto the photographic medium. These phototypesetters have several characteristics that make them ideally suited for producing bar codes. The first is high output speed. Most CRT typesetters are capable of setting a full page of type in just a few seconds. Second, they can contract or expand bar code elements, in increments as fine as 1/7200ths of an inch. Bar width can be easily adjusted, matching the film master image created to the press, ink, and substrate being used. Thus, phototypesetters are widely employed to produce bar code film masters for offset printing, flexo printing on corrugated containers, and finished labels on photographic paper.

To produce labels on photographic paper, the individual labels are exposed on photographic paper, which is chemically processed to develop and fix the images. Next, the back of the paper is coated with an adhesive. A waxed backing sheet is attached, and the paper is die-cut into individual, adhesive-backed labels. For heavy usage and hostile environments, various types of transparent polymer laminates can be applied on top of the label to provide greater durability.

Most CRT typesetters produce character images at resolutions of between 800 and 3600 lines per inch. This degree of precision is sufficient for all existing bar code symbologies. CRT typesetters are naturally suited for computer-controlled production. The resultant labels may contain data taken from a computer tape supplied by the customer, or the encoded information may consist of sequential numbers created by a computer program. Typically, the user can specify the starting number and the amount by which to increment the count. Any check character can also be generated under computer control.

Photocomposed labels offer a unique combination of advantages. The first is quality. With the high print resolution common to these devices, they can produce labels with a precision and clarity available from few other printing technologies. Miniaturization of the label is an important secondary benefit of high print resolution. Photocomposed high density bar codes can fit on extremely small labels.

The second advantage of photocomposition is durability. The photo development process creates an image that is resistant to moisture, chemical change, abrasion, or temperature variations. The third benefit is flexibility. Label adhesives, protective laminations, and packaging of the finished product can be customized for special label applications to maximize utility, durability, and ease of use. The fourth advantage is the computer variability available with any technology that combines computer-compatible input with a high-resolution digital output.[11,12]

Photocomposed labels and labels generated with rotary numbering wheels have both found wide usage in applications such as library systems, fixed asset accounting, circuit board identification, and blood product labeling, with both capable of printing on many substrate compositions, including paper and polymer stocks. Photocomposition has three advantages over rotary numbering wheels. The first is that numbering wheels are mechanical and cannot easily print nonsequential or nonstatic numbers. Computer-generated photocomposition permits printing of random information constrained only by the software of the computer. Second, the mechanical process is limited in its ability to generate certain check characters. Third, since advancement of the numbering machine is accomplished by an actuating pawl located between the character numbering wheels, the thickness of the pawl and its positioning dictates the size of the gap between characters. As an example, Code 39 can be printed at 9.4 characters per inch with an X dimension of 7.5 mils. Using a rotary numbering machine, the X dimension may still be 7.5 mils, but the character density would be diminished to 8.3 characters per inch, or lower, due to the expanded size of the intercharacter gap. Many applications do not require randomized numbering, nor do they require complicated check character computations. The same applications may operate just as well at 8.3 characters per inch as they would at 9.4. Consequently, in many applications, photocomposition and rotary numbering techniques are both viable alternatives for the customer needing high quality bar coded labels from commercial sources.

## Laser Etching

In some applications, a bar coded tag needs to be created that will be attached to a bin, shelving, or raw material metal stock. This tag may identify only the bin location, or it can also identify what product is contained within that location. A bar coded tag can be attached to an ingot, bar, or coil of aluminum, steel, or copper. The metal may be too hot to apply an adhesive label, or it may be subsequently reheated to a point where traditional label stock would burn off or melt. In such applications, laser-etched bar coded tags provide a good solution.

Laser etching actually describes one of two techniques of printing a bar code onto metal. The first technique uses a high power ($CO_2$ or Nd:YAG) laser that actually etches the bar code and human-readable information into the material. The second system uses a lower power (Nd:YAG or a mixture of helium and other gases) laser that burns off the top coating of tag stock, allowing the substrate to show through. The print speed is quite high, but the print area is relatively small (typically less than three inches). Laser etching on metal can provide a narrow element width of from 4 to 80 mils. Most code densities, therefore, can be printed using this technique.

Direct etching on the material to be identified may provide a print contrast that is not sufficient for some bar code reading equipment. Systems which burn off a top coating, on the other hand, have the ability to coat a white substrate with black. The coating that is burned off corresponds with the spaces of the bar code and the remaining coating corresponds with the bars. Laser etch systems yield a very acceptable print contrast that is adequate for most bar code reading equipment. Laser etch systems are expensive and are generally owned by companies providing pre-etched tags to the end-user. Once the tag is etched, however, it is virtually indestructible.

## Off-site Advantages

By selecting an external source for bar code printing, several distinct advantages exist over having the labels printed on-site. Listed below are some of these advantages, some of which apply more to one process than another.

*Print Direct.* In some cases, notably containers and metal cans, the printer can print the bar code directly on the surface of the container. This eliminates the cost of printing and applying labels. By incorporating the bar code printing in the press run, the printer can accurately position the bar code on the container.

*High Volume.* This is where off-site printing techniques really stand out. Some printing processes can print labels at speeds of 1000 feet per minute. In those instances where a large quantity of bar codes must be printed, there can be substantial savings in the cost per label because of the efficiency of the systems.

*Expertise.* Some printers began printing bar code symbols on packaging 10 years ago. Since that time, they have acquired considerable expertise in bar code printing, enabling them to assist their clients in selecting proper substrates, ink colors, and bar code dimensions to comply with the various standards.

*Graphics.* The off-site printer can print additional graphics and color combinations to provide the aesthetic appeal required in some label and direct printing applications. Some presses allow printing of up to eight different colors.

*Responsibility.* The control and responsibility for complying with standards and producing scannable bar codes can be centralized. Vendors can be selected, based upon their expertise in producing bar codes and their familiarity with quality assurance requirements of a particular standard.

*Quality.* The nature of the technology employed in many of the off-site printing processes produces bar codes of very high quality.

*Size.* Image areas of up to 30 by 50 inches are available on some presses for printing additional information and graphics.[10]

# CHAPTER 10

# BRIDGING THE GAP BETWEEN OFF-SITE AND ON-SITE PRINTING

Certain printing techniques can be used both on-site and off-site because of their high speed and relatively low cost. These techniques are electrostatic and ink jet printing.

## Electrostatic Printing

Electrostatic printing techniques change the composition of the image area on the label to be printed or a dielectric cylinder which holds a latent image until the image is transferred to the label. Following that change in composition, the label progresses to a toner station, where the image area attracts a dark dry toner forming the desired image. The label then proceeds to a station that fixes the toner, providing a permanent bar code symbol on the label. Non-impact electrostatic printers can be broadly classified into two categories, namely, electrophotographical and electrographical.

*Electrophotographical (Laser Printing).* Electrophotographical (EPG) printing is most familiar in copying and reproducing machines as opposed to data output printers. Exceptions are the computer-based printers which have the ability to print data as well as forms at the same time; for the printing of these forms would use face-character non-impact printing techniques, rather imprecisely referred to as the "xerographic process."

In contradistinction to face-character processes, most computer non-impact printers employ a dot-matrix character formation. In EPG printing techniques, a latent image is created by making use of the photoelectric characteristics of the materials being used. A typical EPG system might employ a Helium-Neon (He-Ne) laser whose circuitry permits the He-Ne to be pulsed under the control of resident software. The pattern of laser on/off signals corresponds to the information to be printed. The laser beam causes an electrostatic image consisting of charged and uncharged areas to be formed on the surface of a cylindrical drum. A toner consisting of small, black, electrically charged particles is brought near the surface of the drum, and the toner particles adhere by electrostatic attraction to the charged areas of the drum image. Next the media is brought near the drum and a charge is applied to the back of the media to attract toner particles away from the drum and onto the media. The media is moved to a heater station to fix the toner permanently to the media. The final step of the process restores the drum to its original condition. The laser spot is focused to approximately 5 mils (some systems currently focusing to 3 mils), generating a print spot of 5.5 mils in diameter. EPG systems, such as that illustrated in Figure 10-1, can print at 45 pages per minute on plain, letter-sized paper and can place high-quality images anywhere on the page.[13]

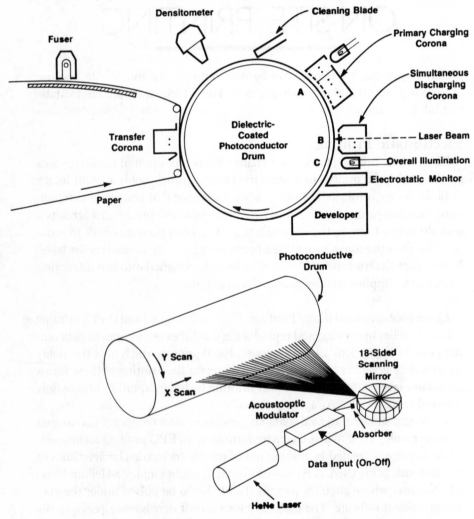

**Figure 10-1. Electrophotographic (Laser) printing technique**

*Electrographical.* In electrographical techniques, the latent character or graphical image is formed by transferring, directly, the electric charge from the writing elements, commonly a linear or matrix array of scanning styli onto the dielectric coating of the recording paper medium or onto a dielectric coated cylinder. One such ion-deposition electrographical device is capable of printing bar codes and other information on substrates such as paper, vinyl, polyester, and tags at speeds of 30 inches per second. The ion-deposition printing station consists of a microprocessor for storing and generating the images, a matrix addressable print head for forming the dot matrix characters and bar codes, and a dielectric cylinder for developing and transferring the toner image to the substrate. The ion-deposition printing station is commonly situated between the feeder section and the first printing station of a four color printing press. This combines the flexibility of microprocessor image development with the graphics, additional colors, lacquering, and die cutting capabilities of the printing press. The system can sequentially number (increment and decrement) human-readable characters and bar codes. The system can print both discrete and continuous bar codes with a minimum "X" dimension of 8 mils.

A similar technique of magnetic or magnetographic printers uses magnetic tape recording technology or writes magnetic images that attract toner, which is then transferred to the substrate to produce the printed image.[10,11]

## Ink Jet Printing

Ink jet printing describes a family of noncontact printing technologies. These technologies are based on the concept of projecting drops of ink at a printing surface and controlling these drops electronically. Ink jet printing has several salient features that render it attractive to the user of automated identification systems. It is noncontact and nonimpact, permitting it to print on contoured, rough, and delicate surfaces of all kinds. It is versatile. Devices can be configured and inks have been developed that can print on bottles, cans, cartons, forms and labels, individual documents, and continuous forms. Ink jet is suitable for high performance requirements, achieving speeds of 100,000 lines of text per minute. And since it is an electronic process, it can be a computer-driven process, offering the ability to print sequential or random information.[11]

In continuous-stream systems, drops are produced in rapid succession from a single nozzle and are either deposited on the paper or deflected away from it and reused, as illustrated in Figure 10-2. Continuous-stream droplet frequency is determined by the stream velocity and the nozzle diameter. A piezoelectric element resonates at a constant frequency to stabilize the drop stream, which passes through a charging electrode and then through a constant electrostatic deflection field. The initial charge level acquired by each droplet determines its deflection and consequent position on the paper or causes it to be deflected into a gutter. In printing an average page of text, only about two percent of the ink hits the paper, and the remaining 98 percent must be caught, filtered, degassed, pressurized, and recirculated through the system.

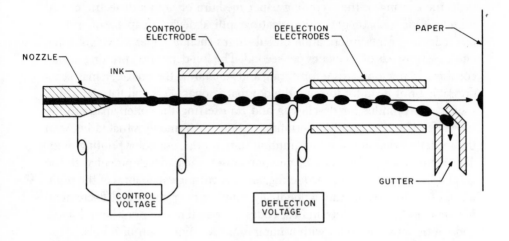

**Figure 10-2. Continuous ink jet**

In drop-on-demand systems, as illustrated in Figure 10-3, an array of nozzles is used in the same manner as the styli in dot-matrix impact printers. Individual nozzles are actuated by piezoelectric element impulses, and drops are produced only when required. As a result, there is no need for a recirculating system.[16]

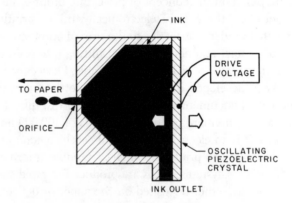

**Figure 10-3. Drop-on-demand ink jet**

Ink jet labels and forms offer a wide range of typefaces and sizes, including an assortment of bar code and OCR fonts. It should be possible to make a selection for virtually any application that will optimize read rates as well as user convenience. In label and forms applications, information typically is printed in small descriptive text, jumbo alphanumerics, and bar codes. This provides the necessary redundancy and assures maximum ease of readability by both human and machine. Computer-controlled printing allows the choice of any sequential or check digit scheme imaginable. In many applications, part numbers and other nonsequential variable parameters are changed "on-the-fly," in conjunction with a selected serial numbering scheme.

Continuous-stream ink jet systems are among the fastest printing devices available. They are frequently used with high speed offset presses. Multiple array systems are capable of producing documents at speeds exceeding 800 feet per minute.[11]

Drop-on-demand ink jet printers are not adapted for use with printing presses. They are designed to print medium and low density bar code symbols at speeds of 250 feet per minute or higher. These systems can create taller bar codes by moving the nozzle away from the printing surface, creating a larger dot size and decreasing the density of the printed symbol. The nozzles can be ganged together to increase bar code height, while not decreasing the density of the bar code symbol. When the heads are ganged together, close attention must be paid to the registration of the heads, so that a uniformly straight bar is produced. Ink jet systems, and particularly continuous jet systems, are gaining in popularity for bar code printing. While the initial investment in these systems may be higher than those that print on label stock, ink jet printing permits application of bar code symbols to product packaging. Direct bar code application eliminates the expense of label stock and applicators, providing an ongoing savings over the systems that print on label stock. Table 10-1 shows a comparison of commercial bar code printing techniques.

**Table 10-1**

**Comparison of commercial bar code printing techniques**

| Characteristic/Technique | Offset lithography | Flexography | Silkscreen | Letterpress | Hot stamp |
|---|---|---|---|---|---|
| Typical substrates | Labels Paper Vinyl Polyester Metal Glass Tags | Labels Paper Vinyl Polyester Corrugated Tags | Plastic Bottles Metal Tags | Labels Paper Vinyl Metal Tags | Labels Paper Vinyl Polyester Foils Tags |
| Variable information | ——With rotary numbering wheel machines (RNWM) or other in-line devices—— | | | | No |
| Special requirements for printed bar codes variable content | ——Symbology must have discrete structure (RNWM) Other in-line devices discrete or continuous—— | | | | N/A |
| Smallest X dimension | 7.5 mils RNWM—6.5 | 7.5 mils RNWM—6.5 | 13 mils RNWM—6.5 | 6.5 mils | 10 mils and smaller |
| Graphics/color capability (stand-alone systems) | Yes | Yes | Yes | Yes | Yes |
| Production speed | High | High | Low | Medium | Medium |
| Special requirements | Printing plate | ——Film master or in-line device—— Printing plate | Screen | Printing plate | Film Master Printing plate |

| Characteristic/Technique | Ink jet | Photo-composition | Laser etch | Rotary numbering | Electrostatic |
|---|---|---|---|---|---|
| Typical substrates | Labels Paper Vinyl Polyester Metal Glass Tags | Photosensitive Label stock Paper Vinyl Metal Tags | Metal Coated metal | Labels Paper Vinyl Polyester Tags | Paper Plastics |
| Variable information | Yes | Yes | No | Yes | Yes |
| Special requirements for printed bar codes variable content | None | None | N/A | Discrete Codes | None |
| Smallest X dimension | 13 mils | 6.5 mils and smaller | 6.5 mils and smaller | 6.5 mils | 6.5 mils and smaller |
| Graphics/color capability (stand-alone systems) | Yes | Graphics—Yes Color—No | No | No | No |
| Production speed | High | Medium | High | High | Medium |
| Special requirements | None | None | None | None | None |

# CHAPTER 11
# DEMAND PRINTING

Commercial printing techniques are satisfactory if the bar code user knows in advance what information is to be printed. When a grocery manufacturer packages a product, a predetermined code is printed on the packaging that identifies the manufacturer and the product. Since many thousands of the same item are manufactured, a printing technique that employs film masters, printing plates, and high speed presses is the most cost-effective. Likewise, a business forms manufacturer needs to number printed forms sequentially. Here, printing plates for the graphics and numbering machines or other in-line devices for the sequentially bar coded numbers are the most cost-effective means of printing long runs of such business forms.

A manufacturer may wish to provide bar coded order books for clients or salespersons. A user may wish to label shelves that contain inventory. The content of the bar code symbols in these cases are known in advance. No variable information is required. Commercial printing techniques are again the most cost-effective means to produce these bar codes.

It may not always be possible to predefine what codes are needed. Even if such definition is possible, it may be too labor-intensive to maintain an inventory of the desired labels. Industrial applications often require random information, such as lot numbers, weight, shift, operator, or production time. Labels are frequently unique, prohibiting their purchase ahead of time. These labels must be produced on-site and in real time. Such unique labels can be produced using demand printers. These printers operate under microprocessor control and can create unique labels as they are needed.

Demand printing systems use one of three methods: character-by-character impact, bar-by-bar, or dot-matrix technologies. This categorization is shown in Table 11-1.

**Table 11-1**
**On-site printing techniques**

Character-by-character impact printers
    Drum printers
    Typewriter element printers
    Rotary encoders
    Chain printers
    Belt printers

Bar-by-bar printers
    Drum impact
    Thermal transfer
    Thermal

Dot-matrix character formation
    Impact
    Thermal transfer
    Ink jet
    Electrostatic
    Thermal

Ink jet and electrostatic printers were discussed in detail in Chapter 10. Bar-by-bar printers can be categorized as either drum or thermal. Consequently, in this chapter we will examine character-by-character and bar-by-bar drum printers, typewriter element printers, rotary encoders, thermal printers, dot-matrix impact printers, and thermal transfer printing systems.

## Drum Printers

Character-by-character drum printers work much like standard office typewriters and generally print high density, discrete bar codes. The characters are etched or engraved in reverse on a drum. Paper, vinyl, or mylar label stock and a dry carbon ribbon pass between the rotating drum and a hammer. Operated by an electromagnet, the hammer forces the paper and ribbon against the drum, causing the image to be transferred from the ribbon to the label. Each hammer stroke forms a complete character.

Around the base of the drum are timing marks counted by an LED/photo-eye unit. When the count is equal to that associated with the correct character, the microprocessor causes the hammer to strike the label and ribbon against the drum. The drum rotates continually at about 500 revolutions per minute, and the hammer operates at 17,000 times per minute, so there is virtually no relative motion between the hammer and drum.

The machine is considered to be a dedicated bar code printer, and label format is limited to the symbols engraved on the drum. One to ten lines of human-readable text may be provided, but the basic purpose of the machine is to provide a bar code symbol. However, various fields within the format can be changed randomly, allowing each label to be different.

Character-by-character printers use label stock which comes in rolls. The stock is either die-cut to size or continuous, in which case it is cut after printing. Paper, vinyl, and polyester stock is available in either plain or preprinted form. It can be backed by an adhesive that meets the particular application need.

Character-by-character impact printing uses a one-time high quality carbon-based printing ribbon, providing instant dry smear-resistant prints. Typical narrow bar widths are about 7 thousandths of an inch. Production speed depends on label length and content. Typically 40 to 60 labels per minute can be produced. Accessories are available to laminate, butt cut, cut off, stack, rewind, and apply the labels. The size of the printer is small enough so that it can be used almost anywhere.[14]

Bar-by-bar printers operate in a manner that is very similar to the character-by-character drum printers, except that each bar, wide or narrow, is printed with the strike of a single hammer, and the sequence of wide or narrow bars/spaces is determined through programming. This process enables the printing of discrete or continuous bar codes. Bar-by-bar drum printers are generally used for medium to low density bar codes.[4]

Character-by-character and bar-by-bar drum printers have a specific engraved format on the drums provided by the bar code printer manufacturer. Consequently, to change the format (the number of human-readable lines of text) or the symbology requires a separate drum.

## Typewriter Element Printers

A second type of formed character impact printer employs a basic typewriter whose characters are formed by means of a type ball or daisy-wheel element. The bar code and human-readable characters are formed on the type element in a reverse image. The image is formed on the substrate by pressing the typewriter key associated with the character desired, causing the element to strike either a carbon-based or cloth-inked ribbon, forming the desired character. Limitations of typewriter element systems include the height of the character to be formed, single densities of the code (approximately 10 characters per inch), and restrictions to only discrete bar codes, such as Code 39 and Codabar. The limitation of character height renders such systems unable to print codes requiring a specific aspect ratio (the ratio of the code height to the code length). Some specifications require a character height of, minimally, 0.025 inch; a requirement difficult to achieve with typewriter element printers. Still other standards recommend a height no smaller than 15% to 25% of the bar code length, e.g., 0.30 inch for a 2-inch-long code, 0.45 inch for a 3-inch long code, etc., further taxing the capabilities of typewriter element printers. Their principal advantage is the minimal investment required to print the bar code, although sometimes it is at the expense of the ease of reading that code, due to the lack of height necessary to accommodate human-assisted scanning.

# Rotary Encoders

One of the older methods of placing variable human-readable information on packaging is the rotary encoder. The process involves movable type that is locked onto a marking wheel. This method of printing has recently been used to print discrete bar codes. The marking wheel containing the bar code symbols is inked. A spring maintains pressure between the wheel and the substrate to be printed. The wheel rotates as the substrate is moved under the wheel, and the bar code image is printed on the substrate. The major advantage of this printing method is its low cost.

This method is particularly useful for printing lot and batch numbers in bar code on corrugated containers. The principal disadvantage of rotary encoders is the mess involved to change the type, because the type contains wet ink after being used. Companies that already employ this method to print human-readable information can easily add bar code printing. Movable-type rotary encoders are restricted to discrete bar codes, such as Code 39, and can generally only achieve a bar resolution of 40 thousandths of an inch, though efforts are underway to improve this resolution.

# Thermal Printers

Thermal printers use heated print heads and special heat activated paper.[15] Two types of thermal printers are available. One employs a print head similar in design to those on dot-matrix impact printers. The print head consists of rectangular or round styli that are selectively heated and cooled under microprocessor control. The heated styli cause chemicals in the paper to turn brown or black or to burn a top coating off. The dot-matrix pattern can vary from a 5 by 7 to 16 by 20 array and is selectable by CRT or computer input.[14] The second variety of thermal printer employs a single bar, much in the way bar-by-bar drum printers operate. Instead of striking an inked ribbon, the bar is heated and cooled as the paper stock moves across the head. This creates the wide and narrow bars which form the bar code symbol.

There are few moving parts in thermal printers, so the printers are inexpensive, quiet, and ideally suited to environments such as libraries and hospitals. Production speed is 10 to 60 labels per minute.[15] The matrix and bar-by-bar character formation permit these printing systems to compose either discrete or continuous bar code symbols. Thermal printers can produce medium and low density bar code symbols with human-readable data in varying sizes. The minimum element size is approximately 4.5 mils. Edge definition of bars is superior to either dot-matrix or formed character impact printing.[14]

Thermal printers have two disadvantages. First, since the label stock is heat-sensitive, label quality may deteriorate over time if the labels are stored in a warm environment. Second, most thermal labels do not present adequate contrast when using light in the B900 band. Since scanning systems use light in either the B633 band or in the B900 band, the labels may not read reliably. The user must ensure that when thermal labels are used, only visible red light scanners are employed. New printing stocks have been developed for thermal printing to achieve adequate contrast in the infrared spectrum. These stocks are the exception, not the rule, in thermal printing.

## Dot-Matrix Impact Printers

Of all the types of printers employed in industry, the most common is the serial dot-matrix printer. The popularity of dot-matrix printing is due to its ability to produce both text and graphics in varying sizes on many types of printing stock. Drum printers are quite acceptable for printing labels up to a certain size, but they do not possess the text and graphics capabilities of dot-matrix systems. Typewriter element systems are considerably constrained in terms of their ability to provide multiple font styles and sizes automatically and are unable to print bar codes in varying heights. Rotary encoders print bar codes only in specialized types of applications. On the other hand, dot-matrix systems provide great flexibility in their ability to print both bar coded labels and forms at low to moderate costs. Table 11-2 compares on-site bar code printing methods.

A dot-matrix print element consists of a series of pins arranged in an array. On some printers the print head is fixed and the label stock moves. Other systems use a moving print head and stationary stock. The pins strike an inked ribbon against the label stock to form the desired characters. The pins are typically 10 mils or larger in diameter. When these pins strike an inked nylon ribbon, the thickness of the ribbon and bleeding of the ink can cause a wire of 14 mils to create a dot that is about 18 mils in diameter. Recently introduced dot-matrix impact printing systems have substantially reduced the size of dot produced, permitting the creation of 14 mil to 15 mil dots and consequently higher density bar codes.

A narrow bar in a bar code is created by printing a set of overlapping dots, and a wide bar is produced by printing a series of overlapping narrow bars. Overlapping can occur either by single vertical half-space form movement or by multipass printing, or a combination of both. The use of overlapping dots results in bar edges that are not as well defined as those edges of bar codes printed by formed character printers. By reducing the size of the dot and using the overlapping technique, edge distortion is minimized. An example of dot-matrix overlap character formation is shown in Figure 11-1.

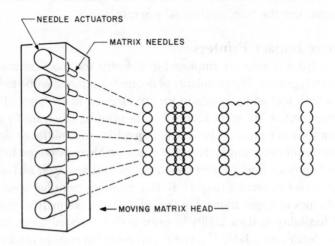

**Figure 11-1. Dot-matrix character formation**

Not all dot-matrix printers have the capability to produce bar codes. Only those printers having graphics capabilities are suited for bar code generation. Many dot-matrix printers that do not have the capability can be equipped with special graphics controller cards to effect bar code and other graphics generation. Dot-matrix printers are able to print documents, sheets of labels, and multipart forms. Typical substrates for dot-matrix impact printers include paper, vinyl, and polyester. At least one manufacturer has printed bar codes on a thin metal substrate using a dot-matrix printer.

## Thermal-transfer Printing Systems

Thermal-transfer printing systems are a combination of dot matrix thermal printing and hot stamp printing technologies. The basic difference between thermal printing and thermal-transfer is that thermal printing employs heat sensitive label stock while thermal-transfer employs a heat sensitive "ribbon." Further, thermal printing requires a specific chemically treated label stock, while thermal-transfer can be employed on virtually any substrate.

In thermal-transfer printing systems a very small stylus, or print wire, is brought in contact with a film ribbon, similar in design to carbon paper. The film can be either sheet fed or resident on a continuous roll. As with thermal printing, the styli are selectively heated and cooled under microprocessor control. The styli are then brought in contact with the film ribbon, which transfers the dot-matrix image to the substrate.

Thermal-transfer can achieve a very fine line of 5 mils and smaller. By combining these lines it is possible to print bar code symbols in their highest densities. The edge definition is crisp and once the image is generated, it is permanent on the label stock. Thermal-transfer is quiet and well-suited for office and hospital environments. The ribbons will not transfer their image without application of heat and consequently will not transfer to the fingers of those coming in contact with the ribbon as is the case with inked ribbons, carbon paper, and electrostatic toner. The styli are under computer control which permits batch, sequential, or random symbol generation.

## Near-term Trends in Demand Bar Code Printing Systems

The two most promising technologies for demand bar code printing are those of thermal-transfer and electrostatic printing systems. Thermal-transfer represents the moderate speed/price alternative while electrostatic will most probably serve the higher speed/price market needs. These two technologies represent the coming generation of bar code printing.

**Table 11-2**

**Comparison of on-site bar code printing techniques**

| Characteristic/technique | Drum printers | Typewriter printers | Rotary encoders | Thermal printers | Dot-matrix impact printers | Thermal-transfer |
|---|---|---|---|---|---|---|
| Typical substrates | Labels Paper Vinyl Polyester | Labels Paper Forms | Corrugated | Labels Heat-sensitive | Labels Paper Vinyl Polyester Forms Metal Tags | Labels Paper Vinyl Polyester Forms Metal Tags |
| Smallest X dimension | 6.5 mils | 7.5 mils | 40 mils | 4.5-10 mils | 7.5-20 mils* | 5-7 mils |
| Graphics capability (other than bar code) | No | No | No | Possible | Yes | Yes |
| Scannable—B633 to B720 | Yes | Yes | Yes | Yes | Yes | Yes |
| Scannable—B900 | Yes | Yes | No | Possible | Yes/no** | Yes |
| Ability to print pages or labels | No | Yes | No | No | Yes | Yes |
| Unlimited format flexibility | No | No | No | Yes/No*** | Yes | Yes |
| Dispense one label | Yes | No | N/A | Yes | Some | Some |

| Characteristic/ technique | Drum printers | Typewriter printers | Rotary encoders | Thermal printers | Dot-matrix Impact printers | Thermal-transfer |
|---|---|---|---|---|---|---|
| Print speed/ minute | 40–100 | 1–5 | Up to 80 | 10–18 | 30–50 | 30 and higher |
| Volume | Medium | Low | Medium | Low | Medium/Low | Medium/High |
| Flexibility | Low | Low | Low | Low | High | High |
| Resolution | High | High | Low | High | Medium/High | High |
| Cost of printer | Medium | Low | Low | Low | Medium | Medium |
| Relative label/ image cost | Low | Low | Low | Medium | Low/Medium | Medium/Low |

\* Dot-matrix impact printers can achieve 10 mil resolution on the highest density printers available. Standard density is around 18 mils. When printing on metal, 20 mils is the highest resolution yet achieved.

\*\* Acceptability of dot-matrix printers in the B900 band is a function of the type of ribbon employed. Cloth ribbons can achieve adequate contrast only in the B633 band. If the printer is equipped with an OCR quality ribbon, having a high carbon content, adequate contrast exists in both B633 and B900.

\*\*\*Note—"Unlimited format flexibility implies dot-addressable graphics. Thermal printers having such graphics have that flexibility; however, bar-by-bar thermal printers limit this flexibility."

# SECTION IV

# BAR CODE READING EQUIPMENT

Bar code readers, or scanners, come in a variety of sizes, shapes, and prices. The most familiar bar code scanner is the checkout scanner used in many grocery stores. This scanner uses a helium-neon (He-Ne) laser. The laser scanner is mounted below a glass plate on the surface of the checkout counter. It reads the UPC bar code symbol on an item as it is drawn across the plate. The decoded value of the bar code is transmitted to a point-of-sale (POS) processor. This information is compared to a list of product numbers stored in the point-of-sale processor. When a match is found, the data, such as description, price, and taxability, are transferred to the checkout terminal for processing.

There are five basic varieties of scanning equipment: hand-held light pens, hand-held lasers, stationary fixed beam scanners, stationary moving beam scanners, and photodiode array (PDA) bar code readers. Table IV-1 compares the types of bar code reading equipment. Common to all varieties of scanning equipment are the three functional elements: opto-electronics, signal conditioning, and digital processing.

Bar codes convey information. The information conveyed depends upon a particular arrangement of bars and spaces. The bars and spaces are translated from their printed form to an analog electrical signal that represents the relative widths of the bars and spaces in the symbol. This is accomplished by illuminating the bar code symbol with a light emitting diode (LED), laser, or other light source and using a light detector to measure the strength of the reflected light. The measurement from a dark area, or bar, will be considerably less than from an adjacent light area, or space. As the light moves from space to bar, the relative intensity of reflection is converted to an analog pattern by the detector, as shown in Figure IV-1.

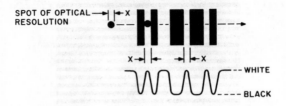

**Figure IV-1. Spatial domain to temporal domain conversion**

The optics of a bar code reader must be matched to the symbol being read. Bar code symbols can be printed over a wide range of densities by varying the widths of the bars and spaces while maintaining the symbol structure and the ratios of the various symbol element widths. Usually, the higher the code density, the narrower are the bar and space widths. High density codes are read with a smaller spot of light than are low density codes. While high resolution scanner systems respond quite well in detecting bar edges, they also respond to imperfections in the bar code symbol. Some imperfections may absorb more light, lessening the intensity of the signal received. They can be interpreted by the scanner as a bar. Voids in the inked areas reflect more light and increase the intensity of the signal received. They can be considered by a scanner to be a space.

When a low resolution reader is employed, the spot of light may be larger than the bar. This causes the reader to have difficulty in reading the symbol. Figure IV-2 shows what happens when the spot is too large for a symbol that has a narrow element width. Figure IV-3 illustrates the problem when the spot is too small.

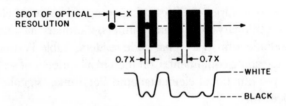

**Figure IV-2. Too large a spot for narrow element width**

# Matrix printer characteristic defects

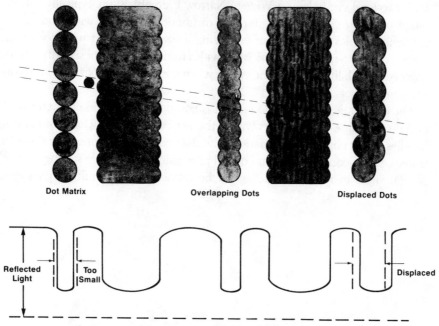

**Dot Matrix**      **Overlapping Dots**      **Displaced Dots**

Reflected Light    Too Small      Displaced

Figure IV-3. Too small a spot for narrow element width

The analog signal from the light detector, representing the light-to-dark and dark-to-light transitions in the bar code symbol, is converted to a digital square wave by signal conditioning circuitry. Thresholds are established to translate the intensity of the analog signal to a square wave. When the threshold is reached, a latch is triggered and the state of the latch is changed.

Following the conditioning of the symbol signal, the digital pattern is passed on for digital processing. The duration of the highs and lows is measured against a predetermined clock frequency of the scanner processor to determine which signals are bars and which are spaces. Adjacent bars are compared to one another, against an established arithmetic average developed over the entire symbol, or by some other algorithm to establish the relative widths of the bars and spaces. Here the ratio of wide to narrow elements becomes of significant importance. Commonly used bar codes have two, three, and four element widths. The fewer the choices permitted within the coding system, the more reliable the decoding. Allowing for defects in printing and imperfect operation of the scanner, print specifications allow printed bars and intervening spaces to be within a range, or tolerance. If the bars and spaces are within this range, and all other conditions acceptable, the symbol will be successfully decoded.

Wide bars and spaces are generally referred to in terms of an X dimension. X represents the width of the narrowest element of the bar code symbol, with larger elements expressed as multiples of X. From these widths are developed, for a two-level symbology, a Wide-to-Narrow Element Ratio, typically within a range of 2:1 to 3:1. The greater the distinction between wide and narrow elements, the less likelihood of confusing a narrow element with a wide element. A wide-to-narrow ratio of 3:1 provides for increased data security and the reduced probability for scanning errors, when considering localized printing and scanning defects.

The electronic image of the symbol is compared to a valid character set to decode the value of characters within the bar code symbol. Digital processing handles check character comparison and data communications. The optoelectronics, signal conditioning, and digital processing of bar code scanners can all be contained in the same package or be resident within multiple packages.

## Table IV-1
## Comparison of bar code reading equipment

| Scanner type | Hand-held or fixed mounted | Spectral response | Printing inks required | Optical throw | Maximum depth of field | Field of view | Cost |
|---|---|---|---|---|---|---|---|
| **Light pens** | | | | | | | |
| Visible red | Hand-held | 630-700 nm | Most | N/A | 20 mils | * | Low |
| Visible white | Hand-held | 450–1080 nm | Most | N/A | 20 mils | * | Low |
| Infrared | Hand-held | 840–930 nm | High carbon content | N/A | 20 mils | * | Low |
| Laser diode | Hand-held | 630-820 nm | Most | Medium to high | Medium to high | * | Low to medium |
| Fixed beam | Either | 630–930 nm | Most; infrared needs high carbon content | Low | Low | * | Medium |
| **Moving beam** | | | | | | | |
| He-Ne laser | Either | 632.8 nm | Most | High | High | High | Medium to high |
| Laser diode | Either | 630-820 nm 820–930 nm | Most High carbon content | High | High | High | Medium to low |
| Visible white | Either | 580 nm peak | High carbon content | Medium | Low | Low | Medium |
| Infrared | Fixed mounted | 840–930 nm | High carbon content | Medium | Low | Medium | Medium |
| Imaging array | Either | 400–1100 nm 850 peak | Most | Medium | Medium | Medium | Medium |

*Note: The field of view for light pens and other fixed-beam readers is the aperture size at any one instant. Over time field of view is restricted only by the distance an operator can stroke continuously.

# CHAPTER 12
# LIGHT PENS

The most common and most popular bar code reading device is the hand-held light pen, or wand scanner. Its popularity stems from its portability and low cost. Use of a light pen requires the operator to find the bar code symbol and move the light pen smoothly over it. The operator locates the quiet zone of the symbol, places the tip in the quiet zone, and sweeps the light pen across the code through the trailing quiet zone. No motors or moving parts are employed, since a human performs the scanning function. This makes the light pen a low cost, small, rugged bar code reading device.

A light pen/wand scanner consists of a pen-shaped housing, a light source which emits light in a specific wavelength band through either a fiber-optic bundle (Figure 12-1), a jeweled tip (Figure 12-2), a lens assembly (Figure 12-3), or an apertured emitter/sensor (Figure 12-4). The operator moves the light pen across the symbol and the reflectance differences between bars and spaces are detected by a photoreceptor. The receptor converts these differences to an analog signal, which is decoded and passed to the host processor.

# REFLECTIVE OPTICAL SYSTEM

### FIBRE OPTIC - SOURCE/APERTURED DETECTOR

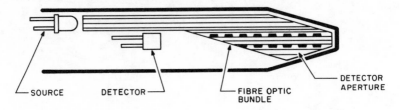

SOURCE  DETECTOR  FIBRE OPTIC BUNDLE  DETECTOR APERTURE

### FIBRE OPTIC - SOURCE AND RECEIVERS

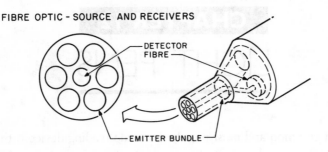

DETECTOR FIBRE

EMITTER BUNDLE

**Figure 12-1. Fiber-optic bundle light pen**

### JEWEL TIP

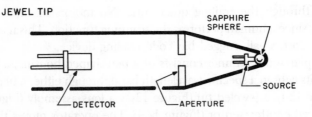

SAPPHIRE SPHERE

SOURCE

DETECTOR  APERTURE

**Figure 12-2. Jeweled tip light pen**

### CONCENTRIC LENS

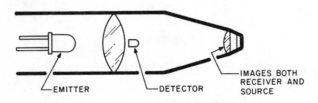

EMITTER  DETECTOR  IMAGES BOTH RECEIVER AND SOURCE

**Figure 12-3. Lens assembly light pen**

98

## BAR CODE SCANNER

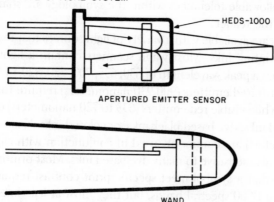

**Figure 12-4. Apertured emitter sensor light pen**

The aperture size is more important in light pen/wand scanners than in moving beam scanning systems. This is because of the single-pass nature of light pens. Poorly printed symbols or incorrect aperture size will result in fewer successful reads.

It takes a typical operator 10 minutes to learn the technique of scanning with a light pen. During this time the operator learns to make a smooth, sweeping stroke, from leading quiet zone through trailing quiet zone, and to orient the light pen within a range of angles perpendicular to the surface of the symbol. While a smooth, sweeping motion is required, the speed can vary anywhere from 3 to 50 inches per second. The operator places the tip of the light pen in contact with the symbol and scans. Most pens, however, allow the tip to be lifted slightly, to accommodate protective coatings or films on the symbol. The distance the tip of the pen can be above the printed surface is referred to as depth of field (DOF).

The "human friendliness" of a light pen is measured by the pen's ergonomic design and its first read rate. The first read rate of a bar code–based system is expressed as a percent of read attempts in which a good scan occurs. If 100 attempts were made and 97 were successful, the first read rate would be 97 percent. The "system friendliness" of a light pen is measured by the system's substitution error rate. This is expressed as the ratio of characters or symbols read to those mismatched (where the data encoded in the printed symbol does not match the data decoded by the reader.) Examples of substitution errors include: where 7B36G14 is read as 7B36G41, where 123456 is read as 123457, and where 9876543 is read as 98765.

The ideal bar code reading system would be one where the first read rate was 100 percent and the substitution error rate was 0 percent. In practice, however, tradeoffs are made to accommodate the varying print qualities that are presented to the reader. The poorer the quality of the printed symbol, the lower the FRR and the higher the SER. Bar code symbologies are designed so that the allowable tolerances within the symbology are shared between the symbol and the reader.

Light pens are available with a variety of light sources that respond differently to various printing inks. Most wand scanners contain a light emitting diode (LED) that has a peak wavelength of 630, 635, 700, 720, 820, or 900 nanometers. In general, infrared emitters (900-930 nanometers) require the use of carbon-based inks, while visible red emitters (633 to 720 nanometers) can be used with carbon-based inks, dye-based black inks, or colored inks. Near-infrared emitters (820 nanometers) are commonly used in conjunction with carbon-based inks, but they are also sensitive to many dye-based inks. Most printing specifications recommend that a symbol meet specific print contrast requirements in both the B633 and B900 spectral bands, but they must at least meet these specific requirements in the B633 spectral band.

When a light pen is moved over a bar code symbol, the reader analyzes the received data according to its design algorithm. If the analyses pass the criteria, the reader sounds a beep or illuminates an LED to tell the operator of a good scan. This audio-visual feedback generally occurs within a half-second, depending upon the reader design and label length.

The absence of audio-visual feedback tells the operator that a good scan has not occurred. A no-read could be caused by the operator missing part of the symbol when scanning, a jerky motion of the wand across the symbol, a printed symbol that did not meet print contrast requirements or bar width tolerances, or reader malfunction. A well-designed system should ensure that the first read rate of the system exceeds 85 percent.

A high number of no-reads reduces the operator's confidence in the system. It produces operator frustration and ultimately results in the failure of the system. Matching the aperture size to the minimum bar width within a symbol and matching the light source to the ink used in printing the symbol results in improved performance of the system. Adding a high print quality to matched resolution and light source elevates the performance of any bar code system, and this is particularly true of light pen–based systems. The considerations that should be made in selecting a given light pen include those listed in Table 12-1.

It would be possible to design a light pen that would function well over the complete range of possible combinations of bar code structure, printing methods, and environment. The cost of such a light pen might be prohibitive. Recent advances in photodiode matrix array technologies provide much hope for a universal light pen capable of functioning over most printing variables. A general purpose scanner that attempted to respond to all situations equally might have a degraded response to a specific set of situations when compared to a scanner tailored to that situation. Manufacturers can supply a wide range of light pens suitable for a wide range of applications. However, the user must have suffi-

**Table 12-1**
**Light pen selection considerations**

| | |
|---|---|
| • Resolution | • Light source wavelength |
| • Degree of tilt permitted | • Depth of field (DOF) |
| • Data output: analog/digital | • Power consumption |
| • Cost | • Service and life expectancy |

cient understanding of light pen operation to select the appropriate device for his/her unique needs.

The small, lightweight, inexpensive, rugged features of light pens permit their use in such diverse applications as entering shipping data into an on-line distribution system, tool crib and asset tracking, work-in-process reporting, quality assurance reporting, warehouse stock location, inventory control, cycle counting, lot tracking, recall isolation, warranty tracking, positive sample identification, document tracking, air freight tracking, labor reporting, patient identification, and hospital materials management.

# CHAPTER 13
# STATIONARY
# FIXED BEAM READERS

Fixed beam readers are close relatives of light pens. They use a stationary light beam to read a moving bar code. Fixed beam readers have no moving parts. They illuminate an area of the symbol with a visible or infrared light source. When a bar code symbol passes through the beam, the reader detects the light reflected from the symbol and reads the bar code. As with light pens, the difference in reflected light is converted to an analog signal, digitized, decoded, and transmitted to the host computer.

Fixed beam readers use broad beam illumination, where a fairly large area of the bar code symbol is illuminated by the reader's light source. However, only a small portion of the reflected light is focused onto the photodetector or matrix array. The light sources utilized in fixed beam readers are either light emitting diodes or lamp based, with emitters and detectors in three spectral bands, yellow at 580 nanometers, red at 630 nanometers, and infrared at 870, 900, and 920 nanometers. As with light pens, a match of light source wavelength to the ink type of the printed symbol is required for a successful bar code reading system. Infrared readers require the use of carbon-based inks. Red or yellow light sources respond well to colored and black-and-white symbols, providing that substantial contrast exists between the bars and the spaces.

Fixed beam readers have one chance to read the symbol as it passes the scanner. Consequently, many fixed beam readers provide an elongated light spot parallel to the bars and spaces. Such configurations are less susceptible to defects than a single round spot the same width as the elongated spot. This allows the reader to sense a larger area of a bar or space, reducing the probability that a random printing defect would cause either a no-scan or substitution error. The principal advantage of fixed beam readers is that they are less expensive than their moving beam counterparts. The principal disadvantage is that the bar code symbol must be relatively close to the reader and this distance must be tightly controlled (see Appendix E, Solving the Problem of Skew).

In any optical system, focus is paramount to the crispness and clarity of the reflected image. An out-of-focus photograph is fuzzy and the outlines of its subjects are indistinct. Fuzzy and indistinct lines distort the reflection of bars and spaces to a point at which the transition between bar and space cannot be discerned. The range of distances where a bar code symbol will be in focus is called depth of field. It is the difference between the maximum and minimum distance at which a bar code symbol can be read. One method is to define the optimum distance (or focal point) from the symbol to reader, and then define the range of distances on both sides of the focal point where the target will be in sufficient focus for the system's signal conditioning circuitry to replicate the bar/space pattern of the symbol. An example would be a reader whose optical focal point is 3 inches and a 1-inch DOF. A second method is to define the depth of field as $\pm 0.5$ inch. Either method yields the same result, i.e., that the reader will be able to resolve a bar code symbol that is between 2.5 inches and 3.5 inches away.

In light pen readers, the depth of field is defined as the maximum distance that the wand tip could be from the symbol and still achieve a good scan. This differs from noncontact readers, where the focal point of the reader is extended further in space through lens assemblies. Just as with a camera, a target could be either too far away or too close. The distance from the reader to the near edge of the depth of field is referred to as optical throw. The combination of optical throw and depth of field is known as a bar code scanner's operating range, as illustrated in Figure 13-1.

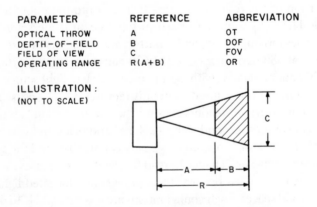

| PARAMETER | REFERENCE | ABBREVIATION |
|---|---|---|
| OPTICAL THROW | A | OT |
| DEPTH-OF-FIELD | B | DOF |
| FIELD OF VIEW | C | FOV |
| OPERATING RANGE | R(A+B) | OR |

ILLUSTRATION :
(NOT TO SCALE)

**Figure 13-1. Scanner terminology of distance**

A fixed beam reader is capable of reading a symbol moving in front of it at speeds of 2 to 200 inches per second (10 to 1000 feet per minute) when the width of the narrow element is 10 mils. Symbols with narrow elements would have to move more slowly than symbols with wider elements. Fixed beam readers usually operate at transport speeds of 18 inches per second (or 90 feet per minute).

Fixed beam readers are used for in-line verification of printed bar codes, envelope sorting, badge reading, test tube tracking, and package identification. They can be used in any application where the orientation and location of a bar code symbol can be closely controlled and where bar code scanning is dependent upon the movement of the symbol past the light source.

# CHAPTER 14

# MOVING BEAM READERS

In the previous discussions of light pens and fixed beam readers, it was required that either the target (symbol) be moved in front of the light source (fixed beam) or that an operator move the light source (light pen) across the target. The motion component of these systems was provided by a source other than the bar code reader, viz., transport system or operator. The discussions in the following paragraphs address bar code readers that provide motion to the light source, automatically and at a constant speed; hence the name, moving beam readers. These readers are further classified as to the light source employed, namely, coherent or incoherent; and as to whether the readers are fix mounted or hand-held. And while most moving beam readers today employ a laser, which is a coherent, monochromatic light source transmitting precisely at 632.8 nm, other moving beam readers are available which do not use lasers, and we will address those types of readers first.

Broad spectrum moving beam readers flood the target area with light from either an infrared (870 nm wavelength) or incandescent light source, then employ a bidirectional optical sweep to read the bar code symbol. A mirror within the reader sweeps an optical sensor beam back and forth across the bar code symbol. Because of this beam movement, the scanner is not dependent upon symbol movement to read the code. The principal advantage of broad-spectrum moving beam readers over fixed beam readers is the multiple pass reading, which increases the overall reliability of the bar code reading system. In the case of a printing defect in the symbol, a fixed beam reader might record a "no-read" or substitution error. A reader that makes multiple passes of the symbol might be able to avoid the defect in subsequent passes and record a "good scan." These readers can operate in a simple bidirectional fashion, moving only on a single axis. For the sake of discussion, let's call that axis the X axis, or horizontal axis.

Or, the movement of the sensor might be horizontal and after the end of each sweep along the X axis, the beam is deflected slightly in the direction of the Y axis, or vertically. The beam then returns in the X direction and is again deflected in the Y direction until it has stepped through a predetermined number of Y deflections. The beam is then deflected back in the opposite Y axis direction until it returns to the original position. In fix mounted systems, such as those on conveyor systems, benefit would be realized from an X and Y axis reader. This is due to the increased label area that could be sampled vertically, and the ability to compensate in future passes for what might, in a single scan, be viewed by the reader as a localized printing defect. This multi-pass compensation would improve the probability of a "good scan" by providing samplings from a wider range of positions in the label than those afforded by the narrow line of an X-axis scanner.

Broad spectrum moving beam readers are commercially available in either fix mounted or hand-held configurations. Their principal advantage is a relatively lower price than Helium-Neon laser based systems, while producing the multi-pass benefits of such systems. Their principal disadvantages are limited operating ranges and depth of fields. Broad-spectrum moving beam readers are generally characterized by an operating range of 3 to 5 inches. with a depth of field less than ±0.5 inch.

One finds the primary application of broad-spectrum moving beam readers in conveyor type applications, e.g., sortation and inventory control, where containers are the same size and their distance from the reader can be closely controlled.

## Laser Based Moving Beam Readers

Laser technology is the science that deals with the generation of coherent light in small but powerful beams. The word laser is an acronym for *Light Amplification by the Stimulated Emission of Radiation*. Laser light has unique properties. A laser beam is one color, or monochromatic. If the light is one color, then it is also of one wavelength. If the wavelengths are stimulated so that they are in phase, the beam is also coherent. Incoherent light is illustrated by an ordinary light bulb, which emits white light. White light is incoherent because it has all visible colors and therefore all visible wavelengths (panchromatic). It is also transmitted in all directions from the light source and cannot be concentrated or controlled. Laser light can be controlled because the beams are of one wavelength and therefore in step (in phase) with each other.

All bar code reading devices have a specified depth of field. The directional and coherent nature of laser light permits an expanded DOF and the power of the laser can well dictate its optical throw, and in combination yield a greater operating range. Lasers further focus the light source while other light sources focus the reflected light. Combining this focused light with the polarized nature of laser light, a polarizing filter can tune the received signal to only that specific wavelength of the laser. This provides for greater immunity to ambient lighting conditions leading to improved signal quality and generally better scanning.

Laser reading provides possibly the greatest benefit to the industrial and commercial community where rapid and accurate data acquisition is needed. The coherent, monochromatic laser light exists in a focused spot, generally less than 10 mils in diameter. This spot is then reflected through lens assemblies and onto a mirrored surface. The mirror can be either rotating in nature or can be rotated left and right, as is the case in flipper mirrors and dithers. This oscillated movement then causes the laser light to appear as a single line of light.

Using once again the similarity of bar code readers and cameras, imagine that two objects are just beyond the limits of the camera's depth of field (DOF). One object is a telephone pole, the other a broom handle. The telephone pole image would be discernible, while the broom handle would not, because the pole is wider than the handle; relative to the total image size, the blur is less pronounced in the case of the pole. Consequently, image width (or nominal narrow element size) and DOF are interrelated—the wider the nominal narrow element, the greater the effective DOF.

The light in a laser beam is extremely directional. It is focused by a lens into a narrow cone and projected in one direction. The direction of the laser beam is the result of optics at the ends or sides of the laser light source. The laser, when focused to a fine, hairlike beam can concentrate all of its power into the beam. Hence, the directionality of the beam has a bearing on its intensity. If the beam were allowed to spread out, it would lose its power. Confinement of large amounts of power into a narrow slit permits the focus of the beam over a greater DOF. With a greater DOF, not as much precision is required in presenting the symbol to the reader.

The beam's focal length (L) is the center of its DOF (or at the beam waist). At the 1.4d points in Figure 14-1, the beam loses its collimation and begins to diverge (and lose illumination power). To reliably read a bar code, the maximum diameter of the beam cannot exceed 1.4 times the minimum bar width. The smaller the X dimension, the less the available DOF. Remember, however, that the DOF can be extended into space by increasing its optical throw. Table 14-1 shows a representative DOF for various X dimensions.

**Figure 14-1. Laser beam waist and optical resolution**

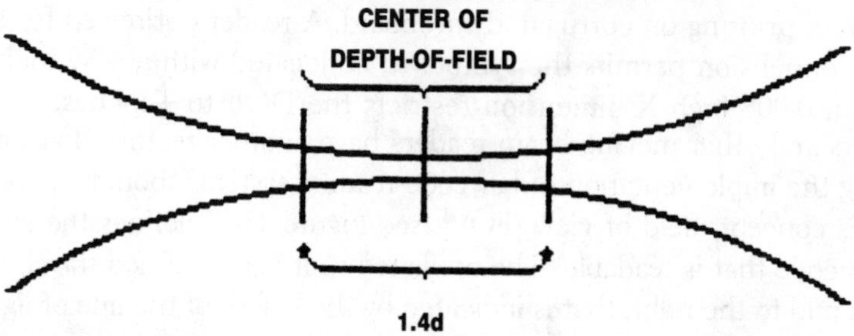

CENTER OF
DEPTH-OF-FIELD

1.4d

- Laser beam spot diameter at waist is the center of the depth of field
- 1.4d points are where diameter has increased to $\sqrt{2}$ times the waist diameter. This is defined as the limits of the depth of field
- $DOF = \dfrac{\pi d^2}{2\delta}$ where: d = waist diameter $\delta$ = wavelength
- Example, 0.008 inch waist diameter and 633 nanometer $(24.92 \times 10^{-6}$ inch) wavelength
- $DOF = \dfrac{3.1416 \times (0.008)^2}{2 \times 24.92 \times 10^{-6}} = 4.03$ inch

Table 14-1 leads us to assume that a nominal narrow element width of 8 mils can be read with a visible-red reader with a spot size of 8 mils and an optical throw of 14 inches. This means that the 8 mil symbol could be read within a range of 14–18 inches from the reader. Using another visible-red reader with a spot size of 20 mils and the same optical throw, reading a 20 mil nominal narrow element, this range would extend from 14–39 inches. Consequently, the relationship between reader spot size, printed nominal narrow element width, and operating range is a dependent one.

**Table 14-1**
**Depth of Field**
(All Table Values Expressed in Inches)

| Optimized X Dimension | Spot Size @ DOF | DOF @ 633 nm | DOF @ 900nm |
|---|---|---|---|
| 0.004 | 0.0057 | 1.009 | 0.709 |
| 0.006 | 0.0085 | 2.269 | 1.596 |
| 0.008 | 0.0113 | 4.034 | 2.837 |
| 0.010 | 0.0141 | 6.303 | 4.434 |
| 0.012 | 0.0170 | 9.077 | 6.384 |
| 0.014 | 0.0198 | 12.355 | 8.690 |
| 0.016 | 0.0226 | 16.137 | 11.350 |
| 0.018 | 0.0255 | 20.423 | 14.365 |
| 0.020 | 0.0283 | 25.213 | 17.734 |
| 0.022 | 0.0311 | 30.508 | 21.458 |
| 0.024 | 0.0339 | 36.307 | 25.537 |
| 0.025 | 0.0354 | 39.396 | 27.710 |

The grocery industry has established a minimum X dimension specified at 0.025 inch when the element is to be part of the Uniform Shipping Container Symbol. This dimension is specified both for labels on shipping containers and direct printing on corrugated cardboard. A reader optimized for a 0.025 inch X dimension permits the symbol to be located within a 39 inch DOF, while an 0.008 inch X dimension restricts the DOF to 4 inches.

Lasers and other moving beam readers have another feature that one considering the implementation of bar code reading systems should be cognizant of. This concept, field of view (FOV) (see Figure 13-1), defines the length of the bar code that is readable. The oscillated spot has a defined travel, both to the left and to the right, that is indicated by the length of the line of light. For a moving beam reader to read a bar code, the entire symbol must be illuminated at the same instant it is being read. Consequently, if the bar code is longer than the line of light, the bar code exceeds the field of view of the reader, and the bar code symbol will not be decodable. As one moves outward from the reader, the angular movement of the moving mirror causes the line of light to become longer, thereby improving the field of view. Since the laser is a focused beam, it too has a defined depth of field. Beyond the limits of the DOF, the line of light will become longer, but cannot be read due to being out of focus and reduced irradiance from the illumination. Hence, there is a direct relationship between the depth of field of a moving beam reader and its associated field of view.

The line of light in moving beam readers can be either horizontal or vertical. Such orientation permits bar code symbols to be placed on packaging where the bars are vertical, called a Picket Fence orientation; or where the bars are horizontal, called a Step Ladder orientation (see Figure 14-2).

**Figure 14-2. Picket Fence and Step Ladder Orientations**

In a conveyor application of moving beam scanning systems, a decision needs to be made as to whether the scanner is going to be alongside the conveyor or whether it is going to be above or below the transport system. If the scanner is going to be alongside the conveyor, then the line of light should be vertical and the bar code symbol in a Step Ladder orientation. If the scanner is going to be above or below the transport system, the line of light should be horizontal and the symbol orientation would be Picket Fence in nature (see Figures 14-3 and 14-4).

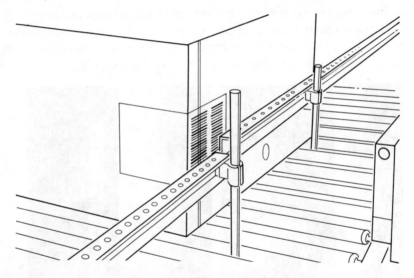

**Figure 14-3. Side Mount/Step Ladder**

The rationale behind the matching of the orientation of the line of light to the symbol orientation is to present the symbol to the reader such that the line of light is perpendicular to the direction of the bars in the symbol, simultaneously intersecting all bars and spaces. Such combination of orientations of symbol and reader permit the calculation of maximum line speeds of the conveyor as functions of the speed of the moving beam scanner and the number of scans required (usually five) to assure a "good scan" as the symbol moves before the reader. This matched orientation additionally allows greater flexibility in the application of the symbol to the package. Since the line of light (which is actually a spot moving at high speed so that the spot appears as a line) must intersect all elements of the symbol at the same instant, registration of the sym-

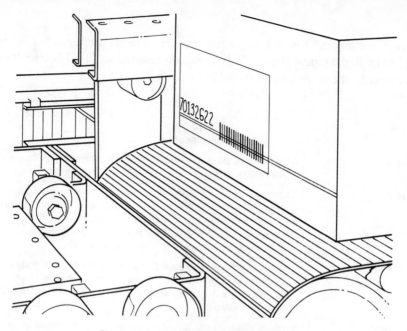

**Figure 14-4. Over-under mount/picket fence**

bol when applied could be critical for future fix mounted scanning. Assuming for a moment that the symbol had an aspect ratio of 1 (the symbol is as high as it is wide) the symbol would be square, permitting the registration tolerance to vary ±45°. For more information on skew and solutions to the problems it causes, see Appendix E.

Lasers are frequently thought of as dangerous light sources with visions of laser beams burning holes in carbon steel or being used in welding operations. Carbon Dioxide ($CO_2$) and Nd:YAG (an yttrium aluminum garnet host crystal and a neodymium activator) lasers are capable of such utilitarian applications and extreme care must be exercised in their use. However, bar code reading lasers are not $CO_2$ or Nd:YAG varieties, but are generally Helium-Neon (He-Ne) or semiconductor based. Both He-Ne and semiconductor lasers emit light at a small fraction of the power of their $CO_2$ and YAG counterparts. In fact laser light is more highly regulated than any light source and the relative safety of lasers is classified. Output and safety aspects of lasers are regulated by the Bureau of Radiological Health (BRH) and are covered in 21 CFR Part 1040, with classifications as follows in Table 14-2.

| Table 14-2 Laser classification | |
| --- | --- |
| **Class I:** | Lasers at visible wavelengths...safe for continuous viewing at irradiance levels of 0.4 microwatts passing through the cornea. |
| **Class II:** | Lasers at visible wavelengths...those lasers that do not have enough power to cause retinal damage during momentary viewing. Warning on product label states "LASER RADIATION—DO NOT STARE INTO BEAM." Prolonged viewing can cause damage no matter what the irradiance levels are. |
| **Class IIIA:** | Lasers which will not cause damage to the eye under normal conditions, but will damage the eye when viewing the beam through optics. These are medium-power lasers in the range of 1.0 to 5.0 milliwatts. |
| **Class IIIB:** | Lasers which cannot cause hazardous diffuse reflection or fire. This medium-power class ranges from 5.0 to 500 milliwatts; they can cause direct eye damage. |
| **Class IV:** | Lasers which are a diffuse reflection and fire hazard. They are classified as high power and range from 500 milliwatts and upward. |

Generally, all lasers used in bar code reading are Class I or Class II products with less than 1 milliwatt of power. YAG and $CO_2$ lasers, sometimes used in laser etching, are generally Class IV products and typically operate between 50 and 1200 watts of power.

Laser scanners are well-suited to a wide variety of industrial and commercial applications. They can be mounted on conveyor and transport systems, can be desk mounted, or can be hand-held. They can be either A.C. powered or powered by batteries for portable data entry terminal applications. Systems exist today where hand-held lasers are interfaced to hand-held batch type terminals and to hand-held wireless (radio frequency and infrared communicating) terminals.

Laser scanners exhibit such features and benefits as shown in Table 14-3.

**Table 14-3**
**Laser scanning features and benefits**

- Redundant Scanning—Multiple pass reading compensates for poorly printed or damaged labels.

- The scanner can read through transparent film, plastic, and glass permitting the bar code symbols to be beneath shrink/stretch wrap, protectors, and windows.

- Laser scanners can read on irregular surfaces, shapes, and curvatures, accommodating many applications.

- Laser scanner's monochromatic, coherent light source is more tolerant of ambient lighting.

- The scanner is more tolerant of the presentation of the symbol in such areas as pitch, tilt, and skew, requiring minimal operator training.

- The enhanced field of view of laser scanners permits them to read longer labels than their broad-beam illumination counterparts.

Moving beam laser scanners operate with a spot forming the laser's line of light at speeds of 40 to 960 scans per second. Hand-held devices generally operate at the lower end of these ranges, as the target is generally stationary. In conveyor applications, the speed of the scanner is directly proportional to the speed of the conveyor and the height of the bar code symbol being read. The faster the conveyor, the faster the scanner and the higher the bar code should be. Unlike light pens and fixed beam readers which have but one opportunity to achieve a "good scan," moving beam laser readers can sample a symbol at least 20 times in the same amount of time required for a single pass with other technologies. This high sample rate can efficiently read a widely varying label quality in a fraction of the time required by light pen and fixed beam technologies. Further, the rapid multiple scanning permits several viewings of the symbol. In addition to reducing operator frustration in low First Read Rate situations through multiple passes across the symbol, a feature under software control can be added to make multiple samples of the symbol and then to compare the samples. If the samples agree, the information is passed to the host processor. If not, the laser scanner continues attempting to read until a sufficient number of samples do agree or the label is deemed unreadable. This feature adds significantly to the data integrity by substantially reducing the substitution error rate of the bar code reading. Finally, laser scanners can be equipped not only with X axis scanning but both X and Y axis scanning (or raster scanning), permitting a larger area of the symbol to be sampled.

The functional structure of a moving beam laser scanner is shown in Figure 14-5. It consists of a light generating medium, which is usually a He-Ne tube (see Chapter 16 for a discussion of laser diodes) that is optically focused within the DOF range of the system. This focused spot is then oscillated by a moving mirror onto the symbol to be read. The irradiance levels reflected back to the system are then subjected to a polarizing filter which blocks all wavelengths other than the 632.8 nanometer wavelength of the scanner. Only the transitions of radiant flux at 632.8 nm, between the bars and spaces, are sensed by the photodetection circuitry; converting these transitions into an analog waveform, this analog signal is then digitized, decoded, and passed onto the host processor system.

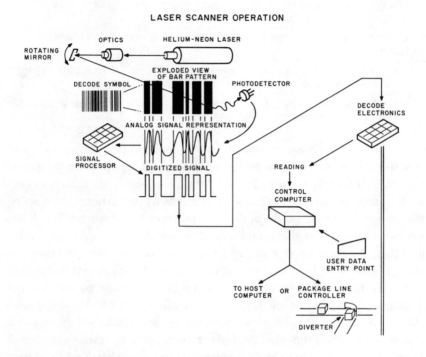

**Figure 14-5. Laser scanner functional structure**

With all of the benefits suggested above in laser scanning devices it would appear that all systems should be laser based. This, however, is not the case. Laser scanners are complex devices with moving parts, whose components are considerably more fragile than their light pen counterparts. Further, laser scanners are significantly more expensive than light pens, often costing more than 10 times as much. Moving beam lasers are restricted as to their field of view, where light pens are restricted only by the ability of the operator. Most fix mounted applications are excellent candidates for laser scanners. Most handheld applications, on the other hand, remain in the domain of the light pen, on the grounds of cost, weight, durability, and ergonomic design. The handheld laser is to the light pen what a Mercedes-Benz is to a Volkswagen. Both can get you to where you want to go, but at what cost? There are numerous applications where a hand-held laser is the perfect tool, but until the cost, weight, and bulk go down and durability goes up, most hand-held applications will remain in the domain of the light pen.

No discussion of moving beam readers would be complete without addressing the retail slot scanner. These systems employ a moving beam laser with similar characteristics and benefits as all moving beam lasers, save one. Where industrial and other commercial implementations of laser bar code readers employ a single line of light and in some cases an X and Y axis (raster) pattern, slot scanners produce a light pattern to optimize the symbology being read, namely, the UPC symbol. This pattern is usually either a crosshatch or starburst, permitting the left-hand portion of the UPC symbol to be sensed by one line and the right-hand portion to be sensed by another, lending to the concept of rotational omnidirectionality. Rotational omnidirectionality implies that a UPC symbol could be placed face down on the scanner, be rotated in any orientation with the face remaining on the glass, and still be successfully read.

Slot scanners are relatively expensive when compared to other bar code readers. These systems read, generally without exception, only the UPC symbol. Principal application areas include those of retail checkout in both grocery and drug stores, with some applications in mass merchandising and grocery/drug wholesalers.

Some of the newer slot scanners provide not only for rotational omnidirectionality, but are also more tolerant to the orientation of the symbol on the sides of the packages, where those sides are not directly in front of the scanning window. These systems employ a technology known as holography, which is the production of three-dimensional patterns with the use of laser beams. These patterns permit the scanner to "see" a symbol that is placed on nearly any panel of the package without the need for orienting the label. While considerably more expensive than other slot scanners, holographic scanners add to the rotational omnidirectionality (X and Y axis) a third Z axis, permitting the orientation on the Z axis upwards to 270° of the plane of the scanning window.

# CHAPTER 15

# IMAGING ARRAY READERS

Each of the preceding bar code reading systems uses a light source and a single photodetector. Relative movement between the scanner and symbol results from operator (light pen), symbol (fixed beam reader), or light source (moving beam reader) motion. The photodector produces a signal representing the bars and spaces of the symbol. Imaging array readers, on the other hand, operate similarly to photographic cameras. The symbol is illuminated by a light source similar to a photoflash (xenon) or by floodlights. The imaging array readers focus the reflected symbol image onto a photosensitive semiconductor device called a linear photodiode array. These arrays typically have 1024, 2048, or 4096 tiny photodiodes. The photodiodes are sampled by a microprocessor to produce an analog of the symbol being read. The analog signal is then conditioned and decoded.

The depth of field of these devices is limited to a few inches. The field of view of imaging array readers is also limited. This precludes their use in reading long bar codes. The number of photodiodes in the array also determines the achievable resolution.

Imaging array readers are available for either fixed mounted or hand-held applications. With their limited field of view, imaging readers are used primarily for reading codes of fixed lengths, such as UPC. These devices can be found in convenience stores and mass merchandise applications where slot scanners, such as those used in grocery checkout systems, would be too expensive.

Generally, hand-held imaging readers use a photoflash for illumination. Sampling rates are limited to 3 to 5 per second. Fixed mounted systems employ constant lighting with sampling rates in a range of 7 to 10 samples per second. The major benefit of imaging array readers is their relative cost as compared to moving beam readers. These systems offer additional benefit over light pens since they are able to sample an entire symbol without movement of the reader. This capability produces less operator frustration than light pens when scanning marginally printed symbols, since rescanning is performed at the push of a button. The imaging array reader's illumination system permits these devices to read colored symbols as well as those with high carbon content.

Matrix array readers represent the next generation of bar code reading devices. Available in both fix mounted and light pen configurations, these bar code readers permit the viewing of an extended vertical portion of the bar code symbol. Such vertical redundancy permits the averaging of localized printing defects; such as spots, voids, and bar edge roughness.

# CHAPTER 16

# LASER DIODES

The light generating medium in a classical moving beam laser installation is a Helium-Neon tube. To cause the He-Ne to lase, or to produce light, the application of 1000 volts or more to the cathode of the laser tube is necessary. A special power supply is required that can develop such output from the application of a 12 volt or 110 volt input. In a hand-held laser scanner, these two components (power supply and laser tube) represent nearly 65% of the Bill of Materials (BOM) cost of the scanner. While semiconductor lasers capable of generating light in the infrared spectrum have been available for several years, the visible red semiconductor laser is a relatively new entrant in the market. Visible light is preferred over infrared light with portable systems, because the operator is able to visually position the line of light over the symbol, an impossibility with invisible infrared illumination. Of course there have been some novel ways of overcoming the invisible nature of infrared lighting. Some manufacturers have installed a pair of orientation LEDs that illuminate the edges of the field of view, with the infrared laser scanning between these two points. Use of a semiconductor laser yields an overall reduction in the BOM costs with the reduced relative cost between the semiconductor component and the laser tube; and the absence of a requirement for a very sophisticated power supply. One can expect to see the introduction of visible semiconductor lasers cause a dramatic reduction in the cost of laser-based bar code reading equipment over the next several years.

As the size and cost of laser moving beam readers are reduced, a substantial crossover from light pen systems to laser-based systems will be witnessed in both the commercial and industrial market segments. The size and cost reduction removes the major benefits of light pen systems and affords the laser benefits of redundant scanning, coherent light sources, and improved operating ranges, not possible with today's light pens.

The advent of visible red laser diodes will see these diodes also placed in light pens with the operator performing the task of light source movement. The advantages of such a system would be those of a focused, coherent, polarized light source leading to improved reading performance in such areas as depth of field and tolerance to a wide range of ambient lighting conditions. The light source advantages would be married to a field of view limited in length only to that achievable by the operator's hand movement.

A moving beam laser diode in a light pen under battery power would permit the addition of data and program memories, yielding a portable data entry terminal that could be placed in a shirt pocket. Light pens with internal memory already exist and have been proven of substantial benefit, though existing implementations employ standard light pen optics and must still come in contact with the symbol being read.

Fixed beam readers having an improved depth of field over light pens already exist in hand-held configurations.

Each of these configurations borrows features and benefits from combinations of light pens, matrix array readers, fixed beam readers, moving beam readers, laser light sourcing, and imaging array readers packaged in such a way as to serve a specific niche of applications in the bar code scanning universe. The possible permutations are limited only by the imagination. The current state of the technology, however, recommends the following:

1. Use of light pens where reader size, weight, and cost are the features most required, and where the number of symbols to be read over a period of time is small in comparison to the overall job requirements of the operator.
2. Use of laser light sources where ambient lighting may be a factor in the overall success of a bar code reading system or where enhanced depth of field is needed.
3. Use of a moving beam reader where label length does not exceed the field of view of the reader. A moving beam reader is more human factored to minimize the number of "no scans" experienced by the operator.
4. Use of matrix array readers where a wide variety in printed symbol printing technique and print quality may be encountered.

# SECTION V
# DATA COLLECTION

# CHAPTER 17

# DATA ENTRY TERMINALS

The purpose of all bar code data collection is to automate the data entry function. This automation improves the speed at which the data can be captured and dramatically reduces the errors associated with key entry. Hand-held readers can be connected directly to a minicomputer or host mainframe. Such configurations generally utilize hand-held readers as an adjunct to key-entry workstations, where the scanner is connected in parallel to the keyboard.

The advent of the microprocessor, and particularly those micros having lower power requirements, has permitted computers to be battery operated. Battery powered microprocessors and their associated semiconductor memories enable the operator to disconnect the power and transmission cables needed in traditional computer data entry systems. With the operator no longer tethered to a host processing system, computing and data collection power can be taken into areas and used in applications where they have previously been unfeasible with traditional computing.

Traditionally, data entry has been accomplished by people recording data by hand with clipboard, pencil, and printed form. These source documents were then hand carried, mailed, or phoned to a transcription and editing center where the data was key-entered into the computing system. This process is shown in Figure 17-1. The use of portable data entry terminals (PDETs), as shown in Figure 17-2, permits the information to be directly transmitted from the point where the data are gathered, to the computing system, bypassing the intermediate error-prone and costly steps.

Portable data entry terminals permit people to become more productive, reducing the data-gathering time by 30 to 60 percent. The elimination of the intermediate clerical functions further reduces the overall cost of getting information to the computer. And, finally, the turnaround time, from data collec-

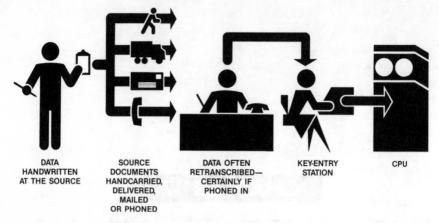

| DATA HANDWRITTEN AT THE SOURCE | SOURCE DOCUMENTS HANDCARRIED, DELIVERED, MAILED OR PHONED | DATA OFTEN RETRANSCRIBED— CERTAINLY IF PHONED IN | KEY-ENTRY STATION | CPU |

**Figure 17-1. Traditional data collection**

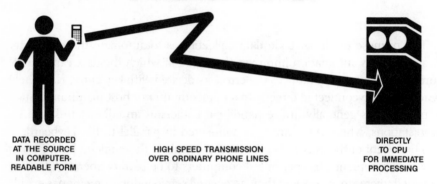

| DATA RECORDED AT THE SOURCE IN COMPUTER-READABLE FORM | HIGH SPEED TRANSMISSION OVER ORDINARY PHONE LINES | DIRECTLY TO CPU FOR IMMEDIATE PROCESSING |

**Figure 17-2. Data collection with portable data entry terminals**

tion until the information is usable by management, is shortened. Equipping the portable data entry terminal with a bar code reading device further reduces the errors during data collection.

## Collecting Data

Once the data has been successfully captured by the bar code reader it must be transmitted to a computer system to create meaningful reports and to influence the control of operations. There are four basic data collection devices available for input to computer systems. The first is an intelligent terminal which is hard-wired to the computer. It has single or multiple line displays, or simply a series of "status lights" to direct the operator. These devices may be used instead of CRTs and at a far lower cost. Several suppliers provide popular keyboard/display emulation which permit their devices to communicate directly with many host processors.

A second device is a "wedge" (or Y-connector) which permits a bar code reader to be connected between the display and its keyboard. While this configuration is generally quite highly regarded, it must be remembered that wedges require CRTs, and it may not always be possible, desirable, or cost-effective to place a CRT wherever data must be captured.

The third type of data collection device is the batch-oriented portable data entry terminal (PDET). These devices are generally handheld and weigh between two ounces and three pounds. Most batch PDETs have a unique communications protocol which requires the use of protocol converters or some other type of front end equipment. Batch PDETs are battery-powered and may have a keyboard or a "scan board," which permits low volume data to be scanned one character at a time (see Figure 17-3). Batch PDETs may range in data storage capacity between 8000 to one million characters. Likewise, they may be able to execute custom programs from ROM, EPROM, EEROM, or RAM. Single- and multiple-line displays are available in either LED or LCD variety. State-of-the-art devices include a recently introduced PDET able to store 16K characters, custom programmable, down-loadable, with a real-time clock, the size of a credit card, $\frac{5}{16}$ of an inch thick, and under \$250 for one unit. Software and supporting communications equipment is available to interface this device to an IBM PC running dBase III for under \$600.

**Figure 17-3. "Scan board," or paper keyboard (Courtesy of Data Documents Systems, Inc.)**

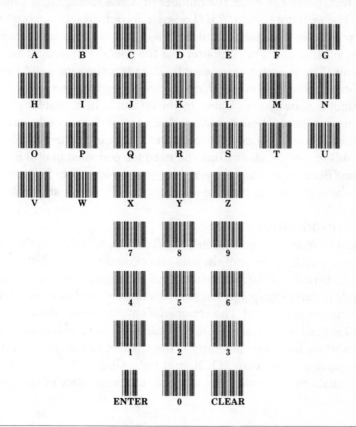

The fourth type of data collection terminal is radio frequency, or RF PDET. These terminals are tied directly back to a processor permitting on-line inquiry and updating of records and files. Presently there are only about a half dozen suppliers of these terminals, though their product offerings are becoming increasingly impressive. One recently introduced RF PDET included the following features: a 2-line by 16-character LCD display, battery-powered, alphanumeric keyboard, bar code reader compatibility, one-mile operating range, $9 \times 3 \times 1.75$ inch dimensions, weight of 2 pounds, and a cost of $2200. The base unit/computer interface supports up to eight such devices per computer interface unit at a cost of $2300.

The marriage of these RF terminals to bar code readers presents some very promising opportunities for inventory control procedures and statistical process control. From the inventory side let us examine a scenario presently in place at several Fortune 500 companies. A material handler scans his bar coded employee identification badge. The system displays, "Good morning, Craig," and directs the handler to storage location 123. Upon arriving the handler scans the shelf tag at storage location 124 and is corrected by the computer system. Scanning shelf tag 123 the operator is prompted to pick 12 of product ABC against work order 789. After the 12 ABCs are scanned as picked, the system prompts the operator to enter the number of ABCs remaining at shelf location 123. The operator keys in "23." The system compares this amount to the amount present in its database and finds a discrepancy: 24 units should be present at location 123. The computer asks the operator to recount and enter the amount. The operator again counts 23, enters the same, and the computer adjusts its inventory noting that a discrepancy exists, who found it, when it was found, the last handler known by the system to be at that location, and the time he was there. These types of systems can perform a cycle count with each pick without the associated paperwork. They can improve inventory accuracy levels to +99%, eliminating the need for periodic physical inventory procedures. Because auditors are very happy to achieve 95 to 97% inventory accuracy, the opportunities available with bar code technology are phenomenal.

## Other Considerations

A typical EDP installation allocates 30 percent of its budget to the data entry function, with 80 percent of the data entry cost directly attributable to the salaries and benefits of data entry personnel. Key operators enter data at an average rate of two to five characters per second. Bar code data entry rates often are 30 characters per second. The key operator averages one error in every 300 characters entered. This error rate can be reduced to one error in every 45 trillion characters when bar code data entry is used. (Refer to Chapter 3, Table 3-1 for a comparison of key-entry, OCR, and bar coding.)

Portable data entry terminals are available in a wide range of sizes, shapes, weights, and capabilities. Some simply record the scanned data. Some have data and program memory and can be programmed for a specific data entry function. Most have a keyboard and display. Most portable data entry terminals are batch oriented. This means that the data are collected in the memory of the terminal and transmitted later as blocks of data to the host computer. Others immediately transmit their data to the host processor, using a radio or optical link. Those terminals that transmit data immediately are said to be on-line with the host processor. On-line portable terminals permit two-way communication between terminals and host. These systems can use data verification and editing to further improve data accuracy.

Some portable data entry terminals incorporate a keyboard, similar to a calculator or typewriter. Some keyboards are configured for strictly numeric data entry, while others accommodate both alphabetic and numeric data. The category of alphanumeric keyboards is further divided into a straight A through Z and 0 through 9 arrangement or a QWERTY-style keyboard as on a typewriter. If the operator is a moderately skilled typist or is familiar with computer data entry, the QWERTY-style keyboard is probably the most appropriate. If the operator is one who "hunts and pecks" it is easier to hunt and peck if the keys are arranged in a sequential manner. With both numeric and alphanumeric keyboards, prospective users should examine whether special characters, such as the decimal point (.), dash (–), or space, are required in the anticipated application and if special function keys are needed.

Some terminals that have been designed around the requirement for bar code scanning employ a novel approach to character data entry by encoding the individual characters in a bar code configuration and using a light pen stroke in place of a keystroke. One advantage of this method is that the keyboard can be remote from the terminal, permitting applications where the operator must also pick up items in addition to entering data. Such character menus can also be formatted with character strings that have a predetermined meaning in the data processing system. Yes and no, skip and enter, back space and delete, and clear and review could each cause the portable data entry terminal to perform in some defined method beyond simple character-at-a-time data entry. This same menu concept could be applied on a much more macroscopic basis where strings collected from different sources in a sequential fashion could yield improved traceability and labor reporting. Consider a manufacturing environment where management wants to establish how much time is required for various employees to perform specific tasks. Or perhaps management wishes to track a specific sold unit back to the conditions under which the unit was manufactured. Any product subject to recall or warranty could be so tracked. Labor standards could be more realistically developed and manufacturing resources could be more effectively utilized. Most manufacturing operations require two pieces of paper for documentation of work; one to open the operation and one to indicate that the operation has been completed. In an assembly which requires five operations, ten pieces of paper will be generated, each requiring some form of subsequent editing and key entry. In this macroscopic menu system, a worker would: read his/her badge number, read the carrier document of the assembly, record the operation being undertaken, record the date and time it was completed and what the disposition of the assembly was, following the workstations operation; all in bar code character strings and without the associated costs of key-entry workstations at each manufacturing position or labor-time lost in shared terminal systems.

Just as the keyboard is defined in terms of what characters are required for data entry, so should the display be defined in terms of types of characters to be displayed and the quantity of characters required to be displayed at one time. Characters are formed either by line segments or by a dot matrix. Line-segment displays consist of either seven segments to accommodate numeric characters or 15 segments that can accommodate most ASCII characters, including alphabetic, numeric, and special characters. Dot-matrix displays employ dots that are usually arranged in a 5-by-7 or 7-by-9 matrix to form ASCII characters.

Display characters are formed by light emitting diodes (LEDs) or liquid crystal displays (LCDs). LEDs have been used for a longer time and provide more crisply formed and, consequently, more readable characters, than do their LCD counterparts. LEDs do have several drawbacks, however, which contribute to the market successes of LCDs. If a terminal having a character display is battery operated, an LED will exhaust the power of the battery far sooner, requiring more frequent recharging or replacement. LED displays generally consume more power than all the rest of the terminal. LCDs are more temperature sensitive than LEDs. LCDs can be used outside in direct sunlight, whereas LEDs are washed out by the intensity of direct sunlight, rendering the LED display unreadable. Applications in dimly lit environments generally favor the readability of LEDs, although backlighting of LCDs has met with some success.

Batch portable data entry terminals store the data that is being collected in random access memory (RAM) or microcassette magnetic tape. RAM is available that stores from 4K to 256K characters of data and more. In addition to data memory, many terminals have a program memory which controls the terminal's display and prompts the operator for specific data in a defined sequence. The program memory also determines how the captured data is to be stored, as well as the time it is stored, and performs various data entry edits on the input data, such as length check, check character, and character string content. Program memories are typically contained in read-only memory (ROM). True ROMs are programmed by the semiconductor manufacturer and the resident program can never be altered. Erasable programmable read-only memories (EPROMS) are generally programmed electrically by the terminal manufacturer and erased by exposure to ultraviolet light. Still another variety of ROM is the electrically erasable programmable read-only memory ($E^2PROM$ or EEPROM). Application programs do not have to reside in ROM. Some portable data entry terminals have a high level interpreter that resides in the ROM, permitting the user to define the application program, prompts, edits, and so on. In these terminals the user enters the programming mode (usually permitting programs to be written in either BASIC or FORTH), writes the program, debugs it, and executes the program straight from the terminal. The application program is resident in RAM and can be saved on a microcassette or protected in memory.

Portable data entry terminals can accommodate other peripherals such as printers, which may be remote from the terminal or integrated within the terminal structure. Portable data entry terminals usually must be connected to communications devices to permit the transmission of the collected data to the host system. Some portables require their own receivers, some are made to look like standard data communication protocols by means of a protocol converter, and still others communicate in a "system friendly" fashion and are easily connected to larger computer systems. The data communications device that takes the stored data and transmits it on conventional telephone lines must also convert the data to standard tones. Such a device is called a modem (MOdulator/DEModulator). A modem is connected directly to the phone line or to the standard telephone handset by using an acoustic coupler.

Some terminals perform better than others in specific environments. Some are designed to operate in an office environment, while others are designed to work in the harsh environment found in the factory. Each has unique environmental specifications relating to temperature, humidity, shock, vibration, and electromagnetic susceptibility. Hand-held portable data entry terminals provide a logical extension of distributed processing by putting computer power directly in the hands of those performing the work. It is important, however, that the system designers carefully evaluate their needs against the capabilities of a specific portable data entry terminal.

In contradistinction to terminals that collect data over a period of time and then transmit all data representative of that period (batch-type terminals) are the on-line PDETs that communicate directly with the host processor at all times, e.g., where management would want to direct an operator based upon the content of the collected data, such as directing a material handler in a warehouse as to storage location for a specific picking operation. Generally, in an on-line configuration, PDETs are linked via a radio link to a controller having the capacity to communicate with numerous terminals. The controller is connected directly to the computer and can receive or transmit messages between the terminal and computer over a wireless, radio-frequency, microwave, or infrared communications channel.

Hand-held terminals can be used for a wide range of scanning applications in a manufacturing environment, from the receipt of raw materials to the final shipment of finished goods. These electronic clipboards are particularly effective for production-line monitoring and lot tracking. Inventory control applications are aided in physical inventory and cycle counting. Finished goods can be tracked through the warehousing of the product and hand-helds with scanners can be used in stock locator applications. Quality control is aided, because the inspector is prompted through each procedure to guarantee completeness and proper sequencing of tests.

Wholesalers employ hand-held scanners and portable data entry terminals as order entry tools. Retailers scan shelf tags and enter the quantity of an item on the shelf. This information is transmitted to a host computer which matches the stock available on the shelves to the sales characteristics of the product, triggering reorder points. Such efficient tracking of stock prevents a lost sale due to an out-of-stock condition, while minimizing the carrying costs of the product.

Some wholesalers provide catalogs of their products which have bar codes printed adjacent to the products. To speed the ordering of a product and to lower the costs associated with product ordering, the catalog product codes are scanned into the portable data entry terminal. The terminal is connected to a modem, which either calls the wholesaler's computer or waits to be called by the wholesaler. The order is transmitted directly, without the costs associated with voice communications, translation errors, transcription errors, and subsequent key entry.

Hospitals use hand-held terminals with scanners to gather and track patient files, for automatic reordering of supplies, drug distribution control, specimen tracking, and statistical record keeping. Bar coded patient wrist bands and unit doses minimize the possibility of administering the wrong drug to the patient. Hospital laboratories use hand-held scanners and portable data entry terminals to collect test data and provide positive tracking of samples, supplies, equipment, and records.

The marriage of the bar code reader and the portable data entry terminal has three effects. It reduces errors, lowers costs, and improves productivity.

# SECTION VI
# SYSTEMS DESIGN

# CHAPTER 18

# JUSTIFYING AND IMPLEMENTING A BAR CODE SYSTEM

Bar codes, by themselves, do nothing! It is the combination of symbol, reader, terminal, communications, and computer software which permits most bar code implementations to achieve a positive return on the investment in them in less than one year. Retail industries have standardized around the fixed-length, fixed-format, and numeric-only UPC code and symbology for units of sale, with an extended-format (though still fixed-length, fixed-format, and numeric-only) and the Interleaved 2 of 5 symbology on shipping containers. The non-retail markets, including manufacturing for retail and non-retail products, have adopted the industry/application-specific format, variable length, and alphanumeric Code 39 symbology. These markets include primary metals, automotive, air transport, government, electronics, machinery, pulp and paper, graphics, and heath care markets. The rationale behind the standards is to foster the enhancement of existing industry software packages and the introduction of new packages which will serve the needs of the marketplace. This is becoming increasingly important in the standardization of mini- and micro-sized computer systems.

Clients often suggest that they wish to connect data collection equipment directly to their mainframe. A quick way to defuse this suggestion is to ask the client what is the existing inquiry response time for the mainframe. Even in traditional batch modes, response times measure 5 seconds, 10 seconds, and even 30 seconds or more. With such extended response times, attempting to collect bar code data in real-time will bring the mainframe to its knees. Capturing data in real-time will entail time-stamping the entry, accessing associated data on disk, and transmitting that data back to the data collection terminal. A moderate to high level of data collection transactions may cause data to begin building up in queues, preventing more data from being captured. Don't forget that both mainframes and the communication links they depend on go down on occasion; when the system is down, data can no longer be collected in mainframe-dependent designs.

The rationale for automated data collection is to approach a paperless environment. When data cannot be collected, and a paper-based back-up system is not immediately available, production must be interrupted. The need for consistent production, and reducing the cost of data collection, has given rise to fault-tolerant, on-line transactional processing computer systems. Such systems may be configured as mainframes, but not without substantial extra cost. With devices such as the AT&T 3B1, DEC Micro-Vax, Epson Equity, HP Vectra PC, ITT Xtra, NCR MicroTower, Xerox 6085, IBM System 36 PC, and IBM PC/ATs, enhanced with co-processor boards to permit faster clock speeds, and multi-user and multi-tasking environments, it is now possible to network two or more systems to provide the redundancy (or fault tolerance) required for electronic data collection in manufacturing environments. Microcomputers like those named above also permit fault tolerance through the operation of simultaneous parallel systems, at a substantially reduced cost to the mainframe solution.

The use of minis and micros on the factory floor permits faster implementation as well. Turning to corporate or institutional MIS departments for software support, one is frequently confronted with three choices:

- To wait two years for the program to be coded;
- To replace an existing high priority project from the same department with the new project; or,
- To use operations department budgets to hire additional programming staff.

Minis and micros can often be on site within three months, complete with the custom software needed to support bar code data collection, provide local operations management, and with an interface to the mainframe which emulates existing data entry methods.

For the most part, bar code technology is thought of as a method of identifying things—a stock keeping unit (SKU), a catalog number, or an airbill. The adage "If it moves – bar code it!", has caused many of us to overlook some of the even greater opportunities that exist in recording transactions. Physical "things" are not all that moves; information moves as well. Often, however, operational data moves far too slowly to be useful for effective management of a business entity. In today's fast-paced business environment, corporate management must have access to information that is as current as can be obtained, preferably information that changes each moment to reflect the changing environment.

Transactional identification technologies permit the capture of information in real time through bar code identification of the essential elements of a transaction. These transactional elements are WHO, WHAT, HOW MANY, WHEN, WHERE, HOW, and WHY. Elaborating further:

**WHO** may identify the individual recording the transaction. The identity is conventionally secured from a bar coded employee identification card, though successful examples exist wherein the employee identification is contained on some other form of bar coded marked medium. **WHO** might identify an operator or a recipient. Figure 18-1A shows a bar coded employee identification badge. Figure 18-1B shows a bar coded patient wristband.

**Figure 18-1A. Bar coded employee ID badge**

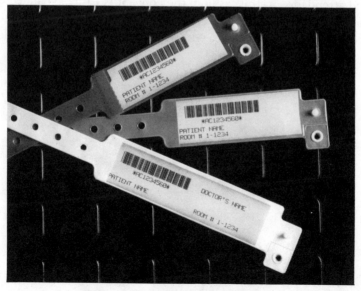

**Figure 18-1B. Bar coded patient wristband**

**WHAT** may be the identity traditionally thought of when considering bar code technology as an item identification technology, viz., the SKU number, the catalog number, or air bill number. This "identity" can also describe a function or series of functions, such as a work order number or quality test report number.

**HOW MANY** may identify the quantity of **WHAT** is being recorded.

**WHEN** may identify the time at which a transaction took place or when it is to occur. Recording the **WHEN** of a transaction is frequently accomplished by the computer time-stamping the data at the time it is entered. **WHEN** could also direct an employee about the time, or within what sequence, a transaction is to be accomplished. For example, in the case of recording statistical process control data, a set of bar code symbols could identify the sequence of data recording.

**WHERE** identifies the location where the transaction took place. Just as the computer can add a time to a transaction, the computer system can maintain an "address" for each data entry terminal which is appended to the transaction. Additionally, **WHERE** can be a bar code marked location sticker affixed to the data entry terminal or to a physical location, such as a storage shelf, a warehouse location, or a room.

**HOW** may identify the steps taken, or the nature of the transaction. A straightforward example of **HOW** would be in a simple time and attendance setting. Bar code symbols representing *Morning clock-in, To break, From break, and Evening clock-out* could serve the same function as a time clock, eliminating the need to process the time cards because each entry is immediately posted to an employee's hourly record. Only a marginal benefit exists in recording time and attendance in this fashion; the concept is easily expanded to provide labor standards reports based on specific tasks. The tasks can be encoded in a bar code symbol generated in a semi-permanent fashion. Only a predefined, limited set of tasks occur at a given location (a "menu" – see Figure 18-2). Or, task definition could be secured from a document that would travel with **WHAT**'s unique to the prescribed task (a "traveler" – see Figure 18-3). In a quality control environment, the tasks might be included within a Quality Control Operations Manual whose pages would contain bar code symbols to represent specific tests and specific types of observations. Manufacturing time and attendance data can be assigned to specific manufacturing orders and tasks by *symbolizing* standard operating procedures and practices on the work order in bar code form.

**WHY** may identify the reason a specific activity is undertaken. The identification may come from a work order or purchase order. **HOW** identifies the process or procedure and **WHY** identifies the authority for the process or procedure.

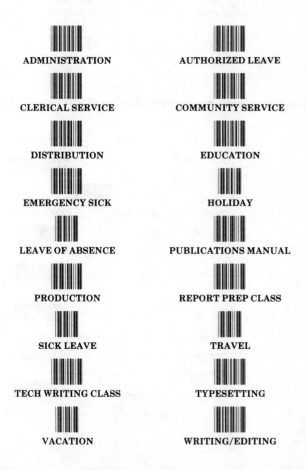

**Figure 18-2A. Sample menu: non-manufacturing (Courtesy of Data Documents Systems, Inc.)**

**Figure 18-2B. Sample menu: manufacturing (Courtesy of Data Documents Systems, Inc.)**

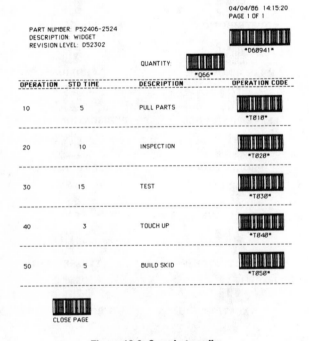

**Figure 18-3. Sample traveller**

The implementation of any bar code system requires close attention to various system issues. These include:
- Training and Education
- Organizational Structure
- Phased Implementation
- Numbering Schemes
- Reporting Techniques

**Training and Education** is critical at all levels within the organization. Senior management needs to be trained because they are responsible for leading and directing the program. Middle and lower management also need this education because they must develop and then execute the programs. And last, but certainly not least, the users must be educated. They must be able to view the program with confidence, to see that they are making a contribution to the success of the program, and to consider bar code technology a friendly tool. The design of the program, and close attention to issues such as print quality, symbol X dimension, reader aperture size, and symbol aspect ratio will ensure that the operator is able to easily achieve a good scan 85 to 90 percent of the time. Lower first-read rates will frustrate the user, destroying any confidence that may exist. Many clerks in the large national department stores have totally lost confidence in the Optical Character Recognition (OCR) systems. This loss of confidence has caused them to abandon the technology and to favor error-prone key-entry methods. While it is highly unlikely that bar code reading rates will ever suffer from the negative performance associated with OCR, careful attention to system design will improve the level of user confidence in the program.

The end user must be able to see his or her contribution to the program. This contribution may be simply making suggestions about where a terminal should be located, but involvement by the end user during system design helps improve acceptance of the program after implementation. Finally, the end user must see bar code technology as a friendly tool and not as some form of automation that will replace him. Bar code technology makes information available more quickly and more accurately. It improves cash flow and helps lower inventory levels. Like most automation, it does not create wholesale lay-offs in personnel. Instead of seeing the bar code program as a threat, the user should be advised that successful use of the technology will substantially reduce the reports he is required to complete. No one likes to fill out the paperwork associated with labor reporting, scheduling, and materials use. Bar code technology can substantially reduce these disliked duties.

**Organizational Structure** is extremely important in bar code system design. To begin with, a corporate bar code task force needs to be assembled, representing *all* departments within the organization. It is the role of this task force to "blue sky" the possible applications within the organization, to select the initial and subsequent pilot programs, to oversee the development of programs in each functional area of the organization, and to transfer technology and lessons learned from department to department. The program responsibility for this task force should rest with a "champion" of the technology. The champion should understand the company functions, both internally and externally. The champion should also have knowledge of the corporate data processing operations and not have any fear of data processing acronyms. The champion should also become the internal resource for information on bar code technology. The champion should have the ability and the authority to define and implement these systems. Finally, the champion needs to be a salesman— able to sell program concepts and requirements to superiors, subordinates, and peers.

The requirement for financial resources is one area where the champion's sales skill may be tested, since invariably management will want to know, "How much will this bar code program save the organization?" One can go to external consultants or to internal industrial engineering departments to find out how much will be saved through the introduction of bar code technology, but the cost of such a study can exceed $40,000. Most bar code systems have paid for themselves in less than one year. Instead of undertaking a massive study to establish how much may be saved, it would be far better to select one highly visible area of the organization and to pilot the technology in that area. Since top management won't be asked to approve the expenditure of hundreds of thousands of dollars, ask management to take a leap of faith regarding the implementation of the pilot bar code system. The highly visible area chosen for the pilot should not be one fraught with problems. Automating a problem-ridden area only causes the problems and inefficiencies to appear more quickly.

The chosen area should be subjected to phased implementation, in which the bar code program has been planned by the task force, piloted in a visible application area, measured against pre-bar code costs and efficiencies, modified to embrace what was learned in the pilot, and expanded to other areas of the organization. Modifications should not occur until the system has had a chance to settle. If the program is inoperative it should be modified to become operational, but if the modification is an enhancement, make sure that most of the modifications considered not be implemented until at least 90 days after the pilot goes live. Since the cost of this program is lower than if the entire organization is brought on-line at the same time, management should be anxious to implement the pilot without overstudying the issue. Phased implementation also permits the organization to take advantage of new technology as it is introduced.

Some organizations have established product numbering systems based on group technology. While flexible manufacturing systems may benefit from group technology, product identification and marking do not. Numbering systems can be thought of as either descriptive or as a license plate. And since it is desirable to mark as low a level of component as possible, it is often desirable to have the product number as small as possible. The license plate approach makes this possible. Code 39 is the dominant bar code symbology in industry; it provides 26 alphabetic and 10 numeric characters in each character position, from which the product may be identified. One character position gives 36 possible permutations, two characters permit 1296, three give 46,656, four yield 1,679,616, and five produce 60,466,176 unique codes. In the license plate approach there is flexibility in numbering, and the computer system maintains descriptive and bill of materials data, while using a small code structure. Numbering schemes are important in bar code technology because the length of the symbol may affect the operator's ability to maintain a smooth, sweeping motion. The size of the printed symbol, the cost of the printed symbol, the time required to print the symbol, and the accuracy with which the symbol can be read (the longer the symbol, the higher the probability of achieving either a no-read or a mis-read) are unaffected by the numbering scheme used.

Bar code technology will also impact reporting techniques, because now it is possible to find out WHO is doing WHAT, WHEN, and WHERE it is occurring, HOW it is happening, and WHY. This information makes immediate intervention possible. With past data-capture systems, intervention was seldom possible because the report followed the activity by days or weeks. Now, corrective action can be taken immediately in much the same way that statistical quality control in manufacturing reduces the amount of rework and scrap. Most businesses today track by exception. If something goes wrong, it is tracked and monitored. Anything that falls in the mainstream is not tracked. Positive tracking is the opposite of exception tracking. In positive tracking, *all* movement and operations are monitored. Federal Express gained tremendously from positive tracking via bar codes. Finally, bar code technology permits immediate on-line inquiry to establish what is going on in manufacturing at this very moment – not what happened last week. The immediate availability of information permits management to *control* operations, not simply review a record of what happened, and find ways to alter similar situations in the future.

A final bar code form, one of a "paper scannable keyboard," serves as a data entry tool encoding values such as 0 to 9, A to Z, ., +, −, $, /, %, and space. Where appropriate—in recording test observations or in reporting yield quantities—such "keyboards" can provide limited variable information entered one character at a time.

In this Transactional Identification System scenario, each type of data element is uniquely flagged. The flag takes the form of a prefix to each data element. An employee identification might be flagged as an "IC," a storage location as a "LW," a manufacturing work order as an "OF," etc. Following these flag characters would be the unique identity of the WHO, WHAT, HOW MANY, WHEN, WHERE, and HOW.

A properly designed Transactional Identification System has the capability of functioning with work stations of the dumb or intelligent variety, and with software that prompts the operator for data elements. The use of flag characters precludes an employee identification from being entered when what was being requested was a warehouse location.

Other industries would be well advised to follow the lead provided by the health care industry, and provide a standard for data element definition (though the health care industry should be more frugal in character assignment, lest we run out of flag characters). One Department of Defense study identified 700 different data elements for recording transactions. These 700 data elements could easily be uniquely represented employing two alphanumeric characters. Proprietary arguments can be made that common data structures might remove some of the competitive considerations.

While agreeing upon a common definition for various data elements for bar code systems is no more deleterious to competition than most of the common Electronic Data Interchange (EDI) formats being suggested today, a common standard would foster the development of less costly computer software throughout all segments of commerce and industry. Today there exists an abundance of bar code equipment to capture data, but a dearth of computer software to transform the captured data into usable information for operations management. Common industry definitions for data elements permit the development of software not only for bar code technology, but for other transactional identification technologies. It would be most desirable for all industries to agree on a common format for intercompany communications including transactional identification technologies. To some extent this is being accomplished through standards for EDI, but as of this writing such efforts are fragmented at best.

Bar code technology, in its item identification form, will permit extensive savings to be realized by organizations implementing the technology. Implementation of transactional identification technologies permits the savings to be even greater. But bar code technology is nothing more than a fourth-generation keyboard with the characteristics of better accuracy, improved productivity, and lower cost than its predecessors. Bar codes symbols and readers, like keyboards and forms, require proven applications software to provide meaningful information to management. Agreement across industry lines to adopt standards relating to both data structures and methods of encodation will permit improved operational efficiency and more cost-effective software.

The costs associated with implementing a bar code system can be found in two areas, start-up costs and ongoing costs:

- Start-up Costs
  - Orientation, education, and training of personnel
  - Label redesign
  - Packaging changes
  - Cost of printers
  - Cost of verification tools (if employed)
  - Cost of applicators (if employed)
  - Computer system change cost (if any)
  - Bar code reading equipment
  - Training costs of field organization
- On-going Costs
  - Cost of labels and supplies
  - Replacement of equipment parts
  - Cost of application (if no applicator is employed)

Offsetting these costs are the benefits realized by the corporation or institution implementing the bar code systems. These benefits include:

- Better Information
  - Information which is standardized;
  - Information which is more timely;
  - Information where manual errors have been eliminated;
  - Information which gives a more accurate product/service identification.
- Cost Savings
  - Data collected more rapidly;
  - Data capture is automated, labor savings over manual data collection;
  - Data is inherently more accurate, necessitating less manual error correction;
  - The materials handling system is more streamlined, requiring less "safety stock";
  - The upstream administrative support is minimized since the data is immediately available from the information system.

# SECTION VII
# APPLICATIONS

# CHAPTER 19

# TIME IS MONEY

## A Network Makes Bar Codes Really Work

BY DONNA BARRON

Time is money—or at least that's what people say. The question, then, is: Does saving time necessarily save you money?

It does if you've got a factory to run, according to Robert McConnell of Rockwell International Corporation. McConnell is project leader of manufacturing systems at Rockwell's Missile Systems Division plant located in Duluth, Georgia, just northeast of Atlanta. The plant, which designs, develops, and manufactures laser tracking devices and tactical missiles (such as the Hellfire missile) for the U.S. Department of Defense and America's allies, recently installed an Intermec Crossbar bar code network as a time-saving device.

Rockwell's Missile Systems Division plant has been around since 1981. It currently employs some 2300 workers at three separate sites. About 500 of these workers comprise two shifts of what McConnell calls "touch labor" people. Touch labor workers are divided into a number of separate work groups, each of which is responsible for all the handwork done on the individual system subassemblies (multi-part units) for a particular project or projects. Each subassembly must undergo a predetermined number of steps to reach completion and must pass through numerous hands as it moves from step to step and worker to worker through the plant. Each subassembly is tracked via its own manufacturing order, which indicates exactly which and how many steps are required for completion of the product, and who's supposed to get the bill.

"We have 100,000 manufacturing orders out on the shop floor, each one for a specific part," says McConnell. With labor charges being made on an hours worked basis and payment for each project coming out of a different pocket, the need for accurate time-keeping records is essential. Add to that the need to keep track of the status of each part—where it is within the plant and what's being done to it by whom—and you can see why McConnell wanted a quick and easy way to input labor charges and status data.

It wasn't as if this was all being done by abacus and carrier pigeon before the Intermec system was installed. The plant has been, and still is, running a Tandem mainframe with TXP processors. Once the information is properly entered into the host, the computer handles all the busywork involved in billing and tracking. The big difference the Intermec system has made is in the input devices. Before the CrossBar network was installed, employees had been entering data exclusively via 130 CRTs located throughout the shop floor.

"Those terminals have both magnetic stripe and bar code readers attached to them," says McConnell. "The employee badges have a magnetic strip on them and our manufacturing orders have bar codes on them. When an employee wanted to charge labor to a manufacturing order, he or she would walk over to a terminal, scan his or her badge, scan the bar code on the manufacturing order, and then hit a function key. It was basically all done through on-line screens."

## The Equation

It sounds like a functional system. Why change? The answer goes back to the original time-is-money equation, says McConnell. Here's how he figures it out. Even with 130 CRTs, in a plant the size of Rockwell's Missile Systems Division a terminal could be as far as 30 feet from an employee's work station. "If you disregard the interruption and break in work flow and look solely at the amount of time it takes a person to get up and walk to a terminal and then get back to his or her work station—even if that's only a one-minute transaction, if that employee does ten transactions a day, that's ten minutes per employee per day. Multiply that times five days a week and you're up to 50 minutes per week per employee," says McConnell. Extrapolate what that means if you've got 500 employees and you come up with enough hours to fill ten 40-hour shifts every week.

Having to lay out the equivalent of ten employees' salaries because workers needed to walk to a CRT simply did not sit right with McConnell. But it wasn't until he visited the company's Cedar Rapids, Iowa, division about a year ago that he came up with a solution. "They were using an earlier form of one of Intermec's satellites," McConnell says. While the Cedar Rapids facility was PC-based, McConnell saw possibilities in tying the Intermec satellite readers into his Tandem system back in Duluth. With satellite readers right at their work stations, McConnell postulated, employees wouldn't have to waste time walking back and forth from the existing CRTs every time they needed to update the status of a manufacturing order.

What he ultimately ended up with is what Intermec calls its hybrid CrossBar bar code network. The hybrid network is composed of Intermec 9512 bar code transaction managers which are hardwired to 9191 satellite wand stations. Transaction managers are essentially programmable bar code readers that can support up to ten satellite input devices. Unlike a stand-alone system, which works independently and provides no access to mainframe data, or a completely interactive on-line system that ties up the mainframe from the beginning to the end of the transaction, the hybrid network allows a Rockwell employee direct access to the host when necessary, yet permits certain validation or verification tasks to be handled by the transaction manager before the employee starts taking up time on the host.

So far Rockwell has installed about 89 satellite wand stations, which currently serve about 150 people. "With a station between every two people, they don't even have to get off their chairs now. Updating the status of the manufacturing orders now takes place within their normal work flow rather than as an interruption," says McConnell.

## Saving Time and Money

The way the system is set up, Rockwell has programmed the 9512 transaction managers to do all the front-end validation for its manufacturing order data entry. An employee who wants to enter a manufacturing order, for example, would scan the bar code menu card at that satellite station, to indicate what kind of entry is going to be made, and would then wand his or her employee badge and the manufacturing order number. The transaction manager would verify the format of the entered data and either reject it as improperly entered or pass it on to the host for processing. The host would then immediately verify the actual data, i.e., whether the employee badge number is valid or whether the manufacturing order number is still open for billing, and return a go-ahead or error signal. If an error signal is received, the employee can make further inquiries of a supervisor or via one of the CRTs to find out why work clearance has been rejected.

"With editing and validation going on at both the transaction manager and mainframe levels, there's no way for anyone to interfere with the information on the mainframe. All anyone can do is collect the data that we're trying to collect. Nothing can be entered that hasn't been preprogrammed for," says McConnell.

One of the things McConnell particularly likes about the satellites is that they have no moving parts beside the wand itself. An optical scanner detects whether the wand is in or out of its holder and a busy signal lights up and beeps if the wand is left off the hook, but nothing has to be manually turned on or off. There are no keyboards and no magnetics. The bar code menu card allows users to indicate what information they plan to enter and to abort the entry if necessary. Four programmed LEDs light up to indicate if the entry is progressing properly and whether or not the data has been accepted and given the go-ahead.

Rockwell's CrossBar network uses a "drop-line" configuration which allows runs of up to 500 feet between a transaction manager and satellite. Intermec 9161A port connectors are used to beef up transmissions between transaction managers and the host computer where necessary, and phone lines are used to connect the remote plant sites to the mainframe.

Only one satellite on a string can be active at any one time, but this is not inconvenient, according to McConnell. "If you have ten people side by side, odds are they're not going to complete something at exactly the same time. Besides, a transaction only takes about ten seconds to complete," he says.

According to McConnell, Rockwell will eventually purchase 250 satellite wand stations. The total cost of the system is estimated at around $230,000. While he won't comment on exactly how long he thinks it will take to amortize installation and hardware costs, if his time-is-money equation holds true, it probably won't take very long.

# CHAPTER 20

# EVEN DOWN EAST

## Scanning Fares Well on the Turnpike

### BY R. MONROE DORRIS

On February 1, 1985, the Maine Turnpike Authority made an important move toward the future. It took tollbooth time clocks so old that parts were no longer available, and data processing equipment installed in the 1960s, and replaced them with a scanning and computer-based automated fare collection system, the first of its kind anywhere in the world. The system has performed so well that 60 tollbooths are being outfitted with the additional capabilities of receipt printing and treadle counting.

The new system enables the Maine Turnpike Authority to account for all toll tickets issued and provides immediate and cumulative data on traffic flow for the entire 100-mile state highway. On-going reporting and analysis of traffic patterns has led to increased short- and long-range planning, especially important in the scheduling of preventive maintenance.

Systems Assurance Corporation, a Yarmouth, Maine, systems design firm, designed the system, delivered it on time and within budget, and continues to maintain and upgrade it. Currently, hardware consists of 15 remote computers, one mainframe at headquarters, and over 90 laser-based bar code scanners. Funding for this equipment and the system's design came entirely from turnpike revenues.

Operating the system is not dramatically different from the original time-clock method for the toll collectors. Each toll ticket given to a motorist carries a bar code containing data on the motorist's point of entry, class of vehicle (automobile, truck, bus, or other type), number of axles, and a seven-digit serial number. The toll collector places the ticket inside a scanner, which automatically reads the bar code and feeds the data to the toll plaza computer, and in turn to the headquarters' mainframe in Portland, Maine. The fare, which is printed on a simple graph on the ticket, is still read manually by the toll collector.

According to Brian Farwell, assistant executive director of the Maine Turnpike Authority, "The system provides us with a remarkably efficient way to collect a comprehensive and accurate database. Using it, we are able to identify peak traffic periods and to determine the times and directions of typical traffic patterns."

Although the system has yielded the average travel times between individual toll plazas, the Authority has expressed its intention not to use it to police the speed limit. In theory, the system could identify violators if each toll booth was equipped with a camera to record the license plates of cars whose elapsed travel times clearly indicate speeds of greater than 55 mph.

"We are extremely pleased with the field operation of the system," says Donald Chase, the president of Systems Assurance Corporation. "In fact, we are now talking with the turnpike authorities of other states and are glad to have such a successful working model to point to."

According to Chase, Systems Assurance pursued several important goals when it designed the system. "First, we sought hardware and software solutions that were as simple and straightforward as possible—the intent was to keep maintenance and development costs down. Next, we wanted a modular design whose hardware and software components could be easily expanded. Then, we made sure that the software would be entirely table-driven to allow for variations in equipment by plaza. And finally, we integrated everything with maximum throughput rates in mind. We didn't want to see traffic slowdowns result from increasing transaction rates."

The system configuration includes a Series 1 IBM computer at each toll plaza. At smaller plazas, a double disk microcomputer system is used. At larger plazas, the computers have a hard disk incorporated. The computer contains the control programs and storage for all plaza-level transactions. Once each day a teller copies the computer's transactions onto a disk for delivery to headquarters. Soon the transactions will be automatically off-loaded via phone lines.

A Lear Siegler ADM 22 CRT with keyboard serves as the operator interface for each Series 1. The teller uses it for data collection and it displays traffic counts upon request.

The data collection key to the system is the laser-based bar code scanner housed in each tollbooth. Systems Assurance subcontracted with Metrologic Instruments, Inc. to develop the special scanner. Metrologic designed the unit with a rugged metal housing, incorporating a card slot, so that it actually resembles the time clocks previously used. A light on the front of the scanner provides visual indication when a good read has been made.

The data collected by each scanner is transmitted to the plaza's S1 computer through a microprocessor controller and a multiplexing unit that permits up to four scanners per controller. The maximum number of scanners (lanes) currently used at any one plaza is 20.

All data is eventually interfaced to an IBM Series 36 computer at the Authority's Portland headquarters. Here, a wide range of vital reports is generated, including: collector tickets/money reports, collector log on/off reports, unmatched reports (all tickets have unique serial numbers), charge account reports, and traffic/lane analysis reports.

There are several plazas where installation of Series 1 computers is physically impractical, so modem hook-ups have been provided. In some cases, a remote S1 controls only that plaza, and in others, one S1 controls two plazas.

In the plazas being equipped with receipt printing and treadle counting, each plaza's Series 1 has been front-ended with additional computers at the lane level in order to ensure that the throughput rates are maintained. An industrialized version of the IBM PC is being used for this purpose. Treadle counting is handled through existing equipment and special software programming. The receipt printer is the same basic model used in Maine's Mega Bucks lottery terminal.

CHAPTER 21

# MICRO CODE

## At Altos, Quality Is First

### BY CHRISTOPHER SEID

When Altos Computer Systems of San Jose, California, manufacturer of 18,000 microcomputers annually, began recently to manufacture customized computers as well as their regular models, they soon found they were shipping incorrectly configured computers to end users. So they got busy tracking the glitch in their system. It didn't take long to find it: human error on the assembly line.

The people at Altos faced numerous problems. Too often customized computers were shipped out with the wrong components: the wrong disk drive, or an incorrect pc board configuration. Other units slipped past operators and test locations altogether. And still others, with incorrect specification codes or no codes at all, were entered in the production folder. This meant that the particular configurations unique to special-order, customized units, of which Altos handles many, were missed completely. The worst part, however, was the inability to track a unit for repair or upgrade once it had left the factory. According to Steve Carpaneto, Altos' MIS manager, "It was a real mess."

After some furious analyses of its problems, Altos decided to integrate a bar code tracking system into the work-in-process shop floor assembly line. The hope was to increase quality by controlling it: to guarantee correct construction of each delicate, often highly customized unit. But how to set about coding the small components of its microcomputers—pc boards, disk drives, tape units, etc.—some with as many as ten or more major sub-assemblies?

## Enter Intermec West

Altos chose Intermec West to help design and implement the assembly-line tracking system. Intermec's long-standing record in the bar code industry is accentuated by its experience handling small components, such as test tubes and unit dose containers for the medical field, where a small, high-density label is required.

Intermec West's John Mercado, one of the original planners of the Altos system, said, "When we walk into a place like Altos and see the antiquated ways in which data is being collected, we know immediately that if they have the funding, we can improve their operation considerably."

The first step in setting up the Altos tracking system was to put together the hardware and software systems. Altos wanted to use its own hardware, and so found a software vendor to develop a database in Unix to run on an Altos 3068 with 4 MB of memory. There are 20 stations in seven work centers on the assembly-line floor, connected to each other and the main computer via an Altos multi-drop network.

## Around the Loop

To get an idea of how the bar code tracking system works for Altos, let's follow a typical Altos computer along its path of assembly. There are seven centers of construction and testing that each unit must pass before it is completed.

Most component parts arrive at Altos from contractors with preprinted bar code labels already attached. The process begins at the Work in Progress (WIP) cage where a CIE 300+ dot matrix printer prints a multipart production folder containing each unit's configuration and three bar code labels representing the unit's part number, serial number, and work order number. These Code 39 labels are placed on the outside of the WIP cage, which contains the unit and all its major components as it moves along the assembly line and stops at each station or workbench.

At the first control point, WIP Cage Kitting, an Intermec 1620 laser scanner scans first the unit part number, then the unit serial number, calling up on the operator's CRT screen all the information—parts, configuration, work history—relevant to that particular unit, as they appear in a Bill of Materials for that computer unit in the database. Then the operator will scan the variety of bar coded parts and serial numbers of each major component, verifying on the CRT that all are in proper order. There's no chance of human error—a wrong part or serial number being entered incorrectly. When all is verified by the operator, the unit is automatically transferred to the next work station when the operator hits the return key.

Throughout the entire assembly and testing process, the unit's part numbers do not change from the form in which they were originally entered into the configuration matrix and folder at the beginning. If a new part is required at any point during the testing process, then the new part's serial number must be entered into the database. If the new part's number is not correct, it won't be accepted when it is scanned, and a correction can be made before the unit is moved onto the next station.

At stations where only a simple pass or fail response is necessary, Altos installed Intermec 1260 wands. The sophistication of a scanner is not necessary at these points. The operator will first wand the unit's serial number, then the pass or fail bar code label at the workbench. If the unit passes, it moves on to the next work station; if it fails, corresponding rejection codes are scanned from preprinted bar code menus and the unit will go back to the manufacturing drop zone for reworking. This procedure is followed at every test station. The unit will follow the loop around as many times as it takes to test out OK. A count of the number of cycles a unit takes before it is accepted is captured by the system.

It's not unusual for a unit's configuration to be changed in the midst of assembly. Say, for example, the company ordering a specific unit changes its mind about what specifications it wants its unit to meet. If this happens, the unit will visit the Reconfiguration work center where it is torn down and rebuilt. If a unit does go that far, all previous information is deleted from the database, a new production folder is made. The original serial number is retained, but all information related to it is changed in the database to reflect the new configuration of the unit.

There is another station indirectly involved in the assembly process, called Sub-Assembly. This is where subcontracted parts, like disk drives, are received and prepared for kitting. These parts often come with the subcontractor's bar coded serial number already attached. The sub-assembly operator will scan the subcontractor's bar code, and an Intermec 3625A thermal printer prints a new bar code label containing the serial number, Altos part number, and manufacturer's code in both Code 39 and human readable form. On sub-assembly units requiring a cover, the new bar coded serial number label is attached to the outside of the cover so it may be scanned easily when the assembly is kitted for a computer.

At the Burn-In station the computers are held 24 hours in warm ovens while undergoing a series of tests. Afterwards, the verdict is a simple pass or fail. If all goes well here, the unit moves on to Button-Up, where another scan and verification of its serial and part numbers is made before the unit is fitted with a plastic cover. End unit labels are then printed, using a CIE 300 + dot matrix printer.

As each unit moves along the assembly line toward its completion, a very thorough history of its test performances, reject codes, number of reworks, and the total time it took to follow the loop to the end is maintained. Where operators conducting tests encounter a unit failing that test, the proper bar code, from a menu, indicating the specific problem is wanded. "The significance of recording this information," explained Tony Kopcych, Altos' MIS director, "is for the future. We can look at the history of a box at any time and see what kinds of problems occurred during its manufacturing."

Kopcych emphasized that it will be this kind of accurate record keeping that will prove to be the biggest payback of the system. "It may help us in the future with the overall design of our product, as well as the ability to fix a particular box out there in the end user's hands.

The last station a unit visits before completion is Final Quality Assurance. Here the computer goes through final electronic testing before a final configuration code is attached to it. Then, at any time in the future, should any questions arise regarding this particular unit, it will only be a matter of entering the serial number into the system to get complete details about its parts and manufacture.

## Payback

It is still too early to tell what kind of payback Altos can expect from the bar code system. By using its own hardware, the company saved about $35,000. Steve Carpaneto believes the system will pay for itself in a little less than a year. But Tony Kopcych is quick to re-emphasize the value this system is going to have in improving not only customer service, "but also our reputation as a leader in multiuser micro systems.

"People should not be afraid of bar code technology," Kopcych said. "It's very simple technology. When the idea first came up to create this system, I was afraid because I wasn't familiar with the technology. But there's really nothing to learn."

# CHAPTER 22

# A BOOT IN TIME

## Grabbing Scofflaws Where It Counts

BY RIP KELLER

The scene is the University of North Florida in Jacksonville, where a new computerized parking ticket system designed by Immediate Business Systems (IBS) is being tested. The campus cops are about to nab a scofflaw—an offender with more than three or four unpaid citations. "Boot" in hand, they are on their way to immobilize the miscreant.

A patrolman who has found a parking violation keys the vehicle's registration number into the FieldPartner and is immediately apprised if more than ticketing is in order. As for the ticket itself, the officer keys in type of violation, time, and other data the municipality requires. The computer is then plugged into the FieldPrinter, and a few seconds later a ticket (option: waterproof) is ready for the windshield.

The FieldPrinter weighs four pounds and is carried on a shoulder strap. It operates from −5 to 130°F, is unaffected by humidity, and withstands three-foot drops to concrete. It prints six dots per millimeter on thermal paper and carries enough stock to print 150 citations.

For unmetered parking-control situations, the computer offers further amenities. The officer on the beat keys in data on each car he passes (license plate, make, color, and what-have-you), including a code for the location of the car. On a later pass, all the patrolman need do is key in the ID data. The computer does the rest: if the vehicle is parked overtime, FieldPartner flashes "POT."

At the end of the day (the computer has a ten-hour power source) the officer plugs the equipment into the precinct's PC and leaves it there. The PC uploads the data automatically and recharges the equipment. At this point, data on the day's drivers is available. The potential revenue from the day's work is available, as are the types of tickets written, locations of violations for analysis of parking and traffic patterns, and officer productivity reports. Furthermore, a list of the day's scofflaws can be called up on the spot, should that be desired. The PC can also print dunning letters, and interfaces with the courthouse computer system. The PC can maintain a reference file of up to 10,000 parking permits, and it can track 50,000 outstanding tickets at any given time.

The First Signal System prints each citation with a bar code. That means that when a ticket is paid, referred to the courts, or in any way changes in status, the change is recorded without paperwork and almost without anyone touching a keyboard.

How do the men in blue feel about the system? Lieutenant John English, who is in charge of the pilot project at the Jacksonville Beach Police Department, is enthusiastic. He wondered, going into the test, whether public attitudes would be an obstacle. One concern was that the new system would arouse hostility; another that people would not recognize the unfamiliar pieces of paper as parking tickets. Neither count has proven an impediment. The trial was begun during the off-season, but response has been so favorable that there is little reason to fear it will not work amidst the tourist deluge.

Lieutenant English endorses the system without reservation. The bottom line benefits are clear, and comments along the line of, "I can concentrate more on my job, now that I don't have so much paperwork to deal with," have been heard from the force. Sergeant Wayne Johnson, of the University's force, concurs, and adds that in the past, people have had to take time from the jobs they were principally responsible for to give a hand with the paperwork glut. "When you have a dispatcher doing clerical filing, you're wasting money. With this system you can generate more activity without losing a handle on it."

This scene wouldn't have taken place with such regularity a few months ago. The problems of enforcing parking laws in the traditional labor-intensive way are considerably more complex than might be imagined. To the cop on the beat, the hassles start even before he pulls out the pad to write a summons. "Is this the same car that was parked here in an unmetered 60-minute zone two hours ago?" he wonders. Then there's the matter of writing a legible summons in the driving rain. In Jacksonville Beach, Florida, which along with the University of North Florida is testing the IBS system, the traditional sequence of events calls for the day's tickets to be physically delivered to the courthouse. There, the flurry of paper has to be sorted, processed, and digested by the legal system.

Doesn't sound so terrible? Consider the following:

One: There is no foolproof way to monitor the unmetered zones. Result: Revenue loss, and encouragement of carefree parking habits among the citizenry.

Two: "I used to avoid writing tickets," a frank patrolman admits, "because of the hassle. I'd see a car parked in a handicapped zone and I'd just let it go." Result: Same as above.

Three: Fifteen percent of handwritten tickets are so illegible they cannot be processed. Result: Revenue loss.

Four: Clerical processing of the large quantity of paperwork costs money. Result: Revenue loss.

Five: By the time someone at the courthouse exclaims, "This so-and-so already has five tickets outstanding!" it's too late to catch the sneak. Result: Revenue loss and a generous dose of police frustration.

In Jacksonville Beach, fate has yet further magnified these difficulties because tourists, in six-figure droves on most summer weekends, swamp the 20,000-inhabitant town. The town takes on part-time meter readers during the high season as a gesture toward coping, but there is no way to gear up the legal machinery by a factor of ten—at least there wasn't until IBS showed up looking for a test market for First Signal.

IBS has marketed portable harsh-environment computers and printers for a number of years. For example, IBS has an on-site billing system that lets utilities employees take a reading, print a bill, and slip it over a doorknob in one operation.

A couple of years ago IBS evaluated the parking ticket market and found it wanting. They joined forces with the Institute of Police Technology and Management (IPTM), which was marketing software to alleviate office-side police problems. The software, Parking Ticket Management System, produces boot- and tow-eligibility and scofflaw data, as well as statistics on personnel productivity. The database package, Team-Up, is produced by another Jacksonville outfit, Unlimited Processing. The hardware IPTM recommends for this office-based management system is the Epson Equity III with 640K RAM and a 20 MB hard disk drive.

IPTM, which is an active force in police training around the country, has undertaken the educational part of implementing IBS's First Signal System for municipalities that choose the system. Training cost is borne by the municipalities and paid directly to IPTM.

Here's what the IBS system looks like. The computer, called the Field-Partner, weighs one pound and measures about 7 by 3 by 2 inches. It has a backlit LCD with four lines of 20 characters and graphics capability. It operates from −20 to 160°F, is waterproof, and withstands six-foot drops to concrete. And it can contain a file of the scofflaws.

## CHAPTER 23

# AN ELEMENTARY SOLUTION

## Solving Book Club Order Errors

BY DEBRA MARSHALL

Most people at some point in their lives join a book club. Book clubs are great fun—once a month or so you receive a catalog in the mail that lists all the books the club is offering. You fill out an order blank with the order number of the books you have selected, and the number of copies of each selection. You send the order off to the book club, and if all goes smoothly, you get a nice big package of brand new, wonderful books.

One of the first book clubs many of us belonged to was operated by Weekly Reader, the publisher approved by educators, whose products many schools distribute. The Weekly Reader book club is joined by schools; once a month during the school year, students may order paperbacks, hardcover books, posters, erasers, and other school-related items, through their home-room teacher.

The Weekly Reader book club is divided by age into three different groups, and each group is offered about 35 titles every few weeks—a total of 600 titles each school year. The different groups are given different club names—the "Buddy" club for youngest readers, the "Goodtime" club for intermediate readers, and the "Discovery" club for fourth grade and up. Students give their orders to their teachers, who compile a master order list and send it in under the club name, their name and their school address.

That's the easy part. The hard part comes when the orders reach Field Publications of Columbus, Ohio, the company responsible for filling the mass of orders in a timely and accurate fashion.

# The Equipment Line-Up

When Field Publications receives a book club order, the order is entered into its on-line system daily. The company uses a computer system, that works with its distribution system called an Automatic Order System (AOS), developed by ESDM Corporation of San Jose, California. The AOS uses a number of dispensers through which the correct number of each title is placed into the carton labeled for the school it is ultimately destined for. Contel Information Systems of Bethesda, Maryland, was the systems integrator for this complicated system, which includes Hewlett-Packard computers, Lord Label Manufacturing Company (Arlington, Texas) on-line imprinters and labelers, Accu-Sort (Telford, Pennsylvania) scanners, and Metromatic scales.

Once an order is entered into the system, an invoice is produced which identifies the order by club, carton size, and teacher. Each club has its own file in the computer. This file is updated and the information transmitted immediately to distribution for processing the next day. After the order has been entered in the system, several things happen.

Orders are filled in the sequence in which they were transmitted. The computer indicates what size carton will be necessary to hold the order for each club. Under computer direction, a carton for a club's order is prepared. More than 200 dispensers, on computer command, load the bestsellers ordered by that club onto a moving conveyor, in the correct quantity and order. Employees will manually add books and items not added by dispenser as the order passes their work station.

While the product orders are being assembled on the moving conveyor, the carton moves under computer direction, on a moving track that travels at a rate of 250 feet per second, to the Lord Label System's thermal printer-applicator. The printer-applicator prepares the mailing label for the shipment. The label is printed in alphanumeric and Code 39, and includes the teacher's name and address, products received, weight of the carton (as determined by the computer system based on the total order), weight for postage, and the amount of postage due. The system also produces a manifest for the post office. The carton weight and the correct bulk mail center number are the only data printed in bar code as well as alphanumerics.

The AOS is synchronized so the carton arrives at the labeler, is labeled, and then arrives at the end of the product conveyor belt in time for the correct order to slide off the belt into the carton.

# A Time for Errors

Book dispensers and timing gadgets aren't perfect. Either one can produce too much or too little of what is desired. When Field Publications is operating at peak production, 8000 cartons per day are filled and shipped. Since Field fills orders for children's hardcover books as well, it averages 65,000 products per day. A mistake can be very hard to detect in that volume.

As a final error check before shipment, the carton proceeds via moving track to the Metromatic scale, tied into an Accu-Sort fixed laser scanner programmed to read the carton weight that appears in bar code on the label. A weight verification program checks the actual weight of the carton with the weight scanned on the label. If the weight falls within a small tolerance variance, the carton is accepted by the system, and is sorted for mailing. If the weight falls outside the variance tolerance, the carton is ejected. Here, quality control personnel step in to manually check each ejected carton. Eighty percent of the time, there is an error in an ejected carton.

To check the accuracy of the system, quality control manually checks 100 cartons per day that were accepted by the system. According to Ernie Spychalski, manager of distribution for Field Publications, less than 0.5 percent of those cartons are found to contain incorrect items. Considering the volume, you could hardly ask for a better record. Spychalski states that complaints have been reduced about 70 percent since the system was instituted.

In a few months, the company will have more conveyors set up. The bar coded bulk mail center code will also be read, and cartons will be automatically sorted and transferred to shipping staging for delivery to post office bulk mail centers. Currently that job is being done by hand, using the alphanumeric number printed under the bar code on the label produced by the Lord Label equipment.

Most book club companies are still doing their shipments the hard way—entirely by hand—and making a good number of errors because of it. The availability of fast-working, heavy-duty bar code imprinting, labeling, and scanning equipment made for use in hostile environments may soon become a bestseller for accurate order fulfillment.

CHAPTER 24

# AT THE END OF THE LINE

## Cellular Phone Technology Meets Bar Code

BY LEONARD GRZANKA

Cellular telephone service companies face strong competitive pressure, and are strictly regulated—factors that lead to experimentation with new technologies, market pressure to use new technology to improve productivity, as well as demands from regulators to keep costs down. It's no surprise then that GTE Distribution Services, a Danvers, Massachusetts, division of GTE Products Corp., recently designed and developed a paperless physical inventory and asset control system for GTE Mobilnet in Houston, which uses the latest technology in bar coding and portable contact wands.

"The key benefits of the system were the elimination of paper and manual data entry, which significantly reduced the processing time for inventory and asset data," says David Armstrong, director of management information for GTE Distribution Services, which operates a nationwide warehousing and distribution network for GTE companies. "We have conducted several surveys of our distribution managers, and high on their list of improvements is the elimination of paper in the warehouse."

In July 1986, GTE Mobilnet management recognized that the company's rapid nationwide growth as a supplier to the burgeoning cellular communications market would complicate taking inventory at year's end. Auditors now had more than 60,000 individual records to check against a physical inventory of electronic cellular communications equipment worth about $130 million, dispersed among a central warehouse and 130 cell sites, each of which stocks more than $800,000 worth of inventory.

"In the past our accounting people would visit each site one at a time, collect the data by hand, manually enter and reconcile it, and then go on to the next one—a very time-consuming process," says Ralph Martinez, GTE Distribution's coordinator of material control. "This was the first time a project of this magnitude had been attempted. We figured it would take an entire month to key in all the data we collected from the cell sites. Bar code was a technology we believed could really help us."

## Configuring the System

GTE manages fixed assets, such as buildings, fences, tools, and antennas, with what it calls an "asset tag." The tag contains a Code 39 bar code label from Intermec in Lynnwood, Washington. Code 39 was selected partly because its alphanumeric characteristics made classifying equipment easier. The company also prepared a menu of bar codes containing the locations of its warehouses, the 130 cell sites, and specific "suites" within the cell sites. The two company inventory takers only had to scan the menu to input location, and scan the asset tags to identify inventory at the location.

GTE Mobilnet needed a portable, programmable bar code scanner that was easy to use and that could be downloaded to a larger system. After considering scanners from numerous vendors, they settled on the Micro-Wand II from Hand Held Products in Charlotte, North Carolina. It's the same device that can be seen in current Federal Express television commercials and print advertisements.

"We evaluated all the devices out on the market and compared the Micro-Wand II to them," Martinez says. "We decided it was the one best suited to our environment. In particular, we liked the compactness and functionality of the unit."

The 7-ounce Micro-Wand II, which measures slightly more than 7 inches in length and about 1 by 2 inches in girth, contains a lot of computer power: 32K of CMOS RAM, 32K of CMOS EPROM, which holds the operating system, and a Hitachi 6303 8-bit microprocessor. The unit communicates with its operator through audio beeps and a two-line, 16-character LCD display. The operator may enter instructions on a 32-character, chicklet-style keyboard. It transmits data and receives programs and other instructions via an optical interface between an LED on the unit and an RS-232 converter. A Bell 202 unidirectional modem on the wand allows direct downloading of data over telephone lines. A rechargeable NiCad battery or a standard 9 V transistor-sized battery powers the unit. The unit is programmed on an IBM Personal Computer with the company's proprietary Universal Data Language (UDL) to read Code 39.

"Much of the success in meeting our tight schedule can be attributed to having a good, solid wand programming language and an interface to a standard IBM PC," says Roger Prouix, GTE Distribution's manager of information management. Prouix was the chief designer of the inventory system, working closely with GTE Mobilnet's material control staff.

# Getting to the Day of Reckoning

It took GTE Distribution Services just six weeks to prepare for the inventory, including purchase of 25 Micro-Wand IIs, programming, training, and documentation. The company developed two applications programs, one for the cell sites, and another for the central warehouse.

Previously, two auditors from the accounting department took inventory at the cell sites, but the new system let the company use on-site GTE Mobilnet technical staff to capture the data. In most cases, two people with a single wand were able to complete the job in 30 minutes. At the central warehouse, three wands checked 14,000 records on $17 million worth of inventory in four days.

"It was very rewarding because the people weren't familiar with this type of technology," Martinez says. "They caught on quickly—it was surprising how fast they ran up the learning curve."

"When we took the system to the warehouse, we were quite amazed," Armstrong says. "We thought there would be some resistance to using a system this high-tech, but in fact what happened was they really latched on to it."

# CHAPTER 25

# EVERYTHING IN ITS PLACE

Voice and Bar Code Keep Things Tidy

BY THAD C. HUNTER

Honeywell's Space and Strategic Avionics Division, located on Florida's southwest coast, comprises eight production plants. These plants operate as individual, build-to-order job shops, producing navigation and flight control computers and inertial instruments. Seven manual and three automated parts stockrooms supplied parts to these plants. Each stockroom was assigned to a specific production program, receiving and disbursing materials used in the program.

In order to reduce costs and improve handling efficiency, Honeywell considered centralizing material management around the automated stockrooms. Doing this would: free plant space by phasing out the manual stockrooms; make all handling procedures consistent; allow efficient scheduling and monitoring of stockroom personnel; and improve paperwork accuracy and kitting cycle time. However, many Honeywell users accustomed to the service provided by personnel in the manual stockrooms voiced fears about centralization. They were concerned that a centralized system would not easily fill program orders in a timely fashion, or be able to reprioritize orders, segregate materials for one program from those for another, or provide the specific handling, tracing, and labeling needs required by each program.

Four bar code systems were already used successfully in Honeywell's production plants. These systems perform the following functions: property control, factory data collection (including labor, work-in-process, tracking, and inspection), time and attendance, and receiving inspection. The new stockroom operational requirements meant new systems would be needed at the work center level. The existing Management Resource Planning mainframe packages and the automation computers, which were used as machine/sensor monitors, could not support the new stockroom functions. A thorough analysis of the centralized supply room requirements indicated the need for a system that used bar code, not a bar code system.

The new system, using work center controllers, needed to do the following:

- Extract data from the MRP host computer
- Return validated feedback transactions to the MRP, and any other appropriate mainframe applications
- Operate autonomously, so as not to be affected by host or data communication failures
- Handle detailed local status queries from employees using screen, hardcopy, and telephone
- Calculate optimum pull sequences
- Collect variable data from bar code or voice systems, add the fixed data, and print the complete information locally in a bar coded form
- Bypass keypad or punched card location and action input, and monitor computer input through a simple keyboard multiplexer device
- Support decision-making and reprioritization after order/pick lists are produced

## The System Works

The system at Honeywell uses a combination of bar code and voice data entry. Boxes and pallets arrive from the receiving inspection area in five to eight batches each day. The stockroom attendant first places them on a shelf, then identifies himself to the work center controller by scanning his bar coded employee badge, via a Computer Identics' ScanStar 100 wand scanner.

These scanners, over 90 of which have been used by Honeywell for two years in the company's factory data collection system, were selected for their decoders' wide array of programmability and unit addressability. (Such features will be important in future network expansion.) Also, a consideration for employee safety led the company to use wand scanners for this function. Employees normally wear their badges attached to their shirt pockets; no one wanted a laser scanner aimed at himself, and removing the badge was too awkward.

The attendant then uses a Micro-Wand II portable scanner from Hand Held Products to log the material in, scanning each item's unique in-ship number as he walks around a 100-foot-square area where the pallets sit. The scanner stores information and the attendant uploads the collected data to the mainframe as soon as he has scanned the entire pallet batch. The mainframe MRP system is then interrogated to determine drawer locations for the batch. Also, a check is made to determine whether the material is on back order. If it is, the material is diverted directly to the user, rather than being stored.

When the attendant is ready to unpack the batch, bag it, and store the parts away, he first scans the in-ship number again with a SpectraPhysics' laser scanner. This scanner was chosen because the attendant stands some distance from the drawer number, and also because the bags in which the parts are stored while in the drawers present a non-rigid surface, making them difficult to scan with any other kind of scanner.

This scan prompts a Data Specialties' Zebra thermal printer to print 3- by 4-inch polybag labels. While the use of preprinted generic labels is preferable to on-site printing, that is not possible here, because variable handling information is required on the packages. The storage location, determined in the first scan, is automatically retrieved. Via a voice recognition system, the attendant then determines exactly where in the storage drawer the package should be placed. Using the laser scanner, he concludes the operation by scanning the bag label and the label of the drawer compartment where the bag has been stored. If the scans match the parts and location IDs determined by the computer, a "restore drawer" command is sent to the automation system. The only further decision that must be made is that the quantity of parts expected from the receiving inspection area is the actual quantity received and stored in the stockroom.

The final, concluding scan is very important in an automated stockroom system because a misplaced item in a system that contains over 1000 drawers is almost impossible to find. Honeywell chose the Hand Held Products scanner for its compact, pocket size. Typical portable units are larger, and too cumbersome to operate while moving boxes and pallets. The stored data from the portable scanner is screened on up-loading. It is very important to ensure the data's validity for the destination application; simply creating a temporary file of collected but not validated data defeats the purpose of automated data collection.

## The Voice Connection

The kitting phase of the system operates in a manner very similar to the stocking phase, except that variable data is collected using Votan VPS 2000 and VTR 6050 voice recognition products.

Honeywell considered a number of factors in implementing a voice system to work with the bar code system. Several potential problems are associated with voice recognition systems:

A lot of disk space is required to digitize templates of user's speech, and messages. The training passes required to create speech templates for each individual who will use the voice system are necessary and take time. However, the speaker-dependancy of the system acts as an inherent security feature, guaranteeing that only the person whose template is currently loaded into the system can use it.

19 K bit rates may be necessary to move messages around—which is a lot of required transfer time. A spin-off function of this, however, is the use of the telephone as a data entry and query station. Before the system was instituted and problems occurred with kitting orders, the attendants had to call a production coordinator and advise him of the problem. Now the system dials the coor-

dinator, waits to receive a correct user ID, then describes the problem. This procedure saves time for the attendant as well as the coordinator. Supervisors can also obtain summarizing reports, status, and attendance information from the system through any phone.

Background noise can interfere with voice recognition. For example, if a stockroom robot located near the attendant begins to move, the noise will make it impossible for the voice recognition system to decipher voice input commands. The work center controller, therefore, must track the position of the robot and synchronize voice input to the robot's position.

Other considerations also affected Honeywell's decision to use voice recognition as part of the automated stockroom system:

Material handling is an eyes-and-hands-busy activity. Voice is a natural interface that lends itself to gathering variable data without using one's hands. Voice is a two-way medium, bar code is not. It is not as reliable as bar code, but can be programmed with verification statements to allow the operator to catch any errors.

Bar coding lends itself to capturing predefined or fixed data fields that are associated with, and preferably attached to, a physical object. Activities associated with the best use of bar coding are repetitive, with a consistent, predictable nature. Feedback in a bar code system should be limited to simple yes/no or pass/fail structures. Voice supports more complex feedback.

Finally, voice technology is far more cost-effective for remote data collection than bar code, and is also physically easier to implement and use. Voice is a simple analog signal that can be inexpensively transmitted, compared to bar code's remote data communications over moduled frequency carriers. Voice requires only a $100 remote microphone and headset to be useful. A microphone and headset are also a lot easier for a stockroom attendant to use, since the attendant frequently travels around a large work area. It would be difficult for an attendant to use a bar code system requiring a CRT terminal for information feedback. The initial cost of bar coding is typically from 40 to 70 percent of a voice option (including scanners and printers), but the recurring printing, paper, and handling costs make bar code technology more expensive to use over the system's entire life cycle.

Good automation designs seek to integrate activities best done by people, with machine control, which is best done by machines. Voice input provided the means for dialog between the two at Honeywell. In this application, people are best suited to determine if a correct quantity of parts is available, and to identify anomalous situations. The machine, in this application, is best suited to transcribe data, input location and action commands to the automated stockroom system, and perform batch transactions.

Bar code and voice recognition have proved to be powerful companions. Voice recognition is not the succeeding generation to bar code technology, so don't wait to evaluate and try voice technology only after you become adept with bar code. Plan your systems with a mind open to implementing both technologies.

## CHAPTER 26

# UNDER CONTROL

## CCD-Array Scanners Handle Curves

BY AMEE EISENBERG

In 1980, state deregulation utterly changed liquor retailing in New Jersey. Prior to the new legislation, the state set liquor prices and retail competition was based totally on service to the consumer. When every store charged $19.95 for a half gallon of Seagram's, the only way to encourage customers to select your store was to provide better service and faster home delivery. Deregulation meant that liquor retailing could become a discounter's dream, a real marketplace where competitive pricing could be used to lure customers.

Robert Rooth, owner of the 17,000-square-foot Patterson/Fair Lawn Super Cellars liquor store, started in liquor retail in 1968 as a delivery boy. It got him through high school, and through college. When the deregulation went into effect, he recognized that the business he'd grown up in was going to offer some new challenges. Volume buying was the only way to ensure price leverage. Handling that volume in a cost-effective way meant watching inventory more closely than ever before. New tools were required if the business was to flourish.

He began looking into computers, searching for a combination of hardware and software that would track inventory and handle the specialized needs of the retail liquor business. In his own words, he spent a year and a half "walking the street," talking to every major and minor computer manufacturer he could find. His research lead him to two major decisions: while the hardware is important in terms of reliability, his purchasing decision had to be based on the software and its ability to meet his needs; and that his best purchase would be made through a consultant who could create, implement, and update a hardware/software system.

Rooth decided to work with a small firm called Innovative Computer Systems (ICS) run by Tony Patiole. ICS specialized in two vertical market applications: one for liquor retail stores, the other for legal offices. In 1982, Patiole and Rooth began the job of bringing Super Cellars on-line. The number one job for the computer, then as now, was inventory control.

When initially implemented, the system relied on inventory control codes generated by the store itself. The system worked, but still required tremendous labor to label each bottle. And it didn't overcome a major inventory bottleneck— the cash register. When a customer arrived at the checkout, the clerk had the major keyboard task of entering the control code. Mistakes happened.

In October of 1986, ICS assisted Super Cellars in breaking the bottleneck by taking advantage of the UPC codes manufacturers include on bottle labels. Keyboardless data entry is, according to Rooth, providing tangible results in the form of fewer mistakes and greater profits.

## Front and Back Door Savings

With a low-volume store it is possible to keep your eye on everything—on accounts payable, inventory, customers, purchasing, and pricing—without a computer. It may be possible, Rooth concedes, to do it with a high-volume store such as his $5 million Super Cellars, but "not with any sort of peace of mind. I don't know what kind of life I'd be living. I'd be working 100 hours a week. If I had to [run the business without computers] I wouldn't be in this business."

At Super Cellars, all six of the full-time managers and assistant managers make daily use of the computer. The eight cashiers have more limited access to the system through the point-of-sale terminals (a.k.a. cash registers). Super Cellars has three computer workstations and four register/terminals, plus an IBM PC hooked onto its computer system. In addition to those eight terminals, the computer runs two printers and a modem.

The heart of the system is an Alpha Micro computer with a 10 MB hard disk, 256K of RAM, and 12 ports. The Alpha Micro is a micro in name only. In operation, it behaves as a small and affordable (starting as low as $8300) minicomputer. Its operating system, AMOS for short, is a true multi-user operating system. Because all the intelligence is centralized, it is possible for all four point-of-sale terminals to access the same inventory records at the same time without any visible degradation in transaction speed.

Since not every product Rooth carries comes with a UPC code printed on its label, some need remains for printing labels. Patiole of ICS selected an Okidata 2410 printer for the job of creating store-generated UPC labels. His selection was based on the facts that the printer had the graphics capability, and had the durability to provide service for years to come.

The workstations watch what Rooth calls the back door. "Inventory is what happens at the back door. If you order 25 cases of Dewars, then you need a reliable way to make sure that 25 cases, not 24, come in." Physical inventories, taken three to five times a year, provide an actual eyeball account of what's on the premises. The computer tracks the merchandise on a day-to-day basis, and can run quick comparisons of paper vs. physical inventories.

Better still, the computer can track trends in customer selections. Merchandise that just sits on the shelf can be very expensive. Thanks to the computer, Rooth and his staff have daily information on what's selling and what's sitting. Instead of buying by the seat of his pants, as he claims he was forced to do in his pre-computer days, his purchasing decisions can be based on the buying patterns of his customers.

The cash register/terminals are the front door, the part of the system the customers see. Each register consists of a Wyse terminal with its keyboard and CRT screen, an Indiana cash drawer, an Okidata receipt printer, and most recently a Bar Code Industries handheld CCD-array bar code scanner from Opticon and decoder box. "It looks a little like a laser gun," says Rooth of the scanner. Because of his store's physical set-up, the scanner of choice was a handheld model rather than the scanning-countertop style used in many supermarkets. A CCD-array scanner was selected because of its durability and ability to read even in tough lighting conditions. In addition, bar code labels placed on bottles curve with the bottle's surface. A CCD-array scanner can easily handle this curve, where a wand-type scanner would fail.

Installing the system was relatively painless. Remember, Rooth had done a year and a half of homework. When he selected the retail software package ICS was offering, he was well acquainted with what was offered in the way of capabilities. "Retail is retail, granted," he says. "There are a lot of systems out there that are geared for, quote, retail, unquote, whether it's selling pens, or ice cream, or liquor. But ICS' system was set up for more of the nuances for the liquor business in New Jersey."

Just as importantly, ICS was prepared upon delivery. When the system was installed, it went up quickly. All the plug compatibility problems had been solved before ICS moved its system in. And the software was designed to evolve as the customer's needs changed or new technology offered better solutions. Says Patiole of his company's mission, "We try to sell a quality system and then provide 110 percent support." The biggest problem Rooth recalls with the initial 1982 installation was overcoming the computer intimidation factor. His people were a little nervous about the machines at first.

Once everyone became accustomed to the new computer inventory system, Rooth started looking for more ways to use his new tool. The first major upgrade in Super Cellars' computer system was the addition of accounts payable programming. Part of the major committment Super Cellars had made to computerization is to keep searching for ways to more fully use the equipment's potential.

Adding the CCD scanners was a way of taking advantage of state-of-the-art technology. Says Rooth, "Anything that will either save me money or make me money, I'm interested in. The scanners will save me money in a couple of ways."

The first is in minimizing errors at the register. Clerks no longer have to type in inventory control codes to "ring up" a sale. Now, they just press the bar code scanner to a bottle's UPC label. The scanner "vacuums up" the information. The computer reads the code, identifies the item, and enters the sale. Information from the UPC code is acted on in a number of different ways: the register prints the item's identity, quantity, and price on a customer receipt; and the computer subtracts that item from the store's inventory.

The second way scanners are helping Rooth save is by rendering unnecessary the time and effort of attaching store labels to every bottle. Rooth is delighted to be out of the label printing business. Before, when a case of liquor was delivered to the store someone had to open it and label it before anything else could be done. A quick inventory clerk might accomplish this task in one or two minutes, but when you're looking at high-volume sales, those minutes add up to hours. Now, because he can take advantage of the UPC codes already on the bottles, cases can be immediately put on sale.

The biggest headache involved with adding the scanners to the system was the initial job of entering his merchandise line. "I carry approximately 3500 different items. So we had to scan all those bottles the first time. That was a big job. It took a few days."

The actual installation of the scanners was both simple and complex. According to Patiole of ICS, selecting the scanner was straightforward. The handheld CCD-array self-scanning bar code reader produced by Opticon was chosen for its reading accuracy and durability. Since the scanners need both a power supply and a decoder box in order to interface with the Wyse terminals, ICS purchased scanner packages from Bar Code Industries. As such, the scanner units just plug into the terminals' RS-232 ports.

To simplify maintenance and ensure constant service, Super Cellars invested in five of the $1400 scanners. At any one time, four are in use while one is kept handy as a backup. If a scanner malfunctions, the backup can be plugged in while the broken scanner is sent for repairs.

More difficult was the job of rewriting software to accept the new data entry source. Patiole estimates it required revision of between 10 and 15 percent of the program code.

# New Tools for Business

The most remarkable aspect of this successful computer/keyboardless data entry system is not the technology that drives it. The application is straightforward enough that we see it daily in this country's larger food markets. Taking advantage of the UPC printed on a product's label is just good business.

What is remarkable here is the obvious delight Rooth has in his computer system. He recognized the need for new tools with which to run his business and he went out to get them. But his committment to his tools didn't end with his well-researched initial purchase decision. He continued to press for improvements, for better reports, increased functionality, and more labor savings.

He also recognized the need to ensure continuing computer expertise. This shaped his decision to purchase a dedicated system from a consultant who was committed to providing service. As a result, real improvements to his system have occurred. Doing this homework has provided Rooth with a computer/ keyboardless data entry system that has increased his store's profitability.

# CHAPTER 27

# TIME AND TIME AGAIN

## Tracking Time and Attendance

BY KATHRYN BROWN COFFEY

Goals with regard to attendance tracking, billing, and project management have changed little within the last few decades, but the methods by which they are tracked are beginning to change significantly. The accounting departments of companies still sort through records at billing time, and must still check records concerning employee working hours, overtime, time off, and holidays taken at payroll time.

Videx, Inc., of Corvallis, Oregon, manufactures the TimeWand, a small, credit-card-sized, portable, wireless bar code reader. Videx is also an end-user of its product, using the TimeWand to track time and attendance for its 30 employees. The seven-year-old company has assigned each of its employees a bar coded identifying number, kept in a database on the computer used by the accounting department. The database also includes information that allows the employees, all of whom are salaried, to indicate during their month-long pay period whether they have taken any time off, sick leave, etc.

The system works like this: it is assumed that each employee works five eight-hour days per week. The accounting department keeps time sheets printed out that include a list of employees, by name, with their bar coded ID numbers and a list of the days of the month, also bar coded. There is a list of activities, exceptions, holidays, and so on that could affect the hours an employee actually works, a list of hours, and a list that allows the employee to account for 15-minute intervals, all in bar code. As often as they like, but at least once a month before the pay period ends, any employee may scan his name, a day of the month, a reason for not working a full day, and the amount of time not worked on that day. The information is stored in the TimeWand's microprocessor and downloaded once a month into the accounting department's computer.

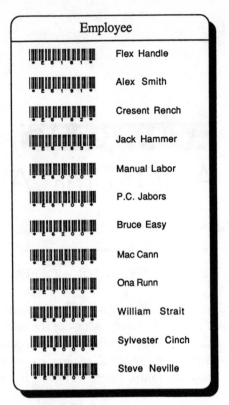

| Employee | |
|---|---|
| | Flex Handle |
| | Alex Smith |
| | Cresent Rench |
| | Jack Hammer |
| | Manual Labor |
| | P.C. Jabors |
| | Bruce Easy |
| | Mac Cann |
| | Ona Runn |
| | William Strait |
| | Sylvester Cinch |
| | Steve Neville |

A sample name card/check-in sheet for time and attendance tracking.

The employees use just one TimeWand to keep track of working time exceptions. A larger company might find it more practical to assign a TimeWand to each department, or even each employee, especially if the time tracking were being used for billing purposes. Once a month, the accounting department at Videx sends a reminder sheet to each employee, stating the hours and days it believes the employee worked; this reminder always indicates a five-day, 40-hour week. After this reminder has been around long enough to prompt employees to enter their exceptions, the TimeWand is downloaded and automatically updates the accounting department's records about sick days, variable time off, vacation days, holidays, and so on. A printout is then made of the information each employee scanned in during the month and given to him to double-check. Any scanning errors can then be corrected. Accounting can also produce printed reports of total time-worked exceptions, allowing the employee to keep an updated record of sick days taken, vacations due, etc.

Videx feels that this method works well for the company because it puts responsibility in the employees hands, and frees them of the psychological burden of checking in and out every day. The system could be altered through the software to keep daily attendance records, or to track time spent on a project by minutes. Information entered into the TimeWand can be cross-referenced by employees to a list that explains what each bar code represents. The system is a tremendous aid and time saver for the bookkeepers.

Videx's own system is simple because its needs are simple, but a company could design a system that printed various reports referenced and cross-referenced in assorted ways, assigning levels (up to 16) to the type of time information gathered and used in the reports. Because the TimeWand has an integral clock that automatically records the time that information is scanned—by date, hour, and minute—real-time applications of time tracking are especially simplified.

Videx spokesmen suggested that this system could be especially useful for organizing the multitude of details involved in construction projects. The Time-Wand can scan a name, followed by a project number for a particular building project. By scanning a start code before beginning the project and a stop code on completion, builders or building inspectors have an accurate record of the time spent inspecting wiring, construction, etc., trips made to and from the project, and time required to complete necessary tasks during construction. "Better time and motion" controls is the way one enthusiast described the use of the TimeWand for this type of project.

## CHAPTER 28

# A MAGIC WAND

## Loan-Tracking Made Fast and Simple

### BY KATHRYN BROWN COFFEY

The problem: to find a means of document control and a way to track information which tends to become lost in the maze of a giant corporation, a bureaucracy, or a smaller company whose various departments are located in branch offices several miles apart.

Valley Federal Savings Bank in Van Nuys, California, solved this problem with a handheld device, a bar code reader that this institution has used successfully to track loan folders. Though Valley Federal Savings is centralized to some extent in the San Fernando Valley, its 800 employees are divided among 52 branches, some of which handle only specific aspects of the loan process.

Valley Federal has increased its efficiency in expediting loan applications and has improved customer relations. The secret behind this, according to some, is a magical device called a TimeWand, which is a product of the Videx company. According to Johnny Munger, vice president of Valley Federal Savings, lowering interest rates and the sudden real estate boom that followed prompted his company to increase the capability of the loan institution to handle the sudden deluge of loan requests that came pouring in.

At any given moment, Valley Federal handles between 200 and 300 loan folders. A home loan takes 90 days to process, and individual folders can contain 100 or more sheets of paper. Construction loan requests sometimes have voluminous files contained in four or five folders. During the 90-plus day waiting period, customers frequently call seeking information on the status of their application.

The folder could be in any number of locations: data processing, appraisal, or loan production. "We were tracking on a Burroughs mainframe, augmented with an IBM personal computer with hard disk, that was not always keeping up with the mainframe," Munger explains. Our "time-compressed" society needs immediate answers, and has too frequently been put off and frustrated with delays and confusion with regard to obtaining information. The ultimate frustration is being hopelessly lost and entwined in red tape and a maze of departments.

Valley Federal sought an end to this confusion with the TimeWand, a small, handheld bar code reader that has a clock calendar within the wand and will internally store scanned bar code information with the time and date of scanning until it is dumped into a computer. The TimeWand resembles a cigarette lighter in size and shape, and is completely cordless.

Historically, handheld wands have been used to keep up with inventory, but document control is another area in which they have "served very well," says Randy Dana-Frigault, who is in charge of customer service at Videx. The company feels that it is an area that will find increasing use as the success rate improves efficiency and customer/consumer relations.

Since the implementation of the TimeWand, a loan can be tracked at any moment. Each loan folder receives a number, determined sequentially, that is tied to the customer's name in the mainframe computer. A bar coded label, representing that number in Code 39, is attached to the folder. Every employee handling the folder scans the number and a location code, and the TimeWand is dumped into the computer periodically, automatically and accurately updating the mainframe's data on each folder. When a customer calls for information, the folder and its status can be located immediately.

Asked if the system has saved time or money, and if it has increased production or reduced error-rate, Munger said that "time, primarily," was the key area in which he saw great improvement. Error-rate was never a major cause of concern or a factor in Valley Federal's decision to implement bar codes.

Recalling the decision to acquire a Videx TimeWand, Munger observed that it was reasonable and cost under $1000. Valley Federal custom-programmed its IBM PC to accept the bar coded data and update the mainframe. "We had a look-alike on the mainframe which was interfaced with DBase III. Using the Time-Wand, we can call up and track the folder on DBase III, and within minutes know its whereabouts."

The introductory price for a TimeWand is between $700 and $850, depending upon the pieces purchased. Valley Federal's cost was under $1000. In addition to computers, the bank already had a Hewlett-Packard laser printer, which is now producing its pressure-sensitive bar code labels.

The loan tracking system affects close to 100 employees. At least 20 individuals use the wand daily. Employees have expressed approval of the system, and no major problems have been cited.

Efficiency of operation has improved with the bar code tracking system, but the incentive for implementing the system, document control, has met with "resounding success" and "primarily, better customer relations."

# CHAPTER 29

# IN PERFECT HEALTH

## Small Hospitals and Bar Code

BY PETER C. DOYLE

A force driving the implementation and use of Health Industry Bar Code (HIBC) standards is a concerted effort by the Voluntary Hospitals of America (VHA) and its 600 member hospitals. By the end of 1986, about 375 of these hospitals were scheduled to have installed a bar code-based, computerized purchasing program, designed and set up by Enterprise Systems, Inc.

Voluntary Hospitals of America, Dallas, Texas, was formed in 1977 by the executives of about 30 nonprofit, locally owned hospitals in order to become more competitive in a rapidly changing hospital environment. The primary source of competition for these locally owned hospitals are groups of investor-owned hospitals. VHA provides its members with management assistance programs, access to capital, educational programs for physicians and nurses, and a materials purchasing arm to reduce costs. VHA is owned by its approximately 600 member hospitals.

The VHA Supply Company, formed in June 1985 to provide cost savings in hospital procurement, is the arm of VHA charged with materials purchasing. Says Richard Rader, vice president of administration for the Supply Company, "The VHA Supply Company is a wholly owned subsidiary of Voluntary Hospitals of America, and it's really the first of its kind in the industry."

Rader goes on to explain that a key feature of the Supply Company is the VHA Plus program, a private label program created in agreement with about 30 manufacturers, including C.R. Bard, Eastman Kodak, Kimberly Clark, Ceddar Roth Bandages, Abbott I.V. Solutions, Minnesota Mining and Manufacturing, and Standard Register Forms. Other manufacturers include pharmaceutical and laboratory products firms. Under the agreement with these manufacturers, the

VHA Supply Company purchases large quantities of products at lower cost, for resale to its members, and is permitted to place its own label on the manufacturers' products.

To facilitate distribution of products from the VHA Plus manufacturers, as well as other manufacturers, VHA has agreements with nine privately owned, regional distributors throughout the country. These distributors are Foxmeyer Co., Dallas, Texas; Burrows, Wheeling, Illinois; Eastern Supply, Stoneham, Massachusetts; Stuarts, Greensburg, Pennsylvania; Owens and Miner, Richmond, Virginia; Interstate Supply Company, Evansville, Indiana; Share Services, Omaha, Nebraska; Trans Health Supply Company, Egan, Minnesota; and Health Materials Network, Tualation, Oregon.

"The VHA Supply Company," says Rader, "offers cost savings. Prior to VHA Supply Company, we had a national materials management purchasing program, but what we have now is similar to what Hospital Corporation of America was trying to do when it attempted to acquire American Hospital Supply Company. But we're doing it differently. We're a company owned and controlled by hospitals and we have our agents in the field. We have an agency arrangement with distributors and manufacturers and we have a joint relationship with a pharmaceutical packaging company."

Rader is not aware of any other such program. "There are," he points out, "many buying groups, but they haven't gotten into their own contracts or gotten private labels."

Some manufacturers are less than enthusiastic about bar coding their products, but Rader believes that the majority have programs in the works to implement scanning. VHA Supply Company is trying to enlist greater support from manufacturers by requiring that they bar code products supplied to the VHA Supply Company.

VHA provides hospitals with a bar code-based materials handling system which is essentially a computer-assisted purchasing system. The system includes HIBC capability and bar code scanners. This allows hospitals to take advantage of the efficiencies found in scanning, and VHA standardizes the system throughout their member hospitals. In addition, all affiliated distributors are using the VHA Supply Company system.

To install the purchasing system, hospitals start by building a database, or item file, of all products that they ever purchase, not just those that come from VHA Supply Company. When they wish to generate a purchase order, they go to the computer and call up the product from the database. This tells them who the vendor is. They enter how much of the product they want to buy, and electronically transmit their order to VHA Supply Company. The vendor or distributor then sends back a printed order confirmation.

Another feature of the system is that using the database they have installed, hospitals can print catalogs and order sheets for each department in the hospital. Department personnel check off the required items and send the sheet to the hospital's purchasing department. Because each item is listed with its bar code adjacent to it on the sheet, purchasing department personnel simply scan in each request to build a purchase order, rather than keyboard items into the computer.

In addition to the basic program, VHA's purchasing system serves as the front end of an optional, total materials management system. With this system, bar code scanning is used to receive products at the docks, or when taking inventory. It's all compatible. With the total management package, hospital administrators have the ability to run various cost analysis and inventory control programs.

While VHA does not provide the total system package, they have a special discounted price from Enterprise Systems, Inc., so the hospital picks up part of the cost and the VHA picks up the balance.

Enterprise Systems, Inc., of Bannockburn, Illinois, is a five-year-old company dedicated solely to materials management applications in the health care industry. They supply hospitals with complete systems, from work stations to software, from training to follow-up support. With about 130 employees and more that 750 systems now installed in hospitals across the country, ESI is the nation's largest such firm.

According to Thomas Pirelli, president of ESI, the two keys to the basic system are building the database, and having the software that does something useful with the information. "The biggest problem we have in health care, and it's a similar situation in other industries, is that there has been too much hype. People seem to think there's magic in bar coding and that all you have to do is to run the wand over the product when it comes in and everything is automated from then on. That kind of myth has done a lot of damage to progress because immediately they buy the equipment without any thought to software support or database reporting, and they're disillusioned. That's the phase we're going through right now.

"The advantage of health industry bar code," says Pirelli, "was not the code itself, but that all the manufacturers now have a standard, and we have a standard database. Instead of having to reassign computer numbers for every hospital and every distributor, we can always use the manufacturer's label code and catalog number. And that's really the key to VHA savings."

According to Pirelli, ESI installs a turnkey system with an IBM PC AT computer in each VHA hospital. Interfaced to the computer is a bar code scanner and a dot matrix printer capable of producing a variety of Code 39. An essential element of each system is the ESI-developed software package.

Expanding upon the process of installing a hospital system, Pirelli says that about a month is required to build the database, using bar coded checklists generated by a Hewlett-Packard LaserJet printer. Hospital personnel check off the items they use and ESI scans the product list into the growing database, adding information on vendors and suppliers. The hospital must manually add specific information, such as charges for each item when they receive their copy of the database. Once the hospital has performed this task, it becomes the hospital's master database and no further alterations need be made unless items are added or charges change.

The client then comes to ESI, which is located in a suburb of Chicago, for two days of training. After that, ESI spends about three days with the client.

"It's about a 60-day process, which is heavily training-oriented," says Pirelli. "People don't scan well without lots of training."

When asked how large a hospital must be to justify a bar code-based purchasing system, Pirelli said that any hospital over 50 beds can justify a system very well. ESI's smallest installation is at the nine-bed Aspen, Colorado, hospital, and it's questionable whether the expense can be justified, except for consistency within a group. ESI's largest installation, at the 1200-bed Baylor University Medical Center, would have no difficulty justifying the system.

With regard to manufacturer's diligence in bar coding product packaging, Pirelli is encouraged, and says that, "By the end of 1987, about 20 percent of all products will contain bar codes. There are something like 300,000 products to be converted, so it's not just inertia holding the manufacturer back. It takes a lot to change all of that artwork on packages."

# CHAPTER 30

# IN AND OUT OF THE CLOSET

## From Closet Confusion to Happier Relations

### BY DEBRA MARSHALL

Large hospitals can be busy, bustling places, and Ball Memorial Hospital in Indiana is no exception. Ball Memorial is one of the largest in the state, with 650 beds spread among a 10-story tower and several smaller buildings. In addition, the hospital is a non-profit teaching hospital, so its interns, residents, and nursing staff are kept very busy around the clock.

The constant activity in the hospital made it difficult to keep a sufficient supply of the stock items used often by the nurses available on each floor. In addition, the nurses had no time to accurately record use of every styrofoam cup and Band-Aid dispensed to patients during a hectic day. Often, when the floors were especially busy, they found little time to record even the expensive, important items used by patients on a routine or one-time-only basis.

The hospital's original system of stocking and reporting was set up around supply closets located on every floor and a labor-intensive system of employees in charge of stocking the supply closets and ordering and receiving materials from the warehouse.

The system worked like this: three orderers would go to the supply closet located at each nursing unit on each floor. They would count all the items remaining in the closet, and write down what items needed to be replaced, and in what quantity. Once all the supply closets had been checked, orders for individual items were totalled, and the totals transferred to a warehouse order sheet. The order sheet consisted of 30 pages of printed forms listing each of 1600 possible items, with a space next to each entry for entering the quantity of the item required. Nurses were supposed to make note of items dispensed from the supply closet to patients, and pass this information on to the accounting department.

Under this system items such as styrofoam cups, moist towelettes, cotton swabs, tape, and so on—items that come in large quantity units and are used for many patients over a long period of time—were not being noted at all, and the hospital was carrying the expense of these bulk items as a loss. Furthermore, expensive supply items, such as hypodermic needles, bandages, and so on, would often go unnoted during times when the nursing staff was especially busy. The supply closet checking system was time-consuming and often resulted in a floor being without some important item for awhile, because of the delay inherent in the system, or because an item missing from the supply closet might be overlooked by the orderers. And finally, bulk items would sometimes be used in quantities that seemed out of proportion to the number of patients on a floor, had to be watched for excessive use, and could not be easily accounted for.

Six years ago, as a partial solution, the hospital acquired an IBM mainframe-based computer system that is in operation around the clock. Terminals located at each nursing station allow the nurses to enter expensive, chargeable items—IV solutions, catheters, hypodermic needles, and so on—as they are taken from the supply closet for a particular patient's use. Bulk items like tape and cups were designated "nonchargeable" items, and the cost of these is figured in a pro-rated manner into the entire cost of the hospitalization service. This didn't eliminate the need to watch the nonchargeable items for overuse, and it didn't eliminate the loss of chargeable items when during a busy time the nurses didn't enter the items into the system, but it did make the losses less frequent. It also saved the labor previously spent regularly tracking down all the nurses on each floor, to determine whether they could remember which patient used which unaccounted-for items. (These entry lapses were discovered during the manual counts taken by orderers, because the new computer system gave them an up-to-date list of the items that should be left in each supply closet.)

## A New System

Something had to change. Too much room for error still existed in the new system, and the ordering staff was still spending too much time sending notes to the nursing staff asking for help in determining the use of missing chargeable items. The nursing staff resented the time and attention taken from their primary responsibility of nursing care. And nonchargeable item use was still uncontrollable.

The solution: Ball Memorial Hospital set up a Supply Processing and Distribution (SPD) system based on software written by SPD Manager Mark Constant, UDI-100 portable bar code terminals with wand readers, and an IBM PC XT to communicate with the hospital's mainframe. Constant, working with Director Imogene Stites and Processing Department Manager Annette Black, wrote

BASIC programs that let the XT communicate with the UDI equipment in a way that best suits the hospital's already-in-place systems, and works well with the hospital's ordering system software.

First the hospital had to find a way to identify all the items that could be found in a supply closet. At that time, individual item packages of health care products were not universally bar coded by the manufacturers. Until a future date when package bar coding becomes standard, the simplest solution for Ball Memorial was to attach bar code labels representing the various items that might be stored in the supply closets to the closet shelves. The bar code is Code 39.

Only one orderer is required to cover all the supply closets at all the nursing stations on all the floors once a day. The orderer makes the rounds during the night shift, when activity is less hectic and supply closets are consequently in use less often. The orderer runs the wand over the bar code label of a needed item, counts the number of that item left in the closet, and manually enters the number of the item required to replenish the stock via the UDI's keyboard. The UDI terminal records the individual entries at each supply closet, and continually updates total quantities entered for each item in its memory. Once the orderer has finished checking all the supply closets, the information is dumped from the UDI terminal into the IBM XT. The computer then prints out what is typically a three- or four-page order sheet for nonchargeable items, and an order sheet for chargeable items.

## Warehouse Benefits, Too

This order sheet, which is in fact a two-part form for warehouse items, has greatly simplified the ordering process by eliminating the 30-page form that used to be sent to the warehouse with each order. The SPD system prints the warehouse orders according to the warehouse bin number system. Warehouse employees can go up and down the warehouse rows, picking the hospital's order quickly and accurately. Warehouse employees note out-of-stock items on the second page of the order form; this page is returned with the completed order to the hospital, providing a record of what items were actually received from the warehouse.

Under the old system, all possible items were listed alphabetically on the 30-page form; it was easy for warehouse employees to miss an item, and they had to skip around the warehouse picking the order in the sequence the items appeared on the form. Also, the 30-page form was returned to the hospital with the order and stored for 30 days. The new form saves much storage space, as well as time, and improves relations with the warehouse employees, who are glad of the easier to read and use new form.

When the supply closet data is dumped into the IBM XT, the information is also transferred to the hospital's mainframe, which compares the quantities of chargeable items entered by the orderer at each supply closet with the chargeable item entries made by each nursing station during the day. The computer then prints a report on item numbers that do not tally. The nursing staff receives a copy of the report each morning, and they use the report to alert them to determine to which patient the missing item should have been charged. Since less than a day has elapsed from the time the item was used and not entered into the system and the time the staff is alerted to the oversight, the nurses can usually recall the incident and reconcile the account. The mainframe keeps an "account" of all missing items "charged" to the nursing station initiating the lapse; when the nurse's reconcilement is received, that station's account is credited with the missing chargeable item and the patient is billed accordingly.

Reports are also generated that list the total number of nonchargeable items used by each nursing station, and the cost of the items. A report concerning the total number of missing chargeable items used and their respective costs is also generated. These reports are used by accounting and by management to keep track of potential problem areas.

## Problems Solved

The biggest problem the hospital has had with the new bar code system is worn bar code labels. Because the hospital chose to use an economical contact wand reader rather than a noncontact reader, and because of the number of scans each label receives daily, they have found it necessary to coat the labels attached to the supply shelves with a clear plastic. In addition, the labels must be completely replaced once a year.

Eventually the SPD system will be connected to the patient billing system, saving even more time for the busy hospital personnel.

Plans are underway now to bar code all pieces of hospital equipment, such as wheel chairs, crutches, and so on, that are loaned to patients for the duration of their stay in the hospital. By scanning the equipment as it is loaned to a patient and entering the patient's name, any piece of equipment could be located at any time, the expected return date found, and the patient using it identified. This is important because equipment has to be inspected regularly, and each piece is on a different inspection schedule, depending on its age and use. The manual system now used for equipment loans only generally identifies the hundreds of pieces of equipment and notes that a piece is in use.

The hospital staff took to the new bar coding system with ease and enjoyment. Besides the benefits of time and accuracy in the ordering system, and the reports that were unavailable to hospital administration prior to implementation of the system, the relationship between SPD staff and nursing staff has improved. The nurses appreciate receiving informative reports in a timely manner. Relations with the warehouse staff have also improved.

None of this surprises Manager Mark Constance, who says he has been saying it all along: it simply isn't necessary for a hospital to buy big, expensive equipment to have a useful, easy-to-operate, accurate system. A microcomputer and bar code equipment is often enough, as Ball Memorial Hospital has proven.

# CHAPTER 31

# THE HEALTH CARE INDUSTRY

## BY CRAIG K. HARMON

Between 1977 and 1984, a proliferation of bar code symbologies and OCR began in the health care industry. The Committee for Commonality in Blood Banking Automation (CCBBA) under the aegis of the American Blood Commission issued its final report to employ Codabar symbols to eliminate errors in blood transfusions. NCR's Color Bar found several applications domestically, and Telepen began being used in Great Britain. UPC had the widest inroads, with UPC encodation of the National Drug Code (NDC), some uses with the National Health Related Items Code (NHRIC), and some grocery-type products coming into hospital food service operations. A majority of products coming into hospitals remained unmarked and prompted the National Wholesale Druggist Association (NWDA) to recommend in April 1983 that all drug items going to pharmacies be UPC encoded. Large distributors, such as American Hospital Supply Corporation and Bergen Brunswig, used UPC in order entry activities within hospital purchasing departments. The UPC implementations were restricted, however, to numeric and fixed length applications. UPC's structure did not address the needs of the many health industry manufacturers who had existing product and lot codes containing alphabetic characters or internal hospital applications that required fields of different lengths and alphabetics.

In 1982, the Secretary of the Department of Health and Human Services issued regulations regarding prospective payments, a method of calculating the reimbursement of various hospital procedures under a concept known as diagnostic related groups (DRGs). With Medicare's prospective payments and other third-party payers soon to follow, hospitals reacted to their inability to continue pricing on a cost-plus basis with the establishment of extensive cost containment and control procedures to lower the overall cost in the delivery of health care. One of these procedures was the development of an industry-wide standard of bar coding.

Between June 1983 and March 1984, the health industry developed and issued a voluntary standard of bar coding that defined the bar code symbology (Code 39); the format for identifying manufacturer, product, and level of packaging; and an optional format for identifying a product's lot number and expiration date. This standard set in motion the use of bar coding at the manufacturing, distribution, and health care provider levels by establishing a uniform system of marking from a manufacturer's point of shipment to a stocking location within a hospital central supply facility.

The selection of Code 39 in the U.S. health care industry as their standard symbology followed closely on the heels of the French pharmaceutical manufacturer's decision to begin product marking with Code 39 and the negotiations within NATO countries to establish Code 39 as the official symbology for logistics marking. Unlike the rigid UPC structure for retail marking, Code 39's variable length, alphanumeric structure permits the health industry maximum flexibility in product identification with superior error rates.

In establishing the oversight organization for health industry adoption of bar code marking, the Health Industry Bar Code Council (HIBCC) included within its membership certain distributors and representatives of the pharmaceutical industry. These organizations supported the use of UPC within their definition of the "health industry," which also included retail drug stores. In an effort to throw the entire weight of the health industry behind the HIBC Standard, the HIBC Council agreed that certain products coming into hospitals might continue to be marked with the UPC symbology, though product packaging provided solely to the hospital market was asked to encode NDC, NHRIC, and UPC Number System 0 codes in the HIBC symbology, Code 39. Consequently, existing products that were so marked were permitted to continue, and it was requested that future packaging be marked with Code 39.

The health industry standardization has led to the creation of the HIBC Provider Applications Standard for bar code marking of patient wrist bands, linking patients and their medications or procedures, etc. The internal marking applications by hospitals and their ability to receive machine-readable marked products from their suppliers is leading to an overall containment of health care costs and an improved delivery of basic health care services.

The introduction of the Health Industry Bar Code (HIBC) Standard presents numerous opportunities for applications in a hospital setting. At the time of admission, the patient chart could include a patient I.D. encoded in bar code markings. Accompanying the patient chart could be a series of pre-printed labels having the same identity as the chart. Specimen samples could be marked with one of the pre-printed labels. Keying from the patient chart, bar code marked medication could be compared to the patient diagnosis, to reduce medication substitution errors.

Machine-readable patient and specimen identification has been researched, indicating that it enhances quality assurance by providing almost complete reliability in the identification of the two most vital ID elements in test performance.

(a) It permits more rapid processing of specimens than can be accomplished by handwritten generation of collection, loading work, or result lists or by manual input of patient/specimen identification through CRTs at multiple stations along the test track. In fact, such lists are no longer necessary since the testing process becomes completely automatic and randomized when an ID reader is coupled to an analytic instrument. Through this linkage, greater accuracy of ID is obtained; it is faster than writing on work lists or entering the specimen ID into CRTs.

(b) Responsibility for ID entry into many analytic systems utilizing turntable or similar batch specimen transport methods may be assigned to laboratory assistants who may load the holders, thus freeing medical technologists for more vital technical and professional activities.

(c) Because machine-readable ID reduces the possibilities for error, duplication of patient distress by repeated venipuncture is eliminated. Waste of personnel time and of expensive test reagents, standards, and quality control materials are avoided.

(d) The system is operational at all times and thus does not require the availability of trained data entry clerks manning CRTs 24 hours a day.[17]

The most immediate benefits that could be achieved in the use of HIBC Standard are in the areas of Materials Management/Central Service. Bar code markings will permit the immediate entry of products received and distributed to hospital functional areas as well as to the patient. In a 1981 survey of 50 percent of all U.S. hospitals, only 67 percent of inventory purchases were carried in hospital's general ledgers. In other words, one-third of hospital inventory was not identifiable under the hospital's standard method of accounting. This one-third included depreciable capital equipment and "unofficial" inventory expensed directly to the departments, without the benefit of centralized inventory management. A method is required to capture these costs and subject them to the same rigors of inventory management. This survey further disclosed that approximately 60 percent of the total "official" hospital inventory is maintained within two areas—materials management and pharmacy. Accordingly, concentrated application of improved inventory management practices in these two areas will have the most significant impact on total hospital inventory investment. Currently, this inventory turns 4.2 times per year, or said another way, the "typical" U.S. hospital maintains an inventory stock for approximately 90 days of use. Each day's stock a hospital is able to reduce from its inventory returns an average $4,951 to cash flow. Were a hospital able to reduce its inventory levels from a 90-day supply to a 30-day supply, some $300,000 could be returned to the hospital's cash flow.[18]

To achieve such an improvement in inventory levels requires the automation of the inventory management function. The inventory management system, like any other system, has three elements: input, process, and output. While process and output deserve the same attention by hospitals as does input, the efforts directed by the HIBC Standard are to take first things first, and the first element is input. In a vast majority of hospitals, data input occurs by recording the proper data elements first to a multi-part carbon copy form and then one of the parts of that form to a computer system by means of a data entry person. It is not uncommon to see delays in excess of three days from the original capture of the data to the time when the data can be processed by the computer. An average 24 percent of a given data processing or MIS budget is dedicated to this delay-prone method of data entry. Further, the typical key operator experiences data entry rates at less than half the speed achievable through automation. This same key operator will average one mistake for every 300 characters entered, not counting transposition and translation errors occurring when the data is initially recorded; or the simple legibility of the form received at data entry, oftentimes as a result of the multi-part form copy's failure to record the information written in a legible manner.

Automated technologies can improve this error rate to one in 45 trillion characters entered, all the way back to the point where the data is originally captured. Such automated technologies regarding data entry reduce errors, improve the timeliness of data processing, increase productivity, and reduce operating costs. Soft benefits are also experienced in such areas as improved traceability, improved patient billing, and the potential for an overall improvement in the quality of health care delivered.

Possibly one of the slowest patient charge items to get posted to the patient charge record are the disbursements from pharmacy, with two weeks' delay from disbursement to posting not uncommon. By applying a bar code marked shelf tag, or preferably a bar code symbol directly on the pharmacy item, disbursement could be posted at computer speed. Combining the pharmacy item machine-readable code with pre-printed labels from the patient chart, as well as ones identifying the authority for the pharmaceutical, permits billing systems to immediately charge the item, inventory systems to relieve inventory, and an audit trail for the disbursement of the item. And while it may be some time before all pharmacy items are source marked by the vendor, hospitals can independently develop such systems through the marking of products and shelves with pressure-sensitive bar code labels. These labels could initially identify the product based upon the hospital's charge item number and convert to the manufacturer's number as the product begins to arrive source marked with the labeler identification and product/catalog number code.

Traceability is an issue familiar with all associated with health care. The HIBC Standard provides a format for a Secondary Bar Code Symbol that encodes the product's expiration date, if applicable, and its lot/batch/serial number.

Hospital purchasing authorities may request such marking on incoming products as a point of negotiation. Some vendors may willingly accommodate such a request, others may flatly refuse, and still others may be willing to provide such marking only at some incremental cost. A hospital could encode unmarked products with supplemental labels that would identify product, expiration date, and lot number. The cost of this activity at the hospital level would surely be higher than if applied by the vendor. And this cost should then be compared with savings that would inure to the hospital with such marking. First Expired First Out (FEFO) inventory methods could easily be applied to date-sensitive products. Recalls could be identified in inventory more easily and the time to relieve or modify inventory greatly reduced.

The HIBC Standard further states that bar code markings be initially employed on master carton packaging with markings on lower levels of packaging phased in as appropriate and as technologically and economically feasible. Technologically and with use of the HIBC Short Symbols, proposed by the author, bar code markings could appear all the way down to "unit of use" for most products. Economically, hospital purchasing authorities need review the cost of recording patient charge items and the willingness of alternate sources of supply to provide marked products.

It is not uncommon in some hospitals for incoming products to have a hospital-generated pressure sensitive label affixed to the product as it leaves Materials Management/Central Service destined for various departments. In the case of OR, the attending nurse removes the label and sticks it to her cap or gown. Following the procedure, these stickers are removed, applied to a patient charge card, and sent to data processing for key entry to the computer system. Were that sticker bar code marked and were a total bar code based information system in place, the labor intensive capture of patient charges at the OR could be replaced with bar code reading systems that would post the patient charge immediately as the item of supply is used. Further benefits could include improved scheduling of OR facilities, labor reporting, patient charge for actual time of OR usage, and a quality control measure of identifying the patient with the activity scheduled in a specific OR.

Exchange cart systems employing bar code marked items have been found in several situations to dramatically reduce labor requirements and to recapture lost patient charges. In one 722-bed hospital a cart exchange system was implemented that required at least two carts for each of the institution's 32 nursing specialty areas. Each cart was stocked with Central Service items in predetermined par level quantities. Carts could carry about 200 different items.

Every day, a fully stocked cart was taken to the nursing area and exchanged for one in use. The latter was taken to Central Service and its supply was brought up to the par levels for the next day's exchange. Time and manpower necessary to implement this system were formidable. Every day, every item on as many as 37 carts was counted, the results recorded, replenishment items ordered, discrepancies reported and many other clerical operations conducted. This operation was further complicated by the presence of both patient charge and non-charge items on the carts. It used to take one-and-one-half hours to complete this procedure on each cart.

Non-charge item usage was recorded in a 15-day cycle. At the end of the cycle, the secretarial staff had to total the counts for every cart and every day, a job that took 55 hours, or 110 hours every month for two cycles. Patient charge item usage also required hours of secretarial time to collect and record. Several hundred hours a month were required to handle the exchange cart system and its related paperwork. In addition to time, there was the question of accuracy and missing charges. Incorrect counts, unrecorded usage, transposed numbers and many other factors contributed to an average of 15 percent loss of patient charges. Because the facility wanted to bring the loss figure down to the three to five percent range, it initiated quarterly audits. This brought it down to the ten percent range, which was better but still unsatisfactory.

Employing a bar code based cart exchange program, the institution was able to save more than 650 hours each month. This comes from a cart replenishment time of approximately one hour, compared to 1.5 hours previously. Taking a cart quantity of 37 and a 30-day month, the facility estimated 555 hours saved there alone. Then there is the reduction of 15-day cycle counts for each cart to 55 hours, or 110 hours a month, down to about 1.5 hours for a saving of 108.5 hours. This savings resulted from the system generating monthly audits which were sent to all appropriate finance, nursing and material management personnel for review. Previously, these reports all had to be done manually. Because of the time factor, they would not always be done daily or even weekly. Totalling non-patient charges, for example, had to be done each 15-day cycle and took 55 hours to complete. Today, the same job can be done in one hour and twenty minutes each month and the figures are for both patient and non-patient charges. Data processing is reduced to once a month instead of twice. Many of the reports now generated were unavailable before. This means that the facility now has a great deal more information at its disposal for use in cost accounting, budget forecasts and similar financial uses.

Another major benefit of the system is accuracy. With the bar code based cart exchange program, the average loss on missing charges dropped to 7.5 percent and one area went as low as 0.4 percent loss. The system itself offers an improved method of checking accuracy by having basic data in a constant, accessible record form—a disk pack.

One area that cannot be overlooked when discussing the advantage of a bar code based cart exchange program is its effect on the staff. Since its inception, the system has helped boost morale by providing greater job satisfaction. The staff worked extra duty to help get the system installed successfully and the staff members now take pride in what they are doing and how they are doing it. The savings illustrated are only the beginning. At the time of this report, only 23 percent of the system's capacity was being exploited. As the hospital's expansion plans call for adding carts, the unused capacity will be available. The bar code based cart exchange program at this specific institution has saved a great deal of time. It has provided a better means of recording information. It has increased accuracy. It has reduced the quantity of missing charges. It provides more complete information about department operations and it has given the Central Service/Distribution Department morale a major boost.[19]

Bar code marked patient records, reports, results, and film could dramatically aid in the tracking of these items from department to department and from person to person. When such items are transferred from one area to another, a departmental or employee ID badge can be scanned along with the symbol identifying the transferred item. When it is received it is logged in in the same manner. The simple entering of the item identification into a computer system could immediately identify the location of that record. Most tracking systems fail because they are overly complex, with employees tending to become lax in the adherence to procedure. It is hard to imagine a more simplified tracking system than one requiring two strokes of a light pen, one for the record and the other for the employee identification.

Consider a clinical laboratory environment where the laboratory personnel want to establish how much time is required for various employees to perform specific tasks or maybe where a specimen might be subjected to several analyses. Most laboratory operations require at least two pieces of paper for documentation of the work; one where the testing was ordered and one containing the results of the testing. In a laboratory analysis which required five operations, ten pieces of paper would be generated, each requiring some form of subsequent editing and key entry. Laboratory personnel would read the badge number, read the bar code marked order document for the test, record the test being undertaken from a laboratory bar code based menu system, record when it was completed and what the disposition of the analysis was following each workstation operation—all in bar code character strings and without the associated costs of key-entry workstations at each laboratory position or the labor time associated in shared terminal systems.

Bar code reading systems combined with hand-held terminals (See Chapter 18) can be used in a wide range of scanning applications within the hospital environment, from the receipt of products from vendors to administering of products to a patient. These electronic clipboards are particularly effective in materials management and exchange cart applications. Inventory control applications are aided in both physical inventory and cycle counting. A patient's ordered prescriptions can be downloaded to a terminal; and when the prescription is administered its identity can be compared to the identity of the drug that was supposed to be administered. Medication substitution errors could go from the present level of nearly 1 in 6 to a point were such errors are virtually eliminated. The same device could serve as a comparator at the patient bed-side to insure that the patient receives the correct unit of blood.

Distributors employ hand-held scanners and PDETs as order entry tools. Hospital purchasing authorities may scan shelf tags and enter the quantity of an item on the shelf. Some manufacturers and distributors provide catalogs of their product that have a bar code printed adjacent to the product description. To speed the ordering of the product and to lower the costs associated with product ordering, the bar code marked catalog product codes are scanned into the PDET. The PDET is then connected to a modem, which in turn calls the distributor's/manufacturer's computer or waits to be called by the distributor/manufacturer; transmitting the order directly, without the costs associated with voice communications, translation errors, transcription errors, and subsequent key entry.

Hospitals use hand-held terminals with scanners to gather and track patient files, automatically re-order supplies, control drug distribution, track specimens, and keep statistical records. Bar code marked patient wrist bands and unit doses minimize the possibilities of administering the wrong drug to the patient. The marriage of scanning systems in health care have three effects: reduced errors, reduced costs, and improved productivity. With 70% of hospital costs directly attributable to labor costs, improvements in productivity, labor reporting, and scheduling will lead the areas of potential savings in health care provider institutions.

On 5 September 1985 the HIBCC issued its combined document *The Health Industry Bar Code (HIBC) Standards,* including a revised HIBC Supplier Labeling Standard and the new HIBC Provider Applications Standard. The HIBC Supplier Labeling Standard defines the formats for bar code markings on various levels of packaging. In 1986 the HIBC Council published the *HIBC Guidelines Manual* to assist in the implementation of bar code technology in all aspects of the health care industry. The American Hospital Association has also published several documents which should assist in implementing bar code systems at the hospital level. These include three case histories: *Patient Information Through Bar Coding* Catalog #101902 (3/86), *Bar Coding in a Radiology Department* Catalog #101900 (4/85), *Integration of Bar Coding Into a Management Information System (Materials Management Department)* Catalog #101901 (9/85), and the 1986 *Directory of Bar Code Users—Hospital Bar Coding* with another survey expected in 1987 to update the 1986 listing of 111 users of bar code technology in health care provide settings.

# APPENDIXES

# APPENDIX A
# SOURCES FOR BAR CODE SPECIFICATIONS

**ABC SYMBOL** (Codabar)
*Committee for Commonality in Blood Banking Automation (CCBBA) Report*
American Blood Commission
1117 North 19th Street, Suite 501
Arlington, VA 22209-1749
(703) 522-8414

**ALUMINUM ASSOCIATION** (Code 39)
ACCS BAR CODE TASK GROUP
*Bar Code Symbology Standard for Code 39*
*Bar Coded Package Identification Standard*
*Implementation Guidelines*
The Aluminum Association
818 Connecticut Avenue, NW
Washington, DC 20006
(202) 862-5100

**AMERICAN NATIONAL STANDARDS INSTITUTE (ANSI)**
(Code 39, Codabar, & Interleaved 2 of 5)
*ANSI MH10.8M-1983 Specification for Bar Code Symbols on Transport Packages and Unit Loads*
(Code 39, Interleaved 2 of 5, Codabar)
*ANSI X3A1.3 Bar Code Print Quality (Draft)*

**AUTOMOTIVE INDUSTRY ACTION GROUP (AIAG)** (Code 39)
*AIAG-B-1 1984 Bar Code Symbology Standard*
*AIAG-B-3      Shipping/Parts Identification Label Standard*
*AIA6-B-6 Standard for Bar Code Data Identifiers*
Automotive Industry Action Group (AIAG)
North Park Plaza Building - Suite 830
17117 W. Nine Mile Road
Southfield, MI 48075
(313) 569-6262

**BOOK INDUSTRY SYSTEM ADVISORY COMMITTEE (BISAC)** (EAN-13) **& SERIALS INDUSTRY SYSTEMS ADVISORY COMMITTEE (SISAC)**
160 Fifth Avenue
New York, NY 10010
(212) 929-1393

**CLUB INTER PHARMACEUTIQUE**
*Marquage des produits Code 39 - Specifications Techniques (Code 39)*
Club Inter Pharmaceutique
32, Rue Poussin - 75016 Paris
FRANCE
33 (01) 524.43.41

## DSSG REPORT
*Recommended Practices for Uniform Container Symbol/UCS Transport Case Symbol/TCS*
Automatic Identification Manufacturers (AIM)
1326 Freeport Road
Pittsburgh, PA 15238
(412) 782-1624

## EMBARC SPECIFICATION (Code 39)
*Electronic Manifesting & Bar Coding of Paper Stock Shipments*
Graphic Communications Association
1730 North Lynn Street - Suite 604
Arlington, VA 22209-2085
(703) 841-8160

## GM MATERIALS MANAGEMENT BAR CODE COMMITTEE
*Shipping/Parts Identification Label Standard*
Room 4-228 General Motors Building
3044 General Motors Boulevard
Detroit, MI 48202-3091

## GRAPHICS INDUSTRY BAR CODE (GIBC) SUPPLIER LABELING STANDARD
(Code 39)
Graphic Communications Association (GCA)
1730 North Lynn Street
Suite 604
Arlington, VA 22209-2085
(703) 841-8160

## HEALTH INDUSTRY BAR CODE (HIBC) STANDARD (Code 39)
*HIBC Supplier Labeling Standard*
*HIBC Provider Applications Standard*
*HIBC Guidelines*
Health Industry Bar Code Council (HIBCC)
111 E. Wacker Drive - Suite 600
Chicago, IL 60601
(312) 644-6610

## HVACR (HEATING, VENTILATING, AIR CONDITIONING & REFRIGERATION) CODE (Code 39)
Air Conditioning & Refrigeration Institute (AAI)
1501 Wilson Boulevard
Arlington, VA 22209
(703) 524-8800

## INTERNATIONAL AIR TRANSPORT ASSOCIATION (IATA)
(Code 39 & 2 of 5 Code)
*Res. 1600t - Specification for Bar Codes in Cargo Applications* (Code 39)
*Res. 606 - Cargo Identification Forms* (Code 39)
*Res. 1720a (ATT. H) - Specification for Bar Codes on Passenger Traffic Documents* (2 of 5 Code)

ATC/IATA *Machine Readable Interline Baggage Tag Study*
International Air Transport Association (IATA)
IATA Building - 2000 Peel Street
Montreal, Quebec, CANADA H3A 2R4
(514) 844-6311

## INTERNATIONAL ARTICLE NUMBERING (IAN/EAN/WPC)
*European Article Number Specifications*
E.A.N. - International Article Numbering Association
Rue Des Colonies, 54
Kolonienstraat
Bruxelles 1000 Belgium
32 (02) 217.45.24

## MOTOR EQUIPMENT MANUFACTURING ASSOCIATION (Code 39/UPC)
Automotive Aftermarket Individual Part Bar Coding Guidelines
222 Cedar Lane
Teaneck, NJ 07666
(201) 836-9500

## NATIONAL RETAIL MERCHANTS ASSOCIATION (NRMA) (UPC/OCR-A)
100 West 31st Street
New York, NY 10001
(212) 244-8780

## PARCEL SHIPPERS ASSOCIATION (Code 39)
Chris Rebello, Current, Inc.
1005 Woodmen Road
Colorado Springs, CO 80901
(303) 593-5990

## TELECOMMUNICATIONS INDUSTRY BAR CODE TASK FORCE (Code 39)
Allan Gilligan/Bell Laboratories
Building WB, Room 2F-109
Holmdel, NJ 07733
(201) 870-7923

## UNIFORM SYMBOL DESCRIPTIONS
USD-1    *Interleaved 2 of 5*
USD-2    *A Subset of Code 39*
USD-3    *Code 39*
USD-4    *Codabar*
USD-5    *Presence/Absence Code*
USD-6    *Code 128*
USD-7    *Code 93*
USD-8    *Code 11*
Automatic Identification Manufacturers (AIM)
1326 Freeport Road
Pittsburgh, PA 15238
(412) 782-1624

## UNIFORM SYMBOL SPECIFICATIONS

| USS-39 | Code 39 |
| USS-1 2/5 | Interleaved 2 of 5 |
| USS-Codabar | Codabar |
| USS-93 | Code 93 |
| USS-128 | Code 128 |

Automatic Identification Manufacturers (AIM)
1326 Freeport Road
Pittsburgh, PA 15238
(412) 782-1624

## UNITED STATES GOVERNMENT (Code 39)

*MIL-STD-1189A (B) - Standard Department of Defense Bar Code Symbology*
*MIL-STD-129J - Military Standard - Marking for Shipment & Storage -*
  *Bar Code Markings*
*FED-STD-123D - Federal Standard - Marking for Shipment (Civil Agencies)*
  *Bar Code Markings*
  Naval Publications & Forms Center
  5801 Tabor Avenue
  Philadelphia, PA 19120
  (215) 697-3321

**Comments and Questions:**
  Director
  AMCPSCC
  ATTN: SDSTO-P (Crouse)
  Tobbyhanna, PA 18466
  (717) 894-7146

## UNIVERSAL PRODUCT CODE (UPC)

*UPC Symbol Specification*
*UPC Location Guidelines*
*UPC Shipping Container Symbol Specifications Manual*
*UPC Industrial Code Guidelines Manual*
*UPC Guidelines Manual*
*UPC Film Master Verification Manual*
  Uniform Code Council (UCC)
  8163 Old Yankee Rd. - Suite J
  Dayton, OH 45459
  (513) 435-3870

---

## INTERMEC

"Code 39"
"Code 11"
"Code 93"

  Intermec
  4405 Russell Road
  P.O. Box 360602
  Lynnwood, WA 98046-9702
  (206) 348-2600

## COMPUTER IDENTICS

"Code 128"

Computer Identics Corporation
5 Shawmut Road
Canton, MA 02021
(617) 821-0830

## KPG-TELEPEN

"Telepen"

KPG, Inc.
6075 Barfield Road, N.E. Suite 204
Atlanta, GA 30338
(404) 252-7366

## WELCH-ALLYN

"Codabar"

Welch-Allyn
Industrial Products Division
Jordan Road
Skaneateles Falls, NY 13153
(315) 685-8351

## PERIODICALS

*ID Systems*
*Automatic Identification Manufacturers & Services Directory*

North American Technology, Inc.
174 Concord Street
Peterborough, New Hampshire 03458
(603) 924-7136

*Scan Newsletter*

*Scan Newsletter*
11 Middle Neck Road
Great Neck, New York 11021
(516) 487-6370

# APPENDIX B
# HOW TO OBTAIN AN IDENTIFIER

There are two prime types of bar code identification systems; one where the identification is purely for internal operations (a "closed system"), and the other where the bar code identification is used not only for internal purposes but also to identify the labeling entity to external parties (an "open system"). Closed systems might identify an employee, a work order, a patient, a specimen, or a fixed asset. These identities are of no consequence to persons or organizations beyond those applying the symbol. Open systems are generally characterized by identifying the labeler, the product, and other information intended to be shared by the labeler and those external parties receiving the item that is labeled. Examples of open system identification include the markings of products retailed in grocery operations, National Stock Numbers for government operations, collection center identification in blood processing, the National Drug Code, the National Health Related Items Code, the Health Industry Bar Code, interline baggage codes, and automobile industry supplier codes. Quite obviously, internal closed system identification codes would be controlled by the organization utilizing the coding structure. Open systems, on the other hand, require a controlling authority to issue identifiers for specific suppliers.

The National Stock Number is a generic code identifying class of equipment, e.g., ADP equipment; the country of origin, e.g., 00 and 01 represent the United States; and, a product code, e.g., a 16K RAM chip. The same product from different manufacturers would have the same NSN and consequently would not have a unique supplier code.

Within the automotive industry, supplier numbers are designated by the specific customer, e.g., specified by General Motors, Ford, Chrysler, American Motors, and Volkswagen of America. At the time of this writing the Automotive Industry Action Group (AIAG) Company Coding Project Team was investigating a uniform coding structure for all automotive product suppliers. AIAG's address and phone number are contained in Appendix A and C.

Labeler Identification Codes (LICs) identifying the supplier of graphics product in the GIBC system can be obtained from:
Graphic Communications Association (GCA)
1730 North Lynn Street, Suite 604
Arlington, VA 22209-2085
(703) 841-8160

Labeler Identification Codes (LICs) identifying the supplier of a health care product in the HIBC system can be obtained from:
Health Industry Bar Code Council (HIBCC)
111 E. Wacker Drive
Chicago, IL 60601
(312) 644-6610

Labeler Codes for medical devices in the National Health Related Items Code (NHRIC) system can be obtained from:
U.S. Food and Drug Administration
Device Registration and Listing Branch HFZ 342
8757 Georgia Avenue
Silver Springs, MD 20910
(301) 427-7190

Labeler Codes for pharmaceutical products in the National Drug Code (NDC) system and Collection Center Identification Codes in the blood identification system can be obtained from:
U.S. Food and Drug Administration
Drug Registration and Listing Branch HFN 315
5600 Fishers Lane
Rockville, MD 20857
(301) 443-7300

Manufacturer Identification Numbers for grocery products in the Universal Product Code (UPC) system can be obtained from:
Uniform Code Council (UCC)
8163 Old Yankee Rd., Suite J
Dayton, OH 45459
(513) 435-3870

# APPENDIX C

# LIST OF
# TRADE ASSOCIATIONS

Air Conditioning & Refrigeration Institute (ARI)
1501 Wilson Boulevard
Arlington, VA 22209
(703) 524-8800

Air Transport Association of America (ATA)
1709 New York Avenue, NW
Washington, DC 20006
(202) 626-4000

Aluminum Association
818 Connecticut Avenue, NW
Washington, DC 20006
(202) 862-5100

American Association for Medical Systems and Informatics (AAMSI)
4405 East-West Highway
Bethesda, MD 20814
(301) 657-4142

American Blood Commission (ABC)
1117 North 19th Street Suite 501
Arlington, VA 22209-1749
(703) 522-8414

American Hospital Association (AHA)
Division of Management and Technology
840 North Lake Shore Drive
Chicago, IL 60611
(312) 280-6137

American Medical Records Association (AMRA)
875 North Michigan Avenue Suite 1850
Chicago, IL 60611
(312) 787-2672

American Production and Inventory Control Society (APICS)
500 West Annandale Road
Falls Church, VA 22046
(703) 237-8344

American Red Cross (ARC)
9312 Old Georgetown Road
Bethesda, MD 20814
(301) 530-6040

Automatic Identification Manufacturers (AIM)
1326 Freeport Road
Pittsburgh, PA 15238
(412) 782-1624

Automotive Industry Action Group (AIAG)
North Park Plaza, Suite 830
17117 West Nine Mile Road
Southfield, MI 48075
(313) 569-6262

Book Industry/Serials Industry
Systems Advisory Committee
(BISAC/SISAC)
1160 Fifth Avenue
New York, NY 10010
(212) 929-1393

Canadian Association of Physical Distribution Management (CAPDM)
One Yonge Street
Toronto, Ontario M5E 1J9
CANADA

Canadian Office Products Association (COPA)
1243 Islington Ave., Suite 911
Toronto, Ontario M8X 1Y9
CANADA

Council of Logistics Management (CLM—formerly NCPDM)
2803 Butterfield Road
Oak Brook, IL 60521-1156
(312) 574-0985

Graphic Communications Association
1730 North Lynn Street, Suite 604
Arlington, VA 22209-2085
(703) 841-8160

Grocery Manufacturers of America (GMA)
1010 Wisconsin Avenue, NW
Washington, DC 20007
(202) 337-9400

Health Care Materials Management Society (HCMMS)
315 Harrison Street P.O. Box 129
Grand Ledge, MI 48837
(517) 627-2144

Health Industry Bar Code Council (HIBCC)
111 E. Wacker Drive Suite 600
Chicago, IL 60601
(312) 644-6610

Health Industry Manufacturers Association (HIMA)
1030 15th Street, NW
Washington, DC 20005-1598
(202) 452-8240

Health Industry Distributors Association (HIDA)
111 E. Wacker Drive
Chicago, IL 60601
(312) 644-6610

Institute of Industrial Engineers (IIE)
25 Technology Park—Atlanta
Norcross, GA 30092
(404) 449-0460

International Article Numbering Association E.A.N.
Rue Des Colonies, 54
Kolonienstraat 28 Bte 8
Bruxelles 1000 Brussel
BELGIUM
(02) 512 34 06

International Air Transport Association (IATA)
IATA Building 2000 Peel Street
Montreal, Quebec, H3A 2R4
CANADA
(514) 844-6311

International Material Management Society (IMMS)
Airport One Suite 103
3900 Capital City Blvd.
Lansing, MI 48906
(517) 321-6713

International Society of Blood Transfusion (ISBT)
Standing Committee on Automation and Data Processing
New York Blood Center
310 East 67th Street
New York, NY 10021
(212) 570-4908

Motor Equipment Manufacturing Association (MEMA)
222 Cedar Lane
Teaneck, NJ 07666
(201) 836-9500

National American Wholesale Grocers' Association (NAWGA)
201 Park Washington Court
Falls Church, VA 22046
(703) 532-9400

National Business Form Association (NBFA)
433 East Monroe Ave.
Alexandria, VA 22301
(703) 836-6232

National Committee of Clinical Laboratory Standards (NCCLS)
771 E. Lancaster Avenue
Villanova, PA 19085
(215) 525-2435

National Electrical Manufacturers Association (NEMA)
2101 L Street, NW, Suite 300
Washington, DC 20037
(202) 457-8400

National Office Products Association (NOPA)
301 N. Fairfax St.
Alexandria, VA 22314-2196
(703) 549-9040

National Retail Merchants Association (NRMA)
100 West 31st Street
New York, NY 10001
(212) 244-8780

National Wholesale Druggist Association (NWDA)
P.O. Box 238
Alexandria, VA 22313
(703) 684-6400

Parcel Shippers Association
Chris Rebello, Current, Inc.
1005 Woodmen Road
Colorado Springs, CO 80901
(303) 593-5990

Pharmaceutical Manufacturers Association (PMA)
1100 15th Street, NW
Washington, DC 20005
(202) 835-3400

Recognition Technologies Users Association
P.O. Box 2016
Manchester Center, VT 05255
(802) 362-4151

Scientific Apparatus Makers Association (SAMA)
1101 16th Street, NW
Washington, DC 20036
(202) 223-1360

Society of Manufacturing Engineers (SME)
One SME Drive P.O. Box 930
Dearborn, MI 48128
(313) 271-1500

Society of Packaging and Handling Engineers (SPHE)
Reston International Center
Reston, VA 22091
(703) 620-9380

Telecommunications Industry Bar Code Task Force
Allan Gilligan, Bell Laboratories
Building WB Room 2F-109
Holmdel, NJ 07733
(201) 870-7923

Uniform Code Council (UCC)
8163 Old Yankee Rd., Suite J
Dayton, OH 45459
(513) 435-3870

Warehousing Education Research Council (WERC)
1100 Jorie Boulevard, Suite 118
Oak Brook, IL 60521
(312) 990-0001

# APPENDIX D
# GLOSSARY OF TERMS

## A

**ABC symbol**—the symbol of the American Blood Commission, developed in 1977 by the Committee for the Commonality in Blood Banking Automation (CCBBA) as a bar code standard for automated systems in the blood service community. The symbology used in the ABC symbol is Codabar.

**AIAG**—Automotive Industry Action Group, North Park Plaza, Suite 830, 17117 West Nine Mile Road, Southfield, MI 48075;a standards body composed of representatives from American Motors, Chrysler Corporation, Ford Motor Company, General Motors, and Volkswagen of America, responsible for the development of a common automotive industry standard relating to bar code symbology and common format. The AIAG standard on bar coding incorporates Code 39 as its preferred symbology.

**AIM**—Automatic Identification Manufacturers, 1326 Freeport Road, Pittsburgh, PA 15238.

**alphanumeric or alphameric**—the character set that contains letters, digits, and usually other characters such as punctuation marks. A machine vocabulary that includes both numerals and letters of the alphabet.

**angle of incidence**—the angle between an incident ray and the normal to a surface at the point of incidence; the angle at the symbol being read. If the reader is perpendicular to the plane of the code, the angle of incidence is 0°.

**anilox roll**—a textured-surface roll, achieved by engraving or ceramic coating, suitable for carrying ink in microscopic cells from a press metering point to the printing plate.

**ANSI**—American National Standards Institute, 1430 Broadway, New York, NY 10018; formerly known as USASI (United States of America Standards Institute), a nongovernmental group responsible for the development of the standard character set of OCR, standard bar code symbology specifications (Code 39, Codabar, and In-terleaved 2 of 5 Code), and other standards relating to government and industry.

**aperture**—the opening in an optical system defined by a lens or baffle that establishes the field of view.

**aspect ratio**—the ratio of height to width of a bar code symbol. A code twice as high as it is wide has an aspect ratio of 2; a code twice as wide as it is high has an aspect ratio of 0.5.

**autodiscrimination**—a feature of certain AIS devices accommodating machine interpretation to define which of a predetermined set of symbologies is being presented to the device. In bar coding, that feature which accommodates the reader in distinguishing, automatically, between various bar codes. Autodiscrimination implies the capability of a reader to read multiple symbologies, such as Code 39, Codabar, Interleaved 2 of 5 code, and UPC, automatically, without deleterious effect to first read rate or substitution error rate. See **multicode reader.**

**automated identification systems (AIS)**—the application of various technologies, such as bar coding, image recognition, voice recognition, and RF/MW transponders, for the purpose of data entry to a data processing system, bypassing the key-entry component of traditional data entry. AIS applications are characterized by data capture at the site of an event with direct transmission to a computer or interim storage device, orders of magnitude reduction in data entry errors, and more timely processing of the captured data.

**automation**—the implementation of processes by automatic means; the theory, art, or technique of making a process more automatic; the investigation, design, development, and application of methods rendering processes automatic, self-moving, or self-controlling; the conversion of a procedure, a process, or equipment to automatic operation.

**average background reflectance**—expressed as a percent, it is the simple arithmetic average of the background reflection readings from at least five different points on a sheet.

**average edge**—an imaginary line bisecting the irregularities of the character edge.

# B

**background**—the area surrounding a printed symbol. See **substrate.**

**background reflectance**—measurement of the brightness of the substrate that a bar code is printed on.

**bar**—one of two types of elements comprising a bar code symbol. A bar element is the element type that has the lower average value of reflectance.

**bar code**—an automatic identification technology that encodes information in an array of parallel, rectangular bars and spaces that vary in width.

**bar code character**—see **character.**

**bar code density**—the number of characters that can be represented in a lineal inch. See **symbol density.**

**bar code label**—a label that carries a bar code and, optionally, other human-readable information; it can be affixed to an article.

**bar code medium gain**—the value equal to the background noise received divided into the code signal received.

**bar code reader**—a device used to identify and decode a bar code symbol.

**bar code symbol**—an array of parallel, rectangular bars and spaces that together represent a single data element or character in a particular symbology. The bars and spaces are arranged in a predetermined pattern following unambiguous rules defined by the symbology.

**barium sulfate**—a chemical compound whose solid form is considered pure white for photometric purposes, yielding 100 percent reflection; used in calibration of photometric devices.

**bar length (bar height)**—the bar dimension that is perpendicular to the bar width. The longer dimension of a bar.

**bar width**—the thickness of a bar measured from the edge closest to the symbol start character to the trailing edge of the same bar.

**bar width ratio**—the ratio between the widest bar or space and the narrowest. In the Uniform Container Symbol (UCS) bar code, the wide bars and spaces are 2.5 times as wide as narrow ones. The recommended bar width ratio for the HIBC symbol and code is 3.0:1.

**bar width reduction (BWR)**—reduction of the nominal bar width dimension on film masters or printing plates to compensate for print gain.

**base line**—a reference line used to specify the desired vertical position of characters printed on the same line.

**bath**—relating to printing press technologies that etch an engraving onto a plate for subsequent printing, the bath is the chemical process that washes away all portions of the plate, with the exception of those that have been exposed as a positive graphic.

**bearer bar**—a printed pattern above, below, and perpendicular to the bars of a bar code symbol. This pattern may be a continuous perpendicular bar intersecting the bar code symbol from the leading edge of the first bar of the symbol to the trailing edge of the last bar. This pattern may also be a rectangular pattern circumscribing the symbol. The sides of the rectangle which is parallel to the bars should be no closer than one quiet zone from the bars in the bar code symbol. The purpose of the bearer bar is to provide printing plate support at critical areas near the symbol and to enhance read reliability by assisting in the reduction of the probability of misreads which may occur when a skewed scanning beam enters or exits the symbol without reading all bars. If the symbol is not printed directly on corrugated packaging material, the bearer bar need only be two times the width of the narrow element and need only appear at the top and bottom of the symbol (butting directly against the top and bottom of the symbol bars). However, when printing directly on the corrugated packaging material, the nominal width of the bearer bar should be 0.19 inch (4.8 mm) and must completely surround the symbol. Rounded corners may be used on the bearer bar if the film manufacturer can supply this feature.

**bidirectional**—the ability to read data successfully, whether the scanning motion is from right to left or left to right.

**bidirectional symbol**—a bar code symbol that permits reading in complementary directions across the bars and spaces.

**bilevel code**—a coding technique in which data bits are presented in two parallel rows.

**binary**—pertaining to a characteristic or property involving a selection, choice, or condition in which there are two possibilities.

**binary code**—A code that makes use of two distinct characters, usually 0 and 1.

**binary coded decimal (BCD)**—Positional notation in which the individual decimal digits expressing a number in decimal notation are represented by a binary numeral; for example, the number 23 is represented by 0010 0011 in the 8-4-2-1 type of binary coded decimal notation and by 10111 in binary notation.

**bit**—an abbreviation for *BInary digiT*; a single character in a binary number; a single pulse in a group of pulses; a unit of information capacity in a storage device.

**byte**—a combination of bits in a predetermined pattern, designed to represent a digit or alphanumeric character.

# C

**calibration mark or bar**—a code bit that provides the scanner with contrast, speed, or code position information, as required.

**carrier sheet**—the backing material on which printing plates are mounted.

**CCD (charge-coupled device)**—an array (linear or matrix) of transductive elements wherein packets of electrons are set in each element as a result of the quantity of light received during an exposure interval, and where these packets are recovered from the array in the form of a pulse height-modulated electric signal.

**center line**—the vertical axis around which character elements are located for letters, numerals, or symbols of an OCR font.

**character**—A letter, digit, or symbol that is used as part of the organization, control, or representation of data. A character is often in the form of a spatial relationship of adjacent or connected strokes. A single group of bars and spaces that represent an individual number, letter, punctuation mark, or other graphic font. A graphic shape representing a letter, numeral, or symbol.

**character alignment**—The vertical or horizontal position of characters with respect to a given reference line.

**character density**—The dimension, in linear inches, required to encode one character; measured in characters per inch (cpi).

**character parity checking**—a self-checking feature of some bar codes which relies upon values being assigned to the various widths of bars and spaces within a bar code representation of a given character. The presence of character parity checking adds security to the bar code, because all the characters share a common specific pattern.

**character reading**—reading of alphabetic and numeric characters and symbols by optical means.

**character set**—those characters which are available for encoding within a bar code system or other type of symbol set, such as OCR-A, OCR-M.

**character skew**—see **skew.**

**character spacing**—the horizontal distance between two adjacent characters.

**check character/checksum/check digit**—a character included within a symbol whose value is based, mathematically, on other characters within the symbol. It is used to perform a mathematical check to ensure the accuracy of the read.

**clear area**—a clear space, containing no dark marks, which precedes the start character of a symbol and follows the stop character. The clear area of a bar code should be 10 times the size of the narrowest bar in the code or .250 inch, whichever is greater. That region of a document reserved for OCR characters and the required clear space around these characters. Also called **quiet zone.**

**clock**—a device that generates periodic signals used for synchronization; a device that measures and indicates time; a register whose contents change at regular intervals in such a way as to measure time.

**clock mark/clock bar**—a timing mark or bar used in certain codes.

**closed system**—one where a central authority has control over the resolution of all bar code readers and the element size of all bar code printers employed within the system.

**Codabar**—a bar code format in which four bars and three spaces are used to represent the digits 0 through 9 and certain special characters. The code is characterized by four unique start/stop codes, variable intercharacter spacing, and code density of up to 10 characters per inch.

**code**—a set of unambiguous rules specifying the way in which data may be represented, such as the set of correspondence in the standard code for information interchange; in telecommunications, a system of rules and conventions according to which the signals representing data can be formed, transmitted, received, and processed; in data processing, to represent data or a computer program in a symbolic form that can be accepted by a data processor. See also **bar code.**

**code density**—see **bar code density.**

**code label**—see **bar code label.**

**code medium**—the material used to construct a machine-readable code. Such materials may be retroreflective, luminescent, magnetic, opaque, transponder, or conductive.

**code medium gain**—see **bar code medium gain.**

**code plate**—a plate to which code marks are affixed in a fixed or adjustable code configuration or pattern.

**code reader/code scanner**—a device that examines a spatial pattern, one part after another, and generates analog or digital signals corresponding to the pattern.

**Code 11**—a code developed by Intermec that encodes 11 different characters (0 through 9 and -). Each character has three bars and two intervening spaces, for a total of five elements. Of these five elements, two are narrow and three are narrow, except for the 0, 9, and - characters, which have only one wide element and four narrow elements. Nominal bar code density is 15 characters per inch.

**Code 39/3 of 9 Code**—a code developed by Intermec that encodes 43 data characters (0 through 9, A through Z, six symbols, and a space). Each character is represented by nine elements (five bars and four spaces); three of the nine elements are wide and six elements are narrow. Nominal bar code density is 9.4 cpi (high density) with other densities of 8.3, 5.7, 3.0, and 1.7 cpi. Code 39 has been recommended for usage or included in standards prepared by the following independent organizations: AIM

(Automatic Identification Manufacturers), ANSI (American National Standards Institute), DOD (Department of Defense/LOGMARS), DSSG (Distribution Symbol Study Group), AIAG (Automotive Industry Action Group), and HIBCC (Health Industry Bar Code Council).

**Code 93**—a code developed by Intermec that includes a character set that is identical to Code 39. Each character is constructed from nine modules arranged into three bars with adjacent spaces. Nominal bar code density is 13.9 cpi.

**Code 128**—a code developed by Computer Identics that encodes the full ASCII character set of 128 characters. Each character is represented by 11 modules and four bar widths.

**contact reader/contact scanner**—a code reader (scanner) which requires physical contact between the code medium and the scanner.

**continuous code/continuous bar code symbol**—a bar code or symbol in which the space between two characters (intercharacter gap) is part of the code, such as USD-1 (Interleaved 2 of 5 Code). A continuous code is the opposite of a discrete code.

**continuous form**—form manufactured from a continuous web of paper that is not cut into units prior to execution. The continuous form may be perforated. Distinguished among bar code printers from cut sheet printers.

**continuous ink jet**—a method of printing which uses print heads that spray a continuous stream of charged ink droplets at the paper. Control of an electromagnetic field between the ink jets and the paper determines whether the ink droplets reach their destination or are electrically deflected and siphoned away by a suction tube. One of two ink jet technologies, the other being drop on demand. Continuous ink jet can give a finer line with greater control of registration of the applied ink. Also called Hertz technology.

**contrast**—amount of difference in reflectance between the dark bars and the light spaces of a bar code; measured by PCS (print contrast signal).

**cut sheet**—form delivered as individual sheets. Distinguished among bar code printers from continuous form printers.

# D

**data acquisition**—the process by which data are moved from the site of an event to an environment in which the data can be processed into meaningful information.

**data collection system**—a system that consists of input devices located at points where data are created. Data are manipulated into these devices and immediately transmitted, by cable, telephone line, or radio signal, to a central location, usually in or near a computer room, where data are automatically recorded. Data may also be transmitted to a storage medium, such as a tape, disk, or semiconductor, and be transferred later to the host computer for data manipulation.

**data element**—a specific item of information appearing in a set of data; in the following set of data, each item is a data element: the quantity of a supply item issued, the unit rate, the amount, and the balance of stock funds on hand.

**decimal**—pertaining to a characteristic or property involving a selection, choice, or condition in which there are 10 possibilities; pertaining to the number representation system with a radix of 10.

**decodability index**—a quantitative measure of cumulative errors contributed by all elements of the bar code system or of one of the system elements, such as the printer or reader. It is expressed as a percentage of the narrow bar/space width.

**decodability limit**—the maximum decodability index that can be allowed by the system design while still ensuring that the bar code symbol will be decodable. The decodability limit is a function of the wide-to-narrow ratio used to create a symbol.

**decoder logic**—the electronic package that receives the signals from the scanner, performs the algorithm to interpret the signals into meaningful data, and provides the interface to other devices.

**delimiter**—An item of lexical information whose form or position in a format or program denotes the boundary between adjacent syntactic components of the format or program.

**demand printer**—a printer that creates individual documents one at a time, as directed.

**densitometer**—an instrument that measures the light reflected from a surface. It is used as a control instrument to check the uniformity of print color.

**density**—the mass of a unit volume; opacity; color strength. See also **symbol density.**

**depth of field**—the distance between the maximum and minimum plane in which the code can be read. See **Figure 13-1.**

**detector**—a device that converts optical energy to electrical energy, such as a PIN photodiode.

**diffuse reflection**—the process by which incident flux is redirected over a range of angles.

**diffusion**—a spreading out or equalized dispersion of a material, force, or condition into the surrounding medium, such as the diffusion of heat by conduction, the diffusion of light through a translucent material, reflection from a rough surface, or the diffusion of gases, liquids, or granular solids into the surrounding medium.

**digital**—pertaining to data in the form of digits. In signals, digital refers to a signal which assumes one of a predetermined set of values, such as 0 to 1, as opposed to a signal which may assume any value over a continuing range of values, such as an analog signal.

**diagnostic verifier**—a device that automatically evaluates the quality of a film master or a printed code. Measures the quality of the symbol against the proper specification for the printing of the symbol, giving relative and absolute measurements of the print contrast signal, absolute light reflectance, absolute dark reflectance, bar widths, space widths, percent decode, and the variance of the printed symbol from the specifications.

**direct product coding**—a type of coding in which the code is marked or printed on the article without using an additional substrate. See **source marking.**

**dirt**—refers to the presence of relatively nonreflective foreign particles imbedded in a sheet of paper. The size and lack of reflectance of the particles may be such that they will be mistaken for inked areas by an optical scanner.

**discrete code/discrete bar code symbol**—a bar code symbol in which the intercharacter gap is not part of the code and is allowed to vary dimensionally within wide tolerance limits.

**Distribution Codes, Inc.**—DCI; an organization that administers labeler codes for the application of the Uniform Container Symbol (UCS) in the United States, now joined with the Uniform Code Council (UCC).

**DRG**—diagnostic related group; a classification system for the establishment of reimbursement to health care institutions covered by third-party payments under prospective payments plans. For example, Medicare has defined 467 procedures with an associated reimbursement for each of the defined procedures.

**DSSG**—Distribution Symbology Study Group; an ad hoc committee formed to specify a practical bar code symbol for corrugated containers. In September 1981, this committee published the recommended practices for Uniform Container Symbol (UCS) and Transport Case Symbol (TCS).

**durometer**—a measure of rubber hardness, usually made with a Shore A durometer gauge.

# E

**each**—the lowest unit of measure within the HIBC standard, identifying the level of packaging that houses an individual unit of a product.

**EAN**—European Article Numbering; now also IAN—International Article Numbering; the international standard bar code for retail food packages corresponding to the Universal Product Code (UPC) in the United States. UPC is a subset of IAN and, where a reader is equipped to read EAN, UPC can also be decoded, but a reader equipped to read UPC may be unable to decode EAN. The EAN and UPC symbols were developed by IBM and introduced into the market in 1971 and adopted domestically in 1973; EAN was adopted in 1976.

**economic feasibility**—a determination of whether a system will return more dollar value in benefits than it will cost to develop and operate, and whether the system development expense is within the resource capability of the organization.

**edge error/edge roughness**—irregularities in the average or nominal edge of a bar code element due to printing.

**electrostatic printing**—the printing process in which information is produced on a dielectric (electrically charged) print head to form an in-

visible image. As paper stock passes through a developing unit, the charged image pulls toner or particle ink to the paper and a visible image is formed. This image is permanently fixed to the label by fusing rollers.

**element**—A single binary position in a character; dimensionally the narrowest width in a character bar or space. A generic term used to refer to either a bar or a space.

**element edge**—the location of the center of the measuring aperture when the aperture is in a position so that the observed reflectance is midway between the maximum reflectance of the adjacent space and the minimum reflectance of the adjacent bar.

**element reflectance uniformity**—the range of reflectance within each bar and space:
ERU (space) = Rs (max) - As (min)
ERU (bar) = Ab (max) - Ab (min)

**emulsion**—a type of mixture wherein two or more immiscible (or unmixable) materials are held together in a homogeneous mixture by the action of a third agent. An emulsifying agent is applied to the material to hold the emulsion. Differs from a solution, in which one material is dissolved into another.

**emulsion side**—the image-bearing side of a film master. Can be identified visually by the slightly raised image. The nonemulsion side is called the base side.

**emulsion up, emulsion down**—orientation of a film master when the human-readable characters read correctly.

**encoded area**—the total lineal dimension consumed by all characters of a code pattern, including start/stop and data.

**engraving**—a general term applied to any pattern which has been cut into or incised on a surface by hand, mechanical, or etching processes.

**etch**—to dissolve the nonprinting areas of a metal plate by the action of an acid, as in the engraving used to mold a plate. See **laser marking.**

**expendable code**—a code label which is disposed of after the completion of its designated use.

**expiration date**—the date past which a product is no longer warranted as effective. In the case of the HIBC standard, the expiration date appears as the first significant field of the secondary symbol and is encoded in a five-digit Julian dating format.

**extraneous ink**—Ink in a scan area that is not intended to be there, such as tracking and splatter.

# F

**FBA**—Fibre Box Association, located at 5725 E. River Road, Chicago, IL 60631.

**FDA**—the Food and Drug Administration.

**feature extraction**—a method of image recognition and specifically of character image recognition in which a processed image is compared in terms of mathematical representations of vertical lines, horizontal lines, loops, and endings to the features of a defined character set and subsequently decoded. Compare to **templating**.

**feet per minute**—abbreviated fpm.

**FEFCO**—European Federation of Manufacturers of Corrugated Boxes.

**fibreboard**—fibre sheets which have been produced or laminated to a thickness that provides a degree of stiffness. Fibreboard used for container production may be corrugated board or solid board; the thicknesses are most commonly 0.060, 0.080, 0.100, 0.120, or 0.140 inch. A generic name applied to many products made of fibreboard.

**field**—any group of characters defined as a unit of information. This differs from a line, as one line may contain several fields.

**field of view**—the lineal dimension defining the length of a code that can be read in one scan; particularly significant in laser, retroflective, and array technologies; of less significance in wand technologies, as the readable code length becomes a function of the ability of the operator to continue the movement of the wand across the code in a smooth fashion in order to successfully read the symbol. See **Figure 13-1.**

**field separator**—a printed mark or symbol that identifies fields to the scanner; also referred to as field mark. See also **delimiter.**

**film master**—a precise negative or positive film transparency of a specific bar code symbol from which a printing plate is produced.

**filter**—a medium that attenuates electrical or optical energy signals of some frequencies more than others. A filter may transmit one band of frequencies and reject all other frequencies.

**firmware**—software that accepts parameters for programming uniquely required by a user.

**first read rate**—FRR; the percentage representing the number of successful reads per 100 attempts for a particular symbol; used as an approximation of "human friendliness" of the bar code reader and symbol to the operational environment.

**fixed base reader**—a bar code reader that is mounted in a stationary fashion to intersect the plane of a bar code symbol passing before the reader. Often employed in conveyor and transport systems. Differs from a hand-held reader.

**fixed beam bar code reader/scanner**—a bar code reader that uses a stationary beam and relies upon the relative motion of the item to be read as it passes before the reader. Compare to **moving beam reader.**

**fixed length (code and field)**—referring to a symbol or code in which the data elements must be of a specific length. Length is fixed to establish field position in the data structure or to provide additional read reliability in scanning.

**flag character**—a character within a data format whose position is fixed and whose contents may vary over a specified range of values; each value representing significant information that is presented to a data processing system.

**flat**—lacking in contrast and definition of tone; dull matte. Opposite of glossy. A full size sheet of engraving metal.

**flexography**—a method of direct rotary printing using resilient, raised image printing plates, affixed to variable repeat plate cylinders, inked by a roll or engraved metal roll that is wiped by a doctor blade, carrying fluid or paste-type inks to virtually any substrate.

**flux**—the combining of photons of light energy to create radiant power. Visible light energy is called luminous flux and is measured in lumens. Radiant light energy is called radiant flux and is measured in Watts. Wavelengths of visible flux fall in the range of 390 to 770 nanometers in length. Wavelengths of radiant flux include all of the optical spectrum, that is, ultraviolet, visible, and infrared wavelengths. Luminous flux is related to radiant flux by a wavelength factor developed by the Commissioner Internationale de'Clairage (CIE) in France in 1924.

**font**—a family or assortment of characters of a given size and style of printer's type.

**format**—the geometric construction rules that define a particular bar code or symbol.

**formed character printing**—an impact printing method similar in nature to an office typewriter. The bars and spaces are engraved or etched in reverse on a rotating drum. Paper, vinyl, or mylar label stock and a dry carbon ribbon pass between the drum and the hammer operated by an electromagnet. The hammer forces the paper and ribbon against the drum, causing the image to be transferred from the ribbon to the label. Each hammer stroke forms a complete character or bar. This technology is used primarily in discrete bar codes and can achieve the highest of the densities for various codes.

**fountain**—a pan or trough on a flexographic press in which the fountain roller revolves, picking up the ink and applying it to the transfer roll.

**four-level code**—a bar code that uses four different element widths in its structure.

# G

**gallium arsenide (GaAs) light emitting diode**—an infrared LED in which most of the material's energy is given up in the form of radiant energy. With forward bias, the diode emits a narrow wavelength of around 900 nanometers.

**gloss**—a phenomenon related to the specular reflection of incident light. The effect of gloss is to reflect more of the incident light in a specular manner, and to scatter less. It occurs at all angles of incidence and should not be confused with the grazing angle, which is specular reflection often referred to as *sheen.*

**go/no go verifiers**—contrasted to the diagnostic verifier, this device tells the user whether the code has been read. If the code has not been read, the go/no go verifier is unable to identify the cause of the no read.

**GPI**—Glass Packaging Institute, 1800 K Street, N.W., Washington, D.C. 20006.

**guard bars**—the tall bars used at the sides and centers of the UPC and EAN bar code symbols to provide reference points for scanning.

# H

**haloing**—a shadow effect around the entire printed segment or around the leading edge of a printed segment, caused by excessive pressure between the printing plate and the printed surface.

**hand-held scanner**—a scanner held and operated by a human, thus enabling the scanner to be brought to the symbol.

**hardware**—physical equipment, as opposed to the computer program or method of use, such as mechanical, magnetic, electrical, or electronic devices. Contrast with **software.**

**helium-neon laser**—the type of laser most commonly used in bar code scanners. Because the laser beam is bright red (a HeNe laser has a wavelength of precisely 632.8 nanometers), bars must not be printed in red ink or they will be indistinguishable from the white spaces.

**HIBC Council**—111 E. Wacker Drive, Suite 600, Chicago, IL 60601. The group responsible for the administration of the HIBC Standard, number issuance and control of Labeler Identification Codes (LICs) within the health industry.

**HIBC Symbol and Code**—the format and symbology for automated data entry within the health industry.

**hickey**—a black mark or area where there should be no ink. Hickeys can interfere with the scanning of bar codes, since they may cause a space to scan as a bar. Compare with **void.**

**horizontal bar code**—a bar code or symbol presented in such a manner that its overall length dimension is parallel to the horizon. The bars are presented in an array that resembles a picket fence.

**hot stamp printing**—a printing technology that uses a dry carbon ribbon or foil to transfer an image from a specific printing plate. Bar widths for this technology rarely go below 0.010 inch and the print quality is excellent. Hot stamping is a marginal technology cost-wise and is mainly used for very high quality multicolor labels. The image is transferred from the printing plate to the label stock when the heated print head containing the printing plate comes in contact with the dry carbon ribbon or foil.

**HRIC**—see **NDC.**

**human-readable**—referring to the representation of the contents of a bar code symbol characterized by alphabetic and numeric characters, as well as special symbols that can be read by a human.

# I

**IAN**—International Article Numbering. See **EAN**.

**image camera**—a photo-optical device used in pattern recognition applications. The received image is compared to the mathematical representation of the correct image or set of images. The received image is decoded based upon stored predetermined representations. This device can be used in quality inspection and optical character recognition applications.

**image orientation**—orientation of the image on a film master; can be emulsion up or emulsion down.

**incandescent lamp**—a lamp in which the light is produced by a filament of conducting material contained in a vacuum and heated to incandescence by an electrical current.

**incident irradiation**—incidence is the amount of flux per unit area that is normal (perpendicular) to a surface or detector. If the flux is not normal (not perpendicular), then the normal component of the angular flux is the incidence. In radiometric terms, incidence is called radiant incidence or irradiance. Irradiance ($E_e$) is measured in watts per square meter using the formula $E_e = W/m^2$.

**infinite pad method**—a method for measuring reflectance, in which the sample substrate being measured is backed with enough thicknesses of the same type of substrate so that doubling the number of sheets does not change the measured value of reflectance.

**information density**—Information density is calculated by raising the character density to a power equal to the number of characters in a character set. Assuming an inch as the given unit length of space and a character density of 5 cpi; a numeric coding structure of 10 characters has an information density of 10 to the 5th power, i.e., 100,000 units and an alphanumeric coding structure of 36 characters has an information density of 36 to the 5th power, i.e., 60,466,176 units. (see character density).

**information system**—the network of all communication methods within an organization. Information may be derived from many sources other than a data processing unit, such as by telephone, by contact with other people, or by studying an operation.

**infrared**—the band of light wavelengths too long for response by a human eye. This band is represented by waves between 750 and 4 million nanometers in length. Photodiodes operating with this light source are usually specified at a peak response of around 900 nanometers.

**ink fill-in**—expansion of a mark beyond specified tolerances.

**ink fountain**—the ink pan or trough on a flexo press.

**ink jet marking/printing**—printing by means of ink droplet electronically propelled directly onto marking surfaces.

**inspection band**—an area of the bar code symbol over which measurements are taken.

**intensity**—the amount of radiant or luminous flux per unit solid angle that is diverging from a light source.

**intercharacter gap/space**—the space between the last element of one character and the first element of the adjacent character of a discrete bar code symbol.

**interelement spaces**—the spaces between bars in bar codes that use only the bars to encode binary data.

**Interleaved 2 of 5 Code**—a code developed by Intermec for Computer Identics that encodes the ten digits 0 through 9. The name Interleaved 2 of 5 is derived from the method used to encode two characters. In the symbol, two characters are paired, using bars to represent the first character and the interleaved spaces to represent the second character. Each character has two wide elements and three narrow elements, for a total of five elements. The specification for this bar code is set forth in MHI/AIM USD-1, and it can achieve a maximum density of 17.8 characters per inch.

**item code**—in the UPC system, the five-digit number that each manufacturer assigns to each product. Corresponds in the HIBC system to product/catalog number (PCN).

**item of supply**—any single, unpacked part, component or end use item.

# J

**Julian date**—A method of dating in which the days of the year are numbered sequentially from 001 to 365, or during leap year, to 366, with January 1 being represented as 001. Julian dating can be in a four-or five-digit format. A four-digit Julian date records the last digit of the year as the first character of the Julian date, followed by the three-digit day code, for example, September 1, 1983 is represented as 3244. In the five-digit format, the last two digits of the year are used as the first two characters of the Julian date, followed by the three-digit day code; in this case, September 1, 1983 is represented as 83244. Julian dating is used in the HIBC standard to encode expiration dates (see Appendix A of the HIBC Standard).

# K

**Kelvin**—abbreviated K; a unit of measure of light temperature. The higher the temperature, the more red the light; the lower the temperature, the more violet the light.

**key mark/trigger**—a code bit that tells the scanner when the code is in position to be read.

**Kilo**—abbreviated K; literally 1000 units. In information processing 1K equals 1,024 bits or bytes (characters) of data.

**kiss impression**—the lightest possible impression which transfers the film of ink from the transfer roll to the plate and from the plate to the material being printed.

# L

**label**—a piece of paper, cloth, polymer, metal, or other material affixed to something and indicating its contents, destination, or other information.

**labeler code**—NDC/HRIC number assigned by the Food and Drug Administration identifying the manufacturer of the product.

**Labeler Identification Code**—A four-character alphanumeric identification in the HIBC System of the labeler of health care products.

**ladder code**—see **vertical bar code.**

**laser**—an acronym for Light Amplification by the Stimulated Emission of Radiation. A coherent, monochromatic light source having the common characteristics of an active material to convert energy into laser light, a pumping source to provide power or energy, optics to direct the beam repeatedly through the active material so that it becomes amplified, and the optics to direct the beam into a narrow cone of divergence. There are four basic laser types: crystal lasers, gas lasers, liquid lasers, and semiconductor lasers. Crystal lasers use a crystal such as a ruby for an active medium. Gas lasers use gases in combination, such as helium and neon, as an active medium. Liquid lasers use organic dyes such as rhodamine as an active medium. The semiconductor laser is made from a material such as gallium arsenide. A laser used in cutting or welding has a power output of hundreds to thousands of Watts, whereas a laser employed in bar code scanning has a power output in the microWatt to milliWatt ranges. Output power and safety considerations of lasers are regulated by the FDA Agency Center for Devices and Radiological Health (CDRH), specifically under 21 CFA 1040, and ANSI Standard Z-136, 1-1980.

**laser diode**—a laser made from a semiconductor pn junction. Historically, laser diodes were of gallium-arsenide composition. These dievices emitted light only in the infrared portion (900 nm) of the light spectrum. Recently advances in laser diode technology have permitted light emission in the near infrared (NIR—780 nm) region. It is expected that visible red laser diode technology will be introduced into the bar code marketplace in 1988. Also called a **semiconductor laser.**

**laser marking**—etching of data by medium to high power lasers directly onto marking surfaces such as metal, wood, and fibreboard.

**laser printer**—a printer employing a pulsed or rastered laser light source to positively charge an image on a dielectric cylinder of electrostatic printing mechanism.

**laser scanner**—an optical bar code reading device using a low energy laser light beam as its source of illumination.

**left-hand justified blank filled**—a common data processing convention for the storage of variable length data in fixed length memory locations. When data of shorter length than the maximum length of the storage location field are input, the data are shifted to the left, so that the first significant character of the input appears in the first reserved memory location of the storage medium. Those memory locations that follow the data field and are unused are filled with blank characters (ASCII hex 20). Also referred to as alphanumeric field convention.

**letterpress**—a printing process that employs a relief, or raised, inked image which comes into direct contact with the material being printed. Letterpress printing can be performed from metal type or plates, or rubber or plastic plates, using a rotary, flatbed, or platen press.

**light pen**—a pen-like, contact reader that is hand-held, typically employing an infrared or panchromatic red light source. See **wand scanner.**

**light source**—light energy is emitted in straight lines from one of two source types, the point source and the extended source. The point source is ideally a single point. The extended source of light energy illuminates a point in space from several directions. Light sources for bar code reading equipment are typically infrared (900 nanometers peak), visible red (630 to 720 nanometers), and incandescent (400 to 900 nanometers). The source wavelength of He-Ne laser light is precisely 632.8 nanometers.

**linear array**—a row and series of transductive elements able to convert the quantity of light received to a relatively-sized modulated electric signal. Distinguished from a matrix array. See photodiode array (linear).

**linkage character/key**—the manner or style of being united, as the quality or state of being a connected structure. With respect to the HIBC Symbol and Code, the process of uniting a Primary and Secondary Symbol in such a way as to minimize a mixing of labels from different products. The Primary Symbol has a character position reserved for a check character, which is derived from an arithmetic computation on the preceding data characters. The Primary Symbol check character becomes the linkage character of the Secondary Symbol for that product. In this way, the Primary and Secondary Symbols of a given product are united, or linked.

**lithography**—a method of printing from a plane surface, such as a smooth stone or metal plate, on which the image to be printed is ink receptive and the nonprinting area ink repellent. Also referred to as planography.

**logistics**—the science of planning and carrying out the movement and maintenance of forces. For LOGMARS purposes, those aspects of military operations which deal with the design and development, acquisition, storage, movement, distribution, maintenance, evacuation, and disposition of material.

**LOGMARS**—the acronym for the Department of Defense (DOD) project on LOGistics applications of automated Marking And Reading Symbols. The LOGMARS project master plan was approved in June 1977, and its final report was issued on September 1, 1981 and adopted by the DOD on September 29, 1981. From the LOGMARS final report, MIL-STD-1189A and MIL-STD-129J were developed.

**logotype**—a name, symbol, or mark used to identify a company; a trademark. Logotype is also a method of application of printed matter onto a carton or surface, where the image to be printed is sequentially placed on a rotary coder, inked, and applied to passing surfaces. Logotype has traditonally printed human-readable characters and is moving toward the printing of discrete bar codes.

**lot/batch/serial number**—LBS; for the purpose of the GIBC and HIBC Standards, identification of a product that groups the product in a unique manner to identify those products manufactured during the same relative time or in the same facilities. Some products have both a serial number and a lot/batch number. In this case, the serial number appears at the eaches level with lot/batch number appearing on higher levels of packaging.

# M

**machine-readable**—that characteristic of printed information that permits the direct transfer of information from a printed surface to a data processing system, without operator intervention. Bar coding and optical character recognition are technologies of machine reading, as is that of image cameras.

**magnesium oxide**—a chemical compound whose solid form is considered pure white for photometric purposes, yielding 100 percent reflection and used in the calibration of photometric devices.

**magnetic code reader**—a remote code reader that reads and identifies by the detection of the presence or absence of a magnetic field.

**magnetic ink character recognition**—MICR; the machine recognition of characters printed with ink that contains particles of a magnetic material. Commonly used in check printing within the banking and financial community.

**magnification factor**—MF; a term used in the UPC and UCS/TCS specifications identifying the size of a printed bar code compared to a standard (nominal) size. A magnification factor of 1.00 (100 percent) is nominal size.

**make-ready**—the preparation and correction of the printing plates, before starting the print run, to ensure uniformly clean impressions of optimum quality; all preparatory operations preceding production.

**manufacturer's identification number**—in the UPC system, the four- or five-digit number assigned to a manufacturer by the Uniform Code Council, Inc. This number appears as the left half of the UPC number. See **item code.**

**margin**—see **quiet zone.**

**marking**—application of numbers, letters, labels, tags, symbols, or colors for shipment or storage.

**mark reading**—automatic optical reading of printed marks. Often used in test scoring of multiple-answer questions.

**mark sensing**—machine reading of marks by using the conductive properties of the marks themselves, such as those made by a Number 2 pencil.

**Material Handling Institute**—MHI; see **AIM.**

**materiel**—equipment, apparatus, and supplies used by an organization.

**matrix array**—a set of rays and columns of transductive elements able to convert the quantity of light received to a relatively-sized modulated electrical signal. Distinguished from a linear array. See photodiode array (matrix).

**matrix printing**—A method of printing that employs a print head to produce a series of dots in a pattern that forms characters or bars. On some printers the head is fixed and the label stock moves. On others the head moves and the stock is fixed. Technologies employing matrix printing include dot-matrix impact, ink jet, thermal, electrostatic and thermal transfer printing.

**maximum bar reflectance**—the maximum reflectance within any bar (Rb max) when the measuring aperture is wholly contained within a bar. Note that the printing tolerance for a particular symbology may result in the measuring aperture being larger than the width of the bar elements. In this case, the maximum bar reflectance is measured when the aperture is centered on the bar.

**maximum space reflectance**—the maximum reflectance within any space (As max).

**mean (arithmetic)**—the value or statistic that is the result of the sum of the statistical observations in a sample divided by the number of observations in the sample.

**measured element width**—the thickness or width of a bar or space as measured from its leading to its trailing edge in accordance with the symbology specification.

**media**—see **substrate.**

**median**—the value of the variable in a statistical sampling that exceeds half of the observations and is exceeded by the other half.

**message (bar code symbol)**—the string of characters encoded in a bar code symbol.

**message code**—a user-specific meaning ascribed to a bar coded message, including message format restrictions and check characters.

**message length**—the number of characters contained in a single encoded message.

**micro**—a unit of measure equal to one millionth of a meter, or about 0.00004 inch; 25 microns equal 0.001 inch.

**mil**—one thousandth of an inch (0.001 inch), or approximately 0.0254 millimeter. Bar code bar widths are commonly referred to as being a certain number of mils wide.

**millimicron**—see **nanometer.**

**minimum bar reflectance**—the minimum reflectance within any bar (Ab min).

**minimum reflectivity difference**—the difference between the smallest minimum space reflectance value and the largest maximum bar reflectance value as measured across the entire symbol.
where: MAD = Min (As min) - Max (Ab max)
      As = Minimum Space Reflectance
      Ab = Maximum Bar Reflectance
Bar, space, and MAD reflectances can be expressed as percentages or in decimal form. If the reflectance of the bars is determined to be 2%, and the reflectance of the spaces is deter-

mined to be 90%, then the MAD equals 88%.
MAD = 90% − 2% = 88%

**minimum space reflectance**—the minimum reflectance within any space when the measuring aperture is wholly contained within a space. Note that the printing tolerance for a particular symbology may result in the measuring aperature being larger than the width of the space elements. In this case, the minimum space reflectance is measured when the aperture is centered on the space.

**misalignment**—Misorientation of the label from its normal, or perpendicular, position.

**miscoding or misencodation**—when the characters which were to be represented in symbol form are not correctly encoded in the bars and spaces; for example, when the desired number is 1–2–3–4 and the number encoded in the symbol is 1–2–5–4.

**misread/bad read**—a condition that occurs when the data output of a reader does not agree with the encoded data presented. see **substitution error.**

**modem**—MOdulator/DEModulator; a device for conversion of one form of a signal to another that is suitable for transmission over communication circuits, typically from digital to analog and then from analog to digital.

**module**—the narrowest nominal bar or space in the code. Wider bars and spaces are often specified as multiples of one module. See **X dimension, unit,** and **element.**

**module resolution**—see **resolution.**

**module width encoding**—a method of bar encoding in which narrow elements represent binary zeros and wide elements represent binary ones.

**modulo check character/digit**—a specific character included in some bar code symbols that is generated from a mathematical computation and the weighting of various characters in the symbol. The use of modulo checking increases the reliability that the bar code will be properly read by signaling the scanner if an error has been made in reading.

**modulus 43 check character**—the method of check character derivation for Code 39. See Schedules A and B of Appendix F—Code 39 Specifications.

**mottled**—a speckled or indistinctly spotted appearance, as in an ink lay, that is attributable to various causes.

**moving beam bar code reader/scanner**—a bar code reader that dynamically searches for code marks by sweeping a moving optical beam through a field of view.

**multicode reader**—also called an autodiscrimination reader. A bar code reader possessing the software or firmware capable of decoding various types of bar codes, such as Code 39, UPC/EAN, Interleaved 2 of 5, and Codabar. Two varieties of multicode readers exist. A switch-selectable, or firmware-based, system permits the selection of the desired code based on switch position (on or off). An autodiscrimination, or software-based, system permits the decoding of any of a specific set of codes automatically, without operator intervention. It is unknown what the substitution error rate of codes which are autodiscriminated will be as compared to the SER of codes read singularly and not in combination with one another.

**multifont**—an OCR reader having the capability to recognize more than one type font automatically, such as OCR-A and OCR-B.

**multiple font**—a firmware-based reader having the capability to recognize more than one type of OCR font, but only one at a time.

**multiple scanning/decoding/reads**—a technique employed within noncontact scanning, and specifically moving beam formats, which adds to the integrity (reduces the probability of a substitution error) of a symbol being read by making two or more reads of the symbol and comparing the reads to ensure agreement before the data is passed to a data processing system.

# N

**nanometer**—a unit of measure to define the wavelength and color of light equal to 10 to the minus 9 meters. One nanometer is equivalent to 10 angstroms. The abbreviation for nanometer is nm.

| Color wavelengths | |
| --- | --- |
| **Color** | **Wavelength (nm)** |
| Ultraviolet | 5–380 |
| Violet | 380–450 |
| Blue | 450–490 |
| Green | 490–560 |
| Yellow | 560–590 |
| Orange | 590–630 |
| Red | 630–760 |
| Infrared | 760–4,000,000 |

**national stock number**—NSN; a 13-character number assigned uniquely to each item of procurement of the U.S. government.

**NDC/NHRIC**—National Drug Code/National Health Related Items Code; a 10-digit code number assigned and administered by the Food and Drug Administration. In the UPC implementation, these numbers use the UPC number system character 3 as the first digit, instead of 0 used by regular grocery items. NDCs can appear in a 4–4–2, 5–4–1, or 5–3–2 format, with the first set of digits representing the manufacturer's identification number and the second set of digits representing the item code. NHRICs can appear in a 4–6 or 5–5 format.

**negative**—a photographic image of an original copy on paper, film, or glass in reverse from that of the original copy.

**nominal**—the exact (or ideal) intended value for a specified parameter. Tolerances are specified as positive and negative deviations from this value.

**nominal size**—the standard size for a bar code symbol; the target width, without tolerances, for a bar width. Nominal for HIBC purposes, refers to the target widths of the wide and narrow bars. Nominal for the UPC symbol refers to percentages of magnification, from 0.80 to 2.12 percent of nominal. See **magnification** factor for further UPC definition.

**nominal ratio**—the ratio of wide bar nominal size to narrow bar nominal size. The HIBC standard recommends a nominal ratio of 3:1 (3.00).

**noncontact**—a method of bar code reading typified by fixed or moving beam scanners having a greater optical throw and depth of field than contact, or wand, scanners. See **Figure 13-1**.

**nonopaque**—a feature of a material that allows light to pass through; transparent, translucent.

**nonreturn-to-zero (NRZ) encoding**—a method of bar code encoding in which binary zeroes and ones are represented by reflective and nonreflective modules, respectively; a series of four binary zeroes, for example, represented by a nonreflective area four modules in width.

**no-read/nonread/nonscan**—the absence of data at the scanner output after an attempted scan due to non code, improper orientation or speed of scan, defective code or scanner, or operator error. Compare to **misread.**

**normal**—perpendicular to a surface or plane.

**number system character**—the first, or left-hand, digit in a UPC number; identifies different numbering systems. Regular supermarket items carry a 0; random weight items such as meat and produce that are marked at the store carry a 2; NDC/NHRIC items carry a 3; non-food items marked in the store carry a 4; coupons carry a 5; and number systems 1, 6, 7, 8, and 9 are unidentified for use at this time. Only number system 0 is valid for the six-digit UPC Version E symbol.

**numeric**—a machine vocabulary that includes only numerals; contrasted to alphanumeric, which includes letters and numerals.

# O

**OCR**—optical character recognition.

**OCR-A**—an abbreviation commonly applied to the character set contained in ANSI standard X3.17-1981. Consists of 26 alphabetic characters, 10 numerals, 60 other graphic shapes, plus the character space. OCR-A was initially chosen as the official symbology of the National Retail Merchants Association (NMRA) and the Canadian Standard Product Code for wine, beer, and liquor items. OCR-A is more stylized than the OCR-B font.

**OCR-B**—an abbreviation commonly applied to the character set contained in ANSI standard X3.49-1975. Consists of 26 alphabetic characters, 10 numerals, 60 other graphic shapes, plus the space character. OCR-B has been adopted by the Uniform Code Council as the human-readable portion of the UPC symbol. The less stylized and more human-readable of the two OCR fonts.

**off-line**—refers to devices that operate independently of a larger central processing unit. An off-line data processing device is one that can stand alone, such as a portable data entry terminal, capture data, and transmit the collected data to a central data processing facility.

**omnidirectional**—refers to a code format that can be read, regardless of orientation to a given plane, such as a bullseye code, or a reader or scanner with the ability to read a bar code symbol from any angle. The combination of the mechanics of a supermarket checkout system slot scanner and the UPC symbol permits omnidirectional reading as long as the bar code passes over the scanner window. Many omnidirectional scanners employ multiple x-axis and y-axis scan patterns to achieve the omnidirectional capability.

**on-line**—an operation in which peripheral devices are connected directly to the processing unit.

**opacity**—the quality or state of substance that causes it to obstruct rays of light. The hiding quality of an ink coating or other substance; the opposite of transparency.

**opacity value**—the calculated value of a material by means of two reflectance measurements, $R_1$ and $R_2$. The first measurement, $R_1$, is taken on a sample of a blank material, backed with enough layers of the same material so that doubling the number of layers does not change the measured value of reflectance. The second measurement, $R_2$, is taken of the same blank material sample except that a black backing is placed behind the material sample instead of the multiple layers. The reflectance value of the black backing should not exceed 5 percent. The calculation of the opacity value is as follows:

$$\text{opacity value} = 1.00 - \frac{R_1 - R_2}{R_1} = \frac{R_2}{R_1}$$

**opaque**—impervious to light rays; a paint exhibiting light obstructive qualities that is used to block out areas on a photographic negative not wanted on the plate; to apply opaque materials.

**open system**—one where printing devices may be specified by one authority and reading devices specified by another authority. Open systems require agreed upon reader resolutions to match printer narrow nominal element widths throughout a system or industry.

**optical character reader**—an information processing device that accepts prepared forms and converts data from them to computer output media via optical character recognition.

**optical character recognition**—OCR; the machine identification of printed characters through use of light-sensitive devices. Contrast with magnetic ink character recognition (MICR) and bar code.

**optical distortion**—change in appearance of objects when viewed through transparent material, adding certain defects such as waviness of surface.

**optical throw**—the distance from the face of the code reader or scanner to the beginning of the depth of field. See **Figure 13-1**.

**orientation**—the positioning of graphic elements relative to a common reference, such as the base of a box, bottle, or can; the alignment of bars and spaces to the scanner. Often referred to as vertical, or picket fence, format or horizontal, or stepladder format.

**orientation bar**—a code bar that provides the scanner with start and stop reading instructions, as well as code orientation. See start/stop characters.

**outer container**—an exterior container that provides protection to items of supply or unit packs for storage and shipment. It may contain similar items or many different items, as in a multipak or repack. A unit pack sometimes serves as an outer container.

**overhead**—the fixed number of characters required for a start, stop, and checking in a given symbol. For example, a symbol requiring start/stop codes and two check characters contains four characters of overhead. Thus, to encode three characters, seven characters are required.

# P

**packaging**—the process of arranging a group or quantity of related objects or material in a form convenient for transportation or consumption. Packaging may contain artwork that identifies the contents of the package, as well as important information regarding the package. Multiple levels of packaging may exist to transport the objects or material to various levels of storage or consumption. An example of multiple levels of packaging is where eaches are individually packaged, and the eaches are placed in a box, the boxes in a carton, the cartons in a case, and the cases unitized on a pallet or slip sheet.

**packaging by product market**—the process whereby the same product is supplied to different markets and the packaging differs between markets. In the health industry, tamper-resistant packaging is required on some items for retail consumption but not for institutional consumption. Here, the manufacturer of a product would have different packaging going to different markets. Also in the health industry, some manufacturers supply products to retail and institutional markets; the retail market is supplied with marking for that market, such as the UPC Symbol, and the institutional market is supplied with marking, such as the HIBC Symbol for that market.

**paper bleed**—an optical phenomenon that causes the bars to appear larger and the spaces narrower than they are actually printed. It is caused by the scattering of incident light rays within the media.

**parity**—a system for encoding characters with odd or even bar code patterns. Even parity characters have an even number of binary ones in their structure, while odd parity characters have an odd number of binary ones in their structure. Parity, for the purposes of data processing and data communications, does not relate to whether the original character is odd or even, but how an individual character is made odd or even with the addition of one more bit (1 or 0). Parity is used to provide a self-checking feature in bar codes and other data transmission techniques.

**parity bit/bar/module**—a parity bit is added to a binary array to make the sum of all of the bits always odd or always even for a fundamental check.

**parity pattern**—used in the shortened six-digit Version E (zero suppressed version) of the UPC symbol; a method of using parity to encode the number system character and the modulo check character.

**periodic binary code**—a binary code format using the same amount of space for each bit; narrow bars are zero and wide bars are one.

**permanent code**—a code that is reused indefinitely in a system.

**photocell/photoelectric cell/photosensor**—a solid-state, photosensitive, electronic device in which use is made of the variation of current-voltage characteristics as a function of incident radiation (light). In conveyor and transport systems, a photocell may serve as a presence sensor, identifying when an item is in view and ready to be scanned.

**photocomposition**—the process of setting type copy photographically, as opposed to using the method of inking and proofing lead type characters.

**photodiode array (linear)**—the grouping of many photodiodes, usually microminiature, in a line that detects photon energy (light) from the radiation that strikes a surface and changes the reflected light into electrical current which can be measured. Photodiode arrays (PDAs) are used in some bar code reading devices which detect saturation (high reflection indicates a light space) and black current (minimal reflection indicates a dark bar). Each photodiode in the array is sampled by a microprocessor, and the image of the bar code is decoded by the microprocessor.

**photodiode array (matrix)**—similar to a linear photodiode array, except having a height in excess of one element, commonly referred to as a 64 × 64 array or a 128 by 128 array. Matrix arrays permit the viewing of more vertical area of a bar code symbol permitting vertical redundancy, to average out localized printing defects. Matrix arrays are less sensitive to changes in element width sizes and acceleration through the symbol.

**photoengraving**—a metal plate prepared by the photochemical process, from which the matrix or rubber mold is reproduced.

**photometer/photometric**—a photometer is a device that measures the intensity and brightness of a light beam.

**photopolymer**—a polymer made so that it undergoes a change on exposure to light.

**picket fence code**—a bar code printed horizontally, with individual bars that look like pickets in a fence. Contrast to **stepladder code**. See also **horizontal bar code**.

**pitch**—the rotation of a code pattern about the x-axis; also called roll. See **Figure D-1** this Appendix. The normal distance between center lines or adjacent characters.

**pneumatic code reader**—a code reader that reads and identifies codes by detecting the presence or absence of pneumatic flow, such as reading perforations in keypunch cards by compressed air flow.

**point-of-sale (POS) data entry system**—a system in which actual transactions are recorded by terminals operating on-line to a central computer, such as supermarket registers. These systems frequently employ optical scanning as a means of capturing data.

**polymer**—a compound formed by the linking of simple and identical molecules having functional groups that permit their combination to proceed to higher molecular weights under suitable conditions.

**portable data entry terminals**—PDET; a microprocessor-based, hand-held terminal capable of capturing data by taking the data capture device to the product as opposed to taking the product to the data capture device. PDETs can be either batch oriented, where the data is captured remotely and later transmitted to a computer, or an on-line device which immediately transfers captured data to the computer through a radiofrequency (RF) or microwave (MW) link. Features of PDETs include the number or characteristics of data entry keys, the attachment of scanning peripherals, program memory, data memory, the number of characters displayed, the method of display, and data transmission techniques.

**positive**—a film master positive has black and white (represented on the film master as clear) areas in the same relationship as the final printed symbol. The background will be white and the human-readable characters will be black.

**preprinted symbol**—a symbol that is printed before being applied on a label or article to be identified. When printed on a label, maintaining printing tolerances is simplified, especially when the package substrate is difficult to print on directly.

**presence sensor**—a device, often a photoelectric device, used in conveyor and transport systems to tell the system that an item is in view and ready to be read.

**Primary Symbol**—for HIBC/GIBC purposes, the recommended Symbol, containing a start code, an HIBC Symbol flag character, a labeler's identification code, a product/catalog number, a unit of measure identifier, a check character, and a stop code. See **Secondary Symbol.**

**printability gauge**—a printer's tool used to determine the amount of print gain under given printing conditions.

**printability range**—the range of print gain found under actual working conditions, based on press sheets selected at random during a press run.

**print contrast signal**—PCS; a comparison between the reflectance of the bars and that of spaces. Under a given set of illumination conditions, PCS is defined as:

$$ PCS = \frac{R_L = R_D}{R_L} $$

where $R_D$ is the reflectance factor of the dark bars and $R_L$ is the reflectance factor of the light spaces, or background. PCS values can be calculated and displayed automatically on suitable instruments. A minimum PCS value is needed for a symbol to be scannable.

**print gain**—gain in bar width in the final printed bar code symbol, compared to the original precision film master; influenced by platemaking and ink spread during printing. Film masters are made with an appropriate amount of bar width reduction (BWR) to allow for print gain.

**printing**—the technique or art of forming a specific mark by the application of pressure of an inked surface to an uninked surface. The printing of bar codes is accomplished in several different ways, as follows:

*commercial printing*—a method used when numerous copies of the same symbol are required, such as printing of labels for items carried in a supermarket. A film master image is incorporated in the artwork of the label prior to the printing of the label. Common methods of commercial printing include:

*intaglio/gravure*—a method that uses an engraved surface or etched design below the surface, such as the cells in an anilox roll or gravure cylinder.

*flexography*—the method of direct rotary printing using resilient, raised-image printing plates that are affixed to plate cylinders of various repeat lengths, inked by a roll or doctor-blade-wiped metering roll, carrying fluid or paste-type inks to virtually any substrate.

*lithography*—a method of printing from a plane surface, such as a smooth stone or metal plate, on which the image to be printed is ink receptive and the nonprinting area is ink repellent. Also called planography.

*letterpress*—a printing process that employs a relief or a raised ink image which comes in direct contact with the material being printed. Letterpress printing can be performed from metal type or plates, rubber plates, or plastic plates, using rotary, flatbed, or platen press.

*demand printing*—a method used when few copies of the same symbol are required and many unique labels may be required, such as assigning unique serial numbers to health-related devices. Common methods of demand printing include:

*formed character printing*—an impact printing technique similar to an office typewriter. The bars and characters are engraved or etched in reverse on a rotating drum. Paper, vinyl, or mylar label stock and a dry carbon ribbon pass between the drum and a hammer operated by an electromagnet. The hammer forces the paper and ribbon against the drum, causing the image to be transferred from the ribbon to the label. Each hammer stroke forms a complete character or bar.

*dot-matrix printing*—a technique that uses a print head to produce a series of dots in a pattern that forms characters or bars. On some printers the head is fixed and the label stock moves; on others the head moves and the stock is fixed. The print head consists of a series of pins arranged in an array to form a 5-by-7 or 7-by-9 matrix. A microprocessor causes the pins to fire in the correct sequence to form the characters. The basic unit of printing is the dot. Impact dot-matrix printing occurs when the print wires in the matrix are activated to form a specific character; the print wires strike a ribbon, which imprints the character onto the label stock. Thermal printing occurs when a heated print head, usually a single bar consisting of 21 dots, is heated and special heat-sensitive paper is passed in front of the head. The dots that form the characters are selectively heated and cooled. Electrostatic printers operate in a manner similar to the thermal printer, except that the dots are charged, rather than being heated, so that when the label is brought through a toner, the toner adheres to the charged area on the label. Ink jet printing replaces the print head wires with ink ports; the ports can either deny or permit the flow of ink (drop on demand), or the print head spray a continuous stream of charged ink droplets at the paper, while an electromagnetic field between the ink jets and the paper determines whether the ink droplets reach their destination or are electrically deflected and siphoned away to the ink reservoir by a suction tube.

*laser etched printing*—two techniques are employed; one requires a high power laser that actually etches into the surface, and the other uses a low power laser that burns off a top coating, allowing the substrate to show through.

**printing plate**—the printing image carrier used on rotary presses, which accepts ink in the image area for printing.

**print quality**—the complete analysis of a printed symbol with regard to reflectance properties, as well as bar and space resolution with regard to symbol specification. The interrelationship of printed material and imprinted material, which affects the optimum performance of the scanner.

**print tolerance**—an absolute measurement of deviation from a nominal print width, expressed as being plus or minus ($\pm$) so many thousandths of an inch. As an example, ANSI MH 10.8M-1983 specifies Code 39's highest density at 9.4 characters per inch with a nominal narrow element width of 0.0075 inch. The tolerance for this width is $\pm 0.0017$ inch when the wide-to-narrow ratio is 2.25:1, which means that the narrow element can be anywhere between 0.0058 inch and 0.0094 inch to be within the printing tolerance.

**product/catalog number**—PCN; for HIBC/ GIBC purposes, that field in the Primary Symbol which identifies the product contents, as opposed to the labeler.

**product code/item code/product identifier/ item ID**—within the UPC system, that string of numeric characters that identifies the product of a specific manufacturer. Similar to the product/catalog number (PCN) for the HIBC system.

**prospective payments**—a method of reimbursement from third-party health care payers based on diagnostic related groups (DRGs). Historically, hospitals have been reimbursed from third-party payers on a retrospective basis with the payers having little control over the determination of essential procedures or length of hospital stay. DRGs classify procedures having a similar form of clinical perspectives into 467 classes, or DRGs. The hospital knows at the beginning of the procedure the amount of reimbursement it will receive, placing a greater emphasis on cost control and containment through the application of technologies developed in general industry.

# Q

**Q.E.D.**—*quod erat demonstrandum*; Latin for "that which has been proven."

**quality**—those characteristics of a production that allow manufacture at a given cost-price relationship, uniformity to meet parameters of customer specifications, and caliber of competitive performance.

**quality control**—the systematic planning, measurement, and control of a combination of people, materials, metrology, and machines, with the objective of producing a product that satisfies the quality and profitability of the enterprise.

**quiet zone**—the area immediately preceding the start character and following the stop character which contains no markings and is free of any extraneous marks; it is quiet in terms of scanning signal produced. For example, the quiet zone of a Code 39 Symbol is 10 times the width of the narrowest element or 0.250 inch, whichever is greater.

# R

**radiant power**—the time rate of flow of electromagnetic energy, measured in Watts (W).

**radiation pattern**—the optical pattern of light that leaves the media surface, as described by the radiated light intensity at various angles.

**radio frequency (RF)/microwave (MW) transponder**—a technology of automated identification systems that operates on the same principle as security tags placed on clothing. The tag signals an alarm if it passes through an antenna field, which is usually located at the door of the establishment. Passive devices are commercially available that will encode and transmit information back to a computer system when in proximity of its associated antenna.

**random errors**—errors introduced by the printer, reader, operator, or other system elements; errors that are encountered during one scan which may not be encountered during the next scan.

**random sample**—in statistics, a sample of a population obtained by a process which gives each possible combination of $n$ items in the population the same chance of being selected.

**range**—in a statistical sampling, the values covered by the frequency distribution, going from the highest to lowest.

**read area**—area covered by a scanner; especially important in material handling applications, such as scanners reading cartons on a conveyor line. Bar codes must reliably pass through the read area with the length of the symbol parallel to the scan plane.

**reader**—a device used for machine reading of bar codes; typically consists of a scanner, a decoder, and a data communications interface.

**reflectance**—the amount of light reflected from a surface; measured under specific conditions, in which a surface coated with barium sulfate or magnesium oxide is considered to be a perfect diffuse reflector of light (diffuse reflection scatters light in all directions).

**reflectance, absolute**—the ratio of the total reflectance by a document to the total light incident on that document.

**reflectance, diffuse**—reflected light whose angle of reflection varies from the angle of incidence of the illuminating light, such as in reflection from a rough surface.

**reflectance, specular**—reflected light whose angle of reflection is equal, or nearly equal, to the angle of incidence of the illuminating light, such as in reflection from a mirror.

**resolution**—in optics, sharpness; the ability to reproduce fine detail; the ability of a scanner to read the narrow bars in bar codes. In printing, a measurement of the narrowest bar that can be printed satisfactorily. The measure of the ability of a lens, a photographic material, or a photographic system to distinguish detail under a specific condition. The dimension of the smallest element that can be printed when employing a particular technique. The narrowest element dimension that can be distinguished by a particular reading device. The measure of this ability is normally expressed in width of aperture in mils, lines per millimeter, or angular resolution.

**retroreflective**—refers to a characteristic of material, causing it to reflect light back to its source, regardless of the angle of incidence.

**reverse image**—a symbol in which the normally dark areas are represented by the material substrate and the light areas are represented by the inked portion of the symbol.

**RF scanner**—that variety of portable data entry terminals possessing the capability of a radio-frequency data link back to a computer system. Also called a **radio-frequency data terminal**.

**right-hand justified zero filled**—a common data processing convention for the storage of variable length numeric data in fixed length memory locations. When data are input of shorter length than the maximum length of the storage location field, the data are shifted to the right so that the last significant character of the input appears in the last reserved memory location of the storage medium. The memory locations preceding the first character of the field being input are unused and filled with zero characters (ASCII hex 30). A convention used for numeric fields.

# S

**sampling**—the statistical process of collecting data or observations.

**scan**—the search for a symbol which is to be optically recognized; a search for marks to be recognized by the recognition unit of an optical scanner. Movement of a light source over a bar code and recognition of the reflective qualities of the signal from that symbol.

**scanner**—a device that examines a spatial pattern, one part after another, and generates analog or digital signals corresponding to the pattern. Scanners are often used in mark sensing, pattern recognition, character recognition, and bar code recognition. The scanner converts bar code symbols to electrical signals for input to a bar code reader decoder for processing and subsequent output through a data communications interface.

**scanning/reading range** (also called Operating Range—OR)—the combined distance of optical ability of a lens, a photographic material, or a photographic system to distinguish detail under a specific condition. The dimension of the smallest element that can be printed when employing a particular technique. The narrowest element dimension that can be distinguished by a particular reading device. The measure of this ability is normally expressed in width of aperture in mils, lines per millimeter, or angular resolution.

**retroreflective**—refers to a characteristic of material, causing it to reflect light back to its source, regardless of the angle of incidence.

**reverse image**—a symbol in which the normal dark areas are represented by the material substrate and the light areas are represented by the inked portion of the symbol.
throw and depth of field. This is typically a function of both scanner performance and code medium employed. See **Figure 13-1**.

**scanning wand**—see wand scanner.

**Secondary Symbol**—for HIBC/GIBC purposes, the Symbol that carries a start code, an HIBC Symbol flag character, an expiration date, a lot/batch/serial number, linkage character, check character, and a stop code.

**segment**—see **element**.

**self-checking bar code**—a bar code that uses a checking algorithm which can be applied against each character such that substitution errors can occur only if two or more independent printing defects appear within a single character. Checking at both the character and the message level (with a modulo check character) greatly minimizes the probability of substitution errors.

**serial number**—that portion of the HIBC/GIBC Secondary Symbol which uniquely identifies an each and distinguishes it from any other each.

**service store**—for military purposes, a consolidated point of distribution for specific expendable supplies to activities that have authorized logistical support at an installation. The following organizational titles are used by the services to refer to this type of operation:
Air Force—Base Service Store
Army—Self Service Supply Center
Marine Corps—Direct Supply Support Center
Navy—Servmart/Seamart

**show-through**—the generally undesirable property of a substrate that permits underlying markings to be seen.

**skew**—rotation about the y-axis; rotational deviation from correct horizontal and vertical orientation; may be applied to a single character, line, or entire encoded symbol. Also called yaw. See **Figure D-1** this Appendix.

**SKU**—(see **Stock Keeping Unit**)

**slot scanner**—the scanning portion of a point-of-sale system embedded within the retail checkout lane counter. Traditionally a helium-neon laser is employed, reflecting the light beam by a series of mirrors to create a pattern which is recognized to read the UPC symbol. The symbol is drawn across the scanner window so that at least one beam of light intersects the entire UPC symbol. Also called **desk scanner** or **checkout scanner**.

**software**—a set of computer programs, procedures, and the associated documentation concerned with the operation of a data processing system, such as, compilers, library routines, manuals, circuit diagrams. Contrast to **hardware**.

**source data automation**—methods of recording data at its source in coded form on paper tape, punched cards, magnetic tape, or tags that can be reused to produce other records without rewriting the original data.

**source marking**—the bar coding of a specific item at the point of initial production of the item; refers to the inclusion of the UPC Symbol in the label artwork of items to be distributed in the grocery marketplace. Also refers to similar marking of the HIBC Symbol. Can mean any item that is bar coded before item tracking begins; for example, printed circuit board encodation in the original artwork of the board.

**space**—the lighter element of a bar code formed by the background between the bars.

**space encoding**—in bar coding, the use of the spaces between the bars to carry encoded information. See **continuous code**.

**spatial**—of or relating to space.

**special symbol/character**—in a character set, refers to a character that is not a numeral, a letter, or a blank, such as -, *, $, /, +, and %.

**spectral**—of, relating to, or made by an array of components of an emission or wave separated and arranged in the order of some varying characteristic, such as wavelength, mass, or energy.

**spectral band**—an arrangement of a specific set of adjacent wavelengths. Spectral Band B633 includes those wavelengths $\pm 5\%$ of the 633 nanometer peak. B900 includes those wavelengths $\pm 10\%$ of the 900 nanometer peak.

**spectral response**—the variation in sensitivity of a device to light or different wavelengths.

**specular/spectral reflection**—reflection of light from a surface at an equal but opposite angle to the angle of incidence, mirrorlike reflection qualities.

**spot size**—the size of the focused image of the emitter as it appears on a surface at the focal point of the optical system. Aperture size is the equivalent term for scanners that use a focused detector image.

**spots/specks**—ink or dirt spots within the spaces or clear areas of a bar code which may reduce the first read rate. Contrast to **void**.

**STAC**—Symbol Technical Advisory Committee to the Uniform Code Council, Inc.

**standalone scanner/bar code reader**—a bar code reader that does not require actual contact with the data to be read. See **fixed base reader**.

**Standard DOD Symbology**—SDS; MIL-STD-1189A, dated 4 September 1984, defines Code 39 as the standard symbology for marking unit packs, outer containers, and selected documents.

**start/stop characters (code)**—distinct characters used at the beginning and end of each bar code symbol that provide initial timing references and direction of read information to the coding logic. For Code 39 purposes, the common character asterisk (*) is employed.

**stationary scanner/bar code reader**—see **fixed base reader**.

**stepladder code**—see **vertical bar code**.

**Stock Keeping Unit**—the standard unit by which a given item is carried in a given organization's inventory.

**striation**—a fine, streaky pattern of parallel lines, usually in the direction of the web of a printing press.

**stroke**—in OCR, a straight line or curve between two nodes of a character. Each character is made up of a variable number of these strokes. Their shapes and arrangement define each individual character of a set. For a character to be read correctly, the quality of printing of each stroke must fall within certain tolerance limits. These limits are usually expressed in terms of stroke width.

**stroke analysis**—in OCR, a technique of recognition in which the strokes and lines of a character are considered descriptive of the character, as opposed to techniques in which the character space is divided into abstractly determined cells.

**stroke average width**—in OCR, the average of actual stroke widths taken at points along the length of the stroke.

**stroke width**—in OCR, the line width of a character stroke. OCR-type fonts express this measurement in terms of a nominal value within prescribed tolerance limits.

**substitution error**—this error can be seen in the misencodation, misread, or human operator error; the correct characters are substituted with erroneous information; for example, 1-2-5-4 for 1-2-3-4. Check characters and character self-checking minimize but do not totally prevent this type of error.

**substitution error rate**—SER; the ratio of the number of invalid or incorrect characters entered into the data base to the number of valid characters entered.

**substrate**—a foundation material on the surface of which a substance is deposited, such as printing or coating.

**sunburst**—a type of circular pattern, made up of uniquely coded preshaped segments available for a character code up to eight characters, plus a start segment and a check digit. Also called a wagon wheel.

**symbol**—a representation of something by reason of relationship, association or convention. Referring to bar codes, a combination of characters, including start/stop and check characters, as required, which form a complete scannable entity.

**symbol density**—the number of characters per lineal inch; limited by the width of the narrowest bar or space.

**symbol length**—the length of the symbol measured from the beginning to the quiet zone adjacent to the start character to the end of the quiet zone adjacent to the stop character.

**symbol reflectance uniformity of bars (SRUB)**—the difference between the largest maximum bar reflectance value and the smallest minimum bar reflectance value as measured across the entire symbol.
SRUB = Max (Ab max) − Min (Ab min)

**symbol reflectance uniformity of spaces (SRUS)**—the difference between the largest maximum space reflectance value and the smallest minimum space reflectance value as measured across the entire symbol.
SRUS = Max (As max) − Min (As min)

**symbology**—representation or expression by means of symbols.

**systematic error**—errors introduced by the printer, reader, or other system elements that are consistent for all bars or all spaces.

# T

**TAPPI**—Technical Association of Pulp and Paper Industry.

**Telepen**—a continuous code developed by S.B. Electronics that encodes the full ASCII character set of 128 characters. Each alphanumeric character is represented by 16 modules and two bar widths.

**templating**—a technique of optical image recognition that compares the read image to a template stored in software to establish the identity of the read character.

**temporal**—of, or relating to, time.

**thermal printing**—see **printing** (*dot-matrix*)

**tilt**—rotation about the z-axis. See **Figure D-1**.

**tolerance**—see **print tolerance.**

**toner**—a dispersion of highly concentrated pigment or dye used to manufacture, strengthen, or modify the color of an ink.

**transcription error**—an error in recording one digit of a number; for example, the substitution of a 3 for the digit 2 in 758792 to produce 758793.

**transfer roll**—a plain roll rotating in contact with another plain roll that transfers variable amounts of ink in an inking system.

**transition point**—the edge of a space or bar where continued movement to an adjacent and complementary module causes a photodetector to reverse its bias from dark current to saturation and vice versa.

**transport case symbol**—TCS; the European nomenclature for the recommendations for the DSSG.

**transport packages**—a package intended for the transportation of one or more individual articles (eaches), small packages, or bulk material.

**transposition error**—an error that occurs when two digits of a number are interchanged, such as interchanging 9 and 2 in 758792 to produce 758729.

**trigger mark**—a code bit that provides the scanner with the instruction that the code is in position to be read. Same as key mark. See also **presence sensor.**

**truncation**—decreasing the length of the bars to reduce the height of the bar code symbol to below the normal UPC specification. Truncation decreases a symbol's ability to be read omnidirectionally and should be avoided.

**two-level code**—a bar code that uses two element widths, wide and narrow, in its structure. Code 39 is a two-level code.

**2 of 5 Code**—A binary coded decimal notation in which each decimal digit is represented by a binary numeral consisting of five bits, two of which are of one kind, conventionally ones; and three are of the other kind, conventionally zeroes. Developed by the Nieaf Company in the Netherlands, it encodes numeric data only and can achieve densities of 15 characters per inch.

**typography**—the style, arrangement, or appearance of typeset matter; the art of selecting and arranging typefaces.

# U

**unidirectional code**—a code format which permits reading in only one direction.

**Uniform Code Council**—UCC (formerly known as the Uniform Product Code Council—UPCC); 8163 Old Yankee Rd., Suite J, Dayton, OH 45459; the organization responsible for overseeing and administering the Universal Product Code in the retail consumer industry.

**Uniform Container Symbol**—UCS; a bar code symbol designed for printing on corrugated board; a result of DSSG.

**Uniform Symbol Description**—USD; specifications set up by AIM for bar codes, as follows:
USD-1 Interleaved 2 of 5 Code
USD-2 subset of Code 39
USD-3 Code 39
USD-4 Codabar
USD-5 Presence/Absence Code
USD-6 Code 128
USD-7 Code 93
USD-8 Code 11

**unit**—a module or segment; the smallest width of bars and spaces in a bar code. See **module.**

**unit load (unitized load)**—a number of filled transport packages or other items that are held together by some means, such as a pallet, slip sheet, strapping, interlocking, glue, shrink wrap, stretch wrap, or net wrap, to make them suitable for transportation, stacking, and storage as a unit. The term is also used to describe a single large item suitable packaged for transportation, stacking, and storage.

**unit of measure**—an identification within the HIBC/GIBC Primary Symbol that establishes a relative level of packaging for the product. This field has a valid range of 1 to 9; 1 is the eaches level of packaging. If products are individually wrapped or packaged, the unit of measure identification, 1, would appear on that level of packaging; 0 in this field is undefined. On higher levels of packaging, a relative measure would appear; an each may be placed in a box, boxes in a carton, cartons in a case, and cases in a unitized load. Here, an each could equal 1, a box could equal 2, a carton could equal 3, a case could equal 4, and a unit load could equal 5. (These identifications are for the purposes of example only.)

**unit pack**—the first tie, wrap, or container applied to an item of supply, which is identified by a national stock number (NSN) of format XXXX - XX - XXX - XXXX, nomenclature, quantity, and unit of issue (U/I).

**Universal Product Code**—UPC; most commonly a 12-digit bar code pattern adopted by the U.S. grocery industry, which identifies the number system character (type of encoded product), five-digit manufacturer number assigned by the UCC, five-digit product code assigned by the manufacturer, and a modulo 10 check digit as the 12th character. The code is numeric, and and there are other versions. Version E accommodates six digits, and Version D is a 12 + n-digit version. Nominal dimensions for the UPC symbol include a module width of 13 mils ($\pm$) 4 mils. Magnification factors range from 0.80 to 2.00 of nominal supporting densities of 10.21 to 4.08 characters per inch, with a nominal of 8.17 characters per inch.

# V

**variable length code**—a code that can be of any length within a range of lengths, commonly with a maximum length specified and frequently with a minimum length also specified.

**variable length field**—a data field or data element that may vary within a prescribed minimum and maximum.

**variable length symbology**—a symbology whose format is not fixed beyond basic requirements for overhead characters, such as start/stop codes. For example, UPC is a fixed length, numeric symbology that supports only six characters (Version E) or 10 characters (Version A). Code 39 is a variable length alphanumeric code which can support any data length from one character up to a maximum dictated by the reading system employed, typically not fewer than 32 characters.

**verification**—the technical process by which a symbol is evaluated to determine whether it meets the specification for that specific symbol. Verification can be accomplished by semiautomated means, with elements measured by a microscope and contrast established by a densitometer. Verification can also be accomplished by automatic means with a device that measures width of elements, contrast, and reflectance, and establishes decodability.

**verifier**—one who is responsible for the verification of a symbol; a device that performs a dynamic analysis of a bar code symbol to ascertain whether the symbol meets specifications. Diagnostic verifiers measure all parameters of the symbol against the standard specification and details the variance from the specification. A go/no go verifier performs a simple read of the code and tells if the code is scannable with that light source, at that acceleration, and at that angle of incidence.

**Version A, Version E**—Version A is the standard 12-digit UPC Symbol, while Version E is a special six-digit shortened version, requiring less space; Version E is formed by the use of zero suppression.

**vertical bar code**—a code pattern presented in an orientation so that the overall coded area from start to stop is perpendicular to the horizon. The individual bars are in an array that looks like the rungs of a ladder.

**vertical redundancy**—viewing an expanded vertical area of a bar code symbol to average out localized printing defects, such as spots, voids, and bar edge roughness. A feature of X&Y-axis moving beam readers and matrix arrays.

**viscosity**—resistance to flow; thickness or thinness measured by the amount of time in seconds for the fluid or paste to flow through a #2 Zahn cup.

**voice recognition**—a process by which a computer or control mechanism can accept data input by spoken command with no intermediate key entry.

**void**—the absence of ink within printed bars or strokes; can cause a bar to scan as a space.

# W

**WB:NB**—the wide-to-narrow bar ratio for a bar code that encodes binary information in its bars and spaces.

**WE:NE**—the wide-to-narrow element ratio for a bar code that encodes binary information in both bars and spaces.

**wand scanner**—a hand-held scanning device used as a contact bar code or OCR reader.

**wavelength**—the amount of space occupied by the progression of an electromagnetic wave; a term describing the frequency of light radiated by the scanner's emitter.

**web**—the paper, foil, film, or other flexible material that comes from a roll as it moves through a machine in the process of being formed, converted, or printed.

**wide-to-narrow ratio**—the ratio between the width of the wide elements and narrow elements in a two-level bar code.

**width error**—the difference between bar (or space) widths, calculated from the scanner's digital output and the optically measured bar (space) widths.

**Wratten 26 filter**—a photometric filter that precisely indicates the color of a helium-neon laser bar code scanner. If a symbol is to be read by a He-Ne, laser verification of the contrast and reflectance of the bars and spaces can be made in a semiautomatic fashion by placing a Wratten 26 filter over the symbol and the measurements can be taken as viewed through the filter.

# X

**X-axis**—a coordinate relating to the orientation and movement of a symbol on a conveyor or transport system. The x-axis is parallel to and in the same direction as the movement of the conveyor or transport system. The deviation from the x-axis is referred to as pitch, or roll.

**X dimension**—the intended width of the narrow bar code element or the equivalent value for the H dimension as dictated by the application standard. Wider elements are generally referred to as multiples of the X dimension.

# Y

**Y-axis**—a coordinate relating to the orientation and movement of a symbol on a conveyor or transport system. The y-axis is perpendicular to the movement and plane of the conveyor or transport system. The deviation from the y-axis is referred to as skew, or yaw.

# Z

**Z dimension**—the midpoint of the range of the narrow bar code element widths. The value may be specified or calculated as follows:
(Narrow Element max) + (Narrow Element min)

**Zahn cup**—a device for measuring viscosity.

**Z-axis**—a coordinate relating to the orientation and movement of a symbol on a conveyor or transport system. The z-axis can be thought of as a plane from which light from a fixed or moving beam scanner will be directed. The deviation from the z-axis is referred to as tilt.

**Zero suppression**—the technique used to shorten UPC codes by omitting certain zeroes from the bar code. If a manufacturer's number ends in 000 or 100 or 200, there are available item numbers between 00000 and 00999 available. The six characters are obtained from the first two characters of the manufacturer's number, followed by the last three characters of the manufacturer's number and the third character of the manufacturer's number. If a manufacturer's number ends in 300, 400, 500, 600, 700, 800, or 900, 100 item numbers between 00000 and 00099 are available. The six characters are obtained from the first three characters of the manufacturer's number, followed by the last two characters of the item number, and ending with the number 3. If a manufacturer's number ends in 10, 20, 30, 40, 50, 60, 70, 80, or 90, the manufacturer has 10 item numbers between 00000 and 00009 available. The six characters are obtained from the first four characters of the manufacturer's number followed by the last character of the item number, ending with the digit 4. If a manufacturer's number does not end in zero, then five item numbers between 00005

and 00009 are available. The six characters are obtained from all five digits of the manufacturer's number, followed by the last character of the item number. Zero suppression is the active coding structure for UPC Version E.

# SOLVING THE PROBLEM OF SKEW

Stationary scanners require that the symbol be brought to the reader. Consequently, these scanners must be positioned within the material flow path. Moving beam scanners oscillate a spot of light at speeds of 40 scans per second and higher. This oscillation makes the moving spot of light appear as a continuous line. For a bar code to be successfully read by one of these devices, all bars and spaces must be intersected by the same scan path, as shown below:

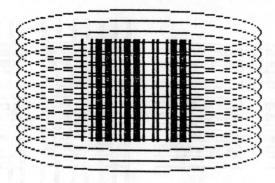

If all bars are not intersected in the same scan, as shown below, a no-scan situation will result.

Since moving beam scanners depend on the symbol being brought to the reader, the manner in which the label is presented to the scanner is also important. If the label is skewed from the normal way in which symbols are usually presented, a no-read situation will occur. Consequently, symbol orientation is a critical matter to stationary readers. The problem of orientation can be overcome by flooding the symbol area with a starburst pattern that can accommodate any orientation. This is a rather neat solution to the problem, but costly. Of all the stationary scanners presently produced, the starburst pattern scanner is by far the most expensive.

Another possible alternative is to ensure that the bar code symbol always appears in the same position relative to the scan path (in many situations a specific distance from the natural bottom of the material bearing the symbol). This solution requires automatic application of the bar code symbol to the material. Accuracy of placement can easily be within $\frac{1}{32}$ of an inch. Further symbol skew, prevalent in human-applied labels, is for all intents and purposes eliminated. The speed of the conveyor and voting algorithms employed by the reader have related impact. Note the figures below.

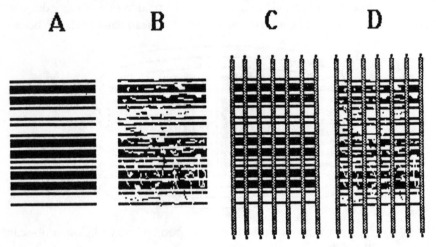

## A      B      C      D

Figure A represents a properly printed bar code symbol. Figure B represents a printed bar code symbol with substantial printing defects. Figure C represents a properly printed symbol oriented in a stepladder fashion to accommodate a conveyor side mounted moving beam reader. Figure D represents the same reader scan lines (shaded vertical lines) positioned over the poorly printed symbol.

Addressing the issue of voting algorithms: moving beam readers are able to take several views of the symbol as it moves in front of the reader. A voting algorithm requires that spatial patterns observed in a given scan line agree with subsequent observation(s)—usually one or two subsequent observations. If the observations agree, the information contained in the spatial patterns are transmitted from the reader. This minimizes the possibility of detecting an erroneous data structure when reading poorly printed symbols (data content of subsequent symbols will not agree unless the data content is correct).

The combined variables of the speed of the conveyor, the scanning speed, and the height of the bar code symbol (in Figures A and C, above, the height of the bars would be the left to right dimension) is shown in the table below:

| Line Speed | Feet/minute | 50 | 75 | 100 | 125 | 150 | 200 | 250 | 300 |
|---|---|---|---|---|---|---|---|---|---|
| | Inches/second | 10 | 15 | 20 | 25 | 30 | 40 | 50 | 60 |
| Scan Speed 45/sec | Inches of bar length required for 5 scans | 1.04 | 1.61 | 2.24 | 2.78 | 3.33 | 4.40 | 5.55 | 6.66 |
| 90/sec | | .52 | .80 | 1.12 | 1.39 | 1.66 | 2.20 | 2.77 | 3.33 |
| 180/sec | | .26 | .40 | .56 | .69 | .83 | 1.10 | 1.39 | 1.66 |
| 360/sec | | .13 | .20 | .28 | .35 | .42 | .55 | .69 | .83 |
| 720/sec | | .07 | .10 | .14 | .18 | .21 | .28 | .35 | .42 |

Since just about every system has some tilt, pitch, or skew, the effective width of the symbol is calculated as it appears to the scanner. Note that one quiet zone has been used. If more than one factor (tilt, pitch, or skew) is present in the system, each calculation must be made separately and the resultant values are cumulative (positive or negative).

$$E_W = E_L(COS \measuredangle) - (S_L + Q)(SIN \measuredangle)$$
Where: $\measuredangle$ = symbol tilt, pitch, or skew

where $E_W$ is the element width, $E_L$ is the element length, $S_L$ is the symbol length, and $Q$ is one quiet zone.

### Selected natural trigonometric functions

| Angle | Sine | Cosine |
|---|---|---|
| 0° | 0.000 | 1.000 |
| 5° | 0.087 | 0.996 |
| 10° | 0.174 | 0.985 |
| 15° | 0.259 | 0.966 |
| 20° | 0.342 | 0.940 |
| 25° | 0.423 | 0.906 |
| 30° | 0.500 | 0.866 |
| 35° | 0.574 | 0.819 |
| 40° | 0.643 | 0.766 |
| 45° | 0.707 | 0.707 |
| 50° | 0.766 | 0.643 |
| 55° | 0.819 | 0.574 |
| 60° | 0.866 | 0.500 |
| 65° | 0.906 | 0.423 |
| 70° | 0.940 | 0.342 |
| 75° | 0.966 | 0.259 |
| 80° | 0.985 | 0.174 |
| 85° | 0.996 | 0.087 |
| 90° | 1.000 | 0.000 |

# CODE 39 SPECIFICATIONS

*These specifications represent an integration of state-of-the-art bar code standards existing as of late 1986. Adherence to these standards will permit the user to realize a cost-effective system of data collection. The specifications in the section on Reflectance, up to and including the note on Symbol Reflectance Uniformity of Spaces, represent specifications for equipment which may, in the very near future, be commercially available. Until such time it may be necessary to rely upon the specifications contained in the section on Bar Edge Roughness, Spots, and Voids (alternate measurement requirement).*

Code 39 (also previously known as Code 3 of 9 and 3 of 9 Code) was developed in 1975 by Dr. David Allais and Ray Stevens of Interface Mechanisms (now Intermec). It is rapidly becoming "the code" for industrial and commercial applications.

The name Code 39 describes both its original character set of 39 characters (currently Code 39 has 43 characters) and the structure of the code, namely, that three of the nine elements per character are wide, and the remaining six are narrow. Each character in Code 39 is represented by a group of five bars and four spaces. The complete character set includes a start/stop character (conventionally represented as an asterisk "*") and 43 data characters consisting of the 10 digits, the 26 letters of the alphabet, space, and the six symbols: −, ., $, /, +, %.

The strong self-checking property of Code 39 provides a high level of data security. With properly designed scanning equipment and an excellent quality of symbol printing, one might reasonably expect only one substitution error out of 100 million characters scanned. Bar codes printed by a well-maintained, better-quality dot matrix printer will provide less than one substitution error in three million characters scanned. For those applications that require exceptional data security, an optional check character is often used. Information regarding Modulus 43 Check Character calculation is contained in Schedule A.

Since the algorithm for Code 39 is highly error resistant, the use of a check character may appear superfluous. A strong incentive for the inclusion of a check character, especially a weighted check character, exists when for some reason the scanner is not able to read the symbol and back-up manual entry is required. Code 39's traditional check character assigns a modulus value to each character in the character set. The sum of the symbol's character modulus values is divided by 43; the remainder is the modulus value of the symbol's check character. This simple equation gives the same check character assignment for the character string 123456 and 123546, namely, 21 or L, which is represented as 123456L and 123546L. The transposition of characters is a com-

## Schedule A
## Modulus 43 Check Character Generation

Some Code 39 data structures employ a Modulus 43 check character for additional data security. The check character is the Modulus 43 sum of all the character values in a given message, and is printed as the last character value in a given message, preceding the stop character. Start and stop characters are not used in calculating the check character. Check character generation is illustrated by the following example.

Symbol data structure: E 5 9 8 9 7 6 9 8 7
Sum of values: $14 + 5 + 9 + 8 + 9 + 7 + 6 + 9 + 8 + 7 = 82$

Divide 82 by 43. The quotient is 1, with a remainder of 39. The check character is the character corresponding to the value of the remainder (see the Table below), which in this example is 39, or "$." The complete symbol data structure, including check character, therefore is:

$$E\ 5\ 9\ 8\ 9\ 7\ 6\ 9\ 8\ 7\ \$$$

---

mon substitution error in key entry, especially as the length of the character string increases. Therefore, a method of "weighting" adjacent characters is necessary so that a transposed message will be rejected by the decoder. Information regarding Weighted Modulus 43 Check Character calculation is contained in Schedule B.

Code 39 is a variable length code, its maximum length determined by the reading equipment used. Code 39 characters are discrete, and a range of intercharacter gaps are permitted. Code 39 is bi-directional, meaning it can be scanned from left to right or right to left. The size of Code 39 varies over a wide range, lending itself to light pen, hand-held laser, and fixed mount scanner reading. A unique character, conventionally interpreted as an asterisk, is exclusively used for both a start and stop character. A Code 39 symbol consists of a leading quiet zone, the start character, appropriate data characters, an optional check character, the stop character, and a trailing quiet zone.

While some industry standards permit the wide-to-narrow ratio to vary between 2:1 and 3:1, this standard encourages a wide-to-narrow ratio of 3:1. The significant parameters of a Code 39 symbol are shown in Figure F-1. The significant recommended printing tolerances and characters per inch with the associated narrow bar and space dimensions at a 3:1 ratio are shown in Table F-1. Figure F-2 shows the Code 39 character set, with its bar/space and bit configurations.

The significant parameters of Code 39 are the nominal width of the narrow elements and the nominal ratio of wide to narrow elements. The minimum nominal width of the narrow element (X dimension) is 0.025 inch (0.635 mm)

## Schedule B
### Weighted Modulus 43 Check Character Generation

Some Code 39 data structures employ a Weighted Modulus 43 check character for additional data security in scanning and key entry. The Weighted Modulus 43 check algorithm described below is not generally implemented in all available reading equipment and may require the user's computer to provide the check algorithm. The same value system as used in Schedule A (Regular Mod 43 Computation), also applies in the Weighted Modulus 43 system. The procedure for computing the weighted check character follows:

1. Starting with the character immediately preceding the check character, multiply the value (from Schedule A) by the weighting constant. The weighting constant is the numerical value from 1 to 43, depending upon the number of character positions in the code. Character position 44 assumes the value of 1, 45 the value of 2, etc. The placement of character weights is from right to left.

2. Sum the result of this multiplication for all data characters.

3. The check character is that character whose value (from Schedule A) is equal to modulus 43 of the sum obtained in Step 2 above.

Check character generation is illustrated by the following example:

| Symbol data structure: | 1 | 2 | 3 | 4 | – | A | B | C | D |
|---|---|---|---|---|---|---|---|---|---|
| Values: | | 1 | 2 | 3 | 4 | 36 | 10 | 11 | 12 | 13 |
| Weighting: | | 9 | 8 | 7 | 6 | 5 | 4 | 3 | 2 | 1 |
| Summation: | | $9 + 16 + 21 + 24 + 180 + 40 + 33 + 24 + 13$ |
| | $= 360$ |

Divide 360 by 43. The quotient is 8 with a remainder of 16. The Check Character is the character corresponding to the value of the remainder, which in this example is 16, or character G. The complete symbol data structure including Check Character, would therefore be:

$$1\ 2\ 3\ 4\ -\ A\ B\ C\ D\ G$$

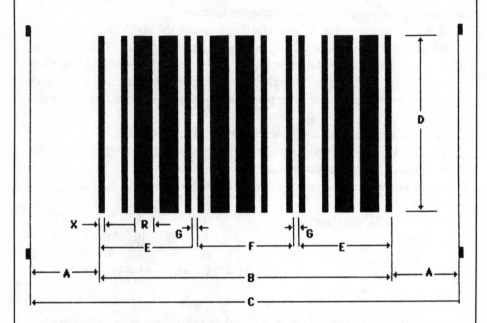

**Figure F-1. Significant parameters of Code 39**

The character "P" is shown in the figure below as a Code 39 symbology message, *P*. The various elements of that message are broken out in the figure.

Notes:

A   Quiet Zone—0.25" or 10 times the X-value, whichever is greater

B   Symbol length excluding Quiet Zone

C   Total symbol length required including Quiet Zone

D   Bar height

E   Start and Stop Code—Asterisk (*)

F   Encodation of the letter P

G   Intercharacter gap which is within a range from 1X to a maximum of 5.3 times the X value (see Table F-2)

R   Wide bar width. Wide to narrow ratio is 3:1

X   The X value, which is the narrowest bar or space of a bar code

## Figure F-2. Code 39 character structure

| CHAR | PATTERN | BARS | SPACES | CHAR | PATTERN | BARS | SPACES |
|------|---------|------|--------|------|---------|------|--------|
| 1 | | 10001 | 0100 | M | | 11000 | 0001 |
| 2 | | 01001 | 0100 | N | | 00101 | 0001 |
| 3 | | 11000 | 0100 | O | | 10100 | 0001 |
| 4 | | 00101 | 0100 | P | | 01100 | 0001 |
| 5 | | 10100 | 0100 | Q | | 00011 | 0001 |
| 6 | | 01100 | 0100 | R | | 10010 | 0001 |
| 7 | | 00011 | 0100 | S | | 01010 | 0001 |
| 8 | | 10010 | 0100 | T | | 00110 | 0001 |
| 9 | | 01010 | 0100 | U | | 10001 | 1000 |
| Ø | | 00110 | 0100 | V | | 01001 | 1000 |
| A | | 10001 | 0010 | W | | 11000 | 1000 |
| B | | 01001 | 0010 | X | | 00101 | 1000 |
| C | | 11000 | 0010 | Y | | 10100 | 1000 |
| D | | 00101 | 0010 | Z | | 01100 | 1000 |
| E | | 10100 | 0010 | - | | 00011 | 1000 |
| F | | 01100 | 0010 | . | | 10010 | 1000 |
| G | | 00011 | 0010 | SPACE | | 01010 | 1000 |
| H | | 10010 | 0010 | * | | 00110 | 1000 |
| I | | 01010 | 0010 | $ | | 00000 | 1110 |
| J | | 00110 | 0010 | / | | 00000 | 1101 |
| K | | 10001 | 0001 | + | | 00000 | 1011 |
| L | | 01001 | 0001 | % | | 00000 | 0111 |

### Table F-1
### Significant dimensional parameters of Code 39
### of various selected X dimensions
### printed at a 3:1 wide-to-narrow ratio

| X Nominal Width of Narrow Bars and Spaces | W Nominal Width of Wide Bars and Spaces | T Bar and Space Width Print Tolerance* | I Intercharacter Gap Range | CPI Character Density Per Inch** |
|---|---|---|---|---|
| **FOR CLOSED SYSTEM USE** | | | | |
| 0.0010 inch | 0.0030 inch | ±0.000350 inch | 0.0010-0.0053 inch | 62.5 |
| 0.0030 inch | 0.0090 inch | ±0.001050 inch | 0.0030-0.0159 inch | 20.8 |
| 0.0040 inch | 0.0120 inch | ±0.001400 inch | 0.0040-0.0212 inch | 15.6 |
| 0.0045 inch | 0.0135 inch | ±0.001575 inch | 0.0045-0.0239 inch | 13.9 |
| 0.0050 inch | 0.0150 inch | ±0.001750 inch | 0.0050-0.0265 inch | 12.5 |
| 0.0060 inch | 0.0180 inch | ±0.002100 inch | 0.0060-0.0318 inch | 10.4 |
| **FOR OPEN & CLOSED SYSTEM USE** | | | | |
| 0.0075 inch | 0.0225 inch | ±0.002625 inch | 0.0075-0.0398 inch | 8.3 |
| 0.0090 inch | 0.0270 inch | ±0.003150 inch | 0.0090-0.0477 inch | 6.9 |
| 0.0100 inch | 0.0300 inch | ±0.003500 inch | 0.0100-0.0530 inch | 6.3 |
| 0.0115 inch | 0.0345 inch | ±0.004025 inch | 0.0115-0.0610 inch | 5.4 |
| 0.0120 inch | 0.0360 inch | ±0.004200 inch | 0.0120-0.0636 inch | 5.2 |
| 0.0145 inch | 0.0435 inch | ±0.005075 inch | 0.0145-0.0769 inch | 4.3 |
| 0.0200 inch | 0.0600 inch | ±0.007000 inch | 0.0200-0.1060 inch | 3.1 |
| 0.0210 inch | 0.0630 inch | ±0.007350 inch | 0.0210-0.1113 inch | 3.0 |
| 0.0400 inch | 0.1200 inch | ±0.014000 inch | 0.0400-0.2120 inch | 1.6 |

\* Note: Bar and Space Width Tolerances specified at 35% of the X Dimension.

\*\* Note: Characters Per Inch (CPI) calculated with the Intercharacter Gap set equal to the X Dimension.

for direct printing on corrugated board. Otherwise, the minimum nominal width of the narrow element (X dimension) is 0.0075 inch (0.190 mm), except for closed system applications where the minimum nominal element is bounded only by the application and by constraints imposed by specific scanning equipment. The maximum nominal width of any element is bounded only by the application and by constraints imposed by specific scanning equipment. The nominal width of the various elements and the nominal ratio of the width of wide to narrow elements must not change within a given Code 39 symbol. Code 39 is a discrete bar code symbol.

The 3:1 ratio for Code 39 permits the printing at smaller X dimensions for increased character density while affording the maximum in read reliability. The minimum of 0.025 inch for direct printing on corrugated is fixed only to permit an increased depth of field for a fixed mount scanner mounted on a conveyor system. A 25 mil X dimension will permit an approximate 39 inch depth of field. To permit uniform fixed mount scanning, an 0.025 inch X dimension is recommended for direct printing on corrugated.

Open systems within the channels of distribution of a given industry must establish some common minimum for X dimensions that may move within distribution channels; 7.5 mils $\pm 2.625$ mils has been established as that minimum. Smaller X dimensions are acceptable in "closed system" applications as long as there is a match between the X dimension of the printed symbol and the resolution of the reader. Users are cautioned not to attempt to read open system symbols with the single detector ultra-high resolution scanners employed in closed systems.

Single detector scanners represent the past and present art of bar code reading equipment. In these systems the diffuse reflection of a small spot of light, typically having a diameter of 0.006 inch, is observed with a single detector. Consequently, as the size of printing defects begin to approach the light, spot size bars may be observed as spaces (voids) and spaces observed as bars (spots). Matrix-array charge coupled device (CCD) readers with the ability to sample a wider and higher segment of the symbol may not be affected by certain printing defects.

## Standard Symbology
### • General
Code 39 is a variable length, bi-directional, discrete, self-checking, alpha-umeric bar code. Its data character set contains 43 characters: 0–9, A–Z, –, ., $, /, +, %, and Space.

### • Symbol
Every symbol consists of:
- a. Leading quiet zone;
- b. Start character;
- c. One or more data characters;
- d. Stop character;
- e. Trailing quiet zone.

**Figure F-3. Encoding the message "1A"**

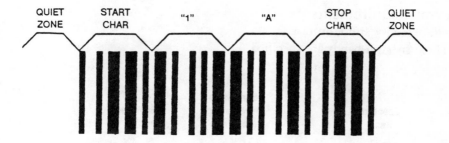

### • Encodation
Each Code 39 symbol consists of a series of characters, each represented by five bars and four intervening spaces. Each character is separated by an intercharacter gap. Figure F-4 illustrates the character A.

**Figure F-4. Code 39 "A" character**

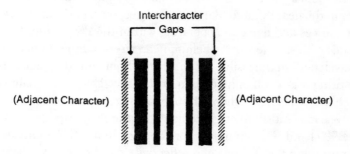

Each bar or space can be one of two alternative widths, referred to as "wide" and "narrow." The particular pattern of wide and narrow bars determines the character being coded. In all cases, each character consists of three wide and six narrow elements.

Table F-2 defines all the Code 39 character assignments. In the table columns headed "BSBSBSBSB," the character 1 is used to represent a wide element and a Ø to represent a narrow element.

- **Start and Stop Character**

The start/stop character, depicted by an asterisk, is used to identify the leading and trailing ends of the bar code. It is a unique character which allows Code 39 symbols to be scanned bidirectionally.

- **Quiet Zone**

The quiet zone is an area clear and free of all printing and marks, preceding the start character and following the stop character.

## Print Requirements
### •Reflectivity and Contrast
Three spectral bands are specified:

| Spectral Band | Maximum Bandwidth Wavelength (Peak nm) | 50% Level (nm) |
|---|---|---|
| B633 | 633 ± 5% | 120 — visible |
| B800 | 800 ± 5% | 40 — laser diode |
| B900 | 900 ± 10% | 40 — infrared |

- **Light Sources**

Bands B633 and B900 represent the spectral response required from the measuring instrument (light source, filter, detector). These responses should be a smooth curve without secondary peaks within the band, and no major part of the response curve can be beyond the specified 50 percent points. Band B900 corresponds to reading devices that use light sources and detectors operating in the near infrared. Band B800 corresponds to reading devices that use light sources and detectors operating within the B800 band. Band B633 corresponds with scanners using helium-neon lasers or other sources emitting a peak wavelength in the visible red spectrum. Some printing processes, such as those using inks containing carbon, will easily achieve adequate contrast in all three spectral bands. Other printing processes, such as those using various colored dyes, may satisfy the requirements for the B633 band but not for the B800 or B900 band. As a minimum for "open systems," the printed bar code symbol must meet the contrast and reflectivity requirements for band B633.

# Table F-2
## Code 39 configuration (Courtesy of Intermec)

| CHAR. | PATTERN | BARS | SPACES | CHAR. | PATTERN | BARS | SPACES |
|-------|---------|------|--------|-------|---------|------|--------|
| 1 | | 10001 | 0100 | M | | 11000 | 0001 |
| 2 | | 01001 | 0100 | N | | 00101 | 0001 |
| 3 | | 11000 | 0100 | O | | 10100 | 0001 |
| 4 | | 00101 | 0100 | P | | 01100 | 0001 |
| 5 | | 10100 | 0100 | Q | | 00011 | 0001 |
| 6 | | 01100 | 0100 | R | | 10010 | 0001 |
| 7 | | 00011 | 0100 | S | | 01010 | 0001 |
| 8 | | 10010 | 0100 | T | | 00110 | 0001 |
| 9 | | 01010 | 0100 | U | | 10001 | 1000 |
| 0 | | 00110 | 0100 | V | | 01001 | 1000 |
| A | | 10001 | 0010 | W | | 11000 | 1000 |
| B | | 01001 | 0010 | X | | 00101 | 1000 |
| C | | 11000 | 0010 | Y | | 10100 | 1000 |
| D | | 00101 | 0010 | Z | | 01100 | 1000 |
| E | | 10100 | 0010 | - | | 00011 | 1000 |
| F | | 01100 | 0010 | . | | 10010 | 1000 |
| G | | 00011 | 0010 | SPACE | | 01010 | 1000 |
| H | | 10010 | 0010 | * | | 00110 | 1000 |
| I | | 01010 | 0010 | $ | | 01010 | 1110 |
| J | | 00110 | 0010 | / | | 00000 | 1101 |
| K | | 10001 | 0001 | + | | 00000 | 1011 |
| L | | 01001 | 0001 | % | | 00000 | 0111 |

The * symbol denotes a unique start/stop character which must be the first and last character of every bar code symbol.

## • Measurement Methodologies

Measurements are made on the bar code symbol in its final packaging configuration whenever possible. All measurements are made with a system with a peak response of 633 nanometers $\pm 15$ percent, which also has a half-power band width no greater than 120 nanometers (in which there are no secondary peaks). Among possible source filter-photodetector combinations that can be used are those employing a He-Ne laser, appropriate red LEDs, or the CIE Source A illuminant (incandescent source), along with an S-4 response photodetector and a Wratten 26 red filter.

Reflectivity measurements are made with a source of incident irradiation of 45° from the normal to the surface and in a plane containing the source irradiation element that is both normal to the surface and parallel to the bars. The reflected flux shall be collected within a 15° angle center about the normal. A measuring aperture of 0.006 inch (0.152 mm) is used. For conveyable shipping cases, a measuring aperture of 0.020 inch (0.508 mm) may be used. For other X dimensions, the spot size or aperture diameter of the measuring instrumentation must be no greater than 0.8 times the nominal width of the narrowest element to be measured. Reflectivity is measured with diffuse light relative to barium sulfate or magnesium oxide, which is 100%.

## • Opacity

Opacity is the ratio of diffuse reflection ($R_2$) of a sample sheet of substrate, backed with a black surface of not more than 5% reflectance, to the diffuse reflectance ($R_1$) of the same sheet backed with a white surface that has a minimum reflectance of 89%. The concern is limiting the see-through phenomenon. Opacity is calculated as follows:

$$\text{Opacity} \, ^5 \, R_2/R_1$$

The infinite pad method is used for measuring reflectance for non-opaque substrates when it is not possible to measure the reflectance in the final configuration. In this case, the calculated opacity value of a material is determined from two reflectance measurements. ($R_1$) is taken on a blank material sample backed with enough layers of the same material so that doubling the number of layers will not change the measured value of reflectance.

## • Reflectance Values

The maximum allowable reflectivity of the dark bars is related to the reflectivity of the light spaces. Bar code symbols with spaces that are less reflective will require bars that are "darker" (less reflective). Table F-3 illustrates the maximum bar reflectance $R_D$ as a function of pace reflectance $R_L$. The minimum space reflectance is 50% for bar code symbols with an X dimension less than 40 mils and 25% for bar code symbols with an X dimension of 40 mils or more.

**Table F-3**
**Bar reflectance allowable values**

| Space Reflectance $R_L$(%) | Maximum Bar Reflectance $R_D$(%) |
|---|---|
| <25 | Substandard |
| 25 | 6.25 |
| 30 | 7.50 |
| 35 | 8.75 |
| 40 | 10.00 |
| 45 | 11.25 |
| <50 | Substandard for X dimensions <40 mils |
| 50 | 12.50 |
| 55 | 13.75 |
| 60 | 15.00 |
| 65 | 16.25 |
| 70 | 17.50 |
| 75 | 18.75 |
| 80 | 20.00 |
| 85 | 21.25 |
| 90 | 22.50 |
| 95 | 23.75 |
| 100 | 25.00 |

**Note:** The minimum ratio of $R_L/R_D$ is 4.0 and the minimum print contrast signal (PCS) is 75%. The PCS is defined as:

$$PCS = \frac{R_L - R_D}{R_L}$$

## • Ink Recommendations (Corrugated)

Based upon testing conducted by the Distribution Symbology Study Group (DSSG), Table F-4 presents Glass Packaging Institute (GPI) (Edition VII natural) colors that provide acceptable PCS values (defined in Table F-3) when printed on a variety of currently available corrugated liner boards. This does not mean that all inks with these GPI designations will give acceptable values, as the light reflectance will depend on the specific ink formulation. Reflectance values should be determined as defined in the Reflectivity and Contrast section above. Although natural kraft liner boards look dark to the human eye, their reflectance values, when measured with a light of 633 nm wavelength, are sufficiently high to be used as a substrate for bar codes when used with properly applied inks. Lighter color substrates, such as mottled and bleached liner boards, provide even higher reflectance values, which may allow selection of a broader range of colors than those shown in Table F-4.

### Table F-4
### Ink colors (GPI Edition VII Natural)

| Color (GPI) | | Typical Ratio ($R_L/R_D$) |
|---|---|---|
| 394 | Blue | 4.80 |
| 33 | Blue | 5.00 |
| 32 | Blue | 5.00 |
| 31 | Blue | 5.50 |
| 3086 | Blue | 5.00 |
| 387 | Blue | 5.00 |
| 38 | Blue | 4.17 |
| 3213 | Aqua | 5.60 |
| 24 | Green | 5.00 |
| 21 | Green | 5.00 |
| 20 | Green | 5.00 |
| 2008 | Green | 5.00 |
| 22 | Green | 4.17 |
| 2014 | Green | 4.17 |
| 523 | Brown | 4.50 |
| 52 | Brown | 4.17 |
| 90 | Black | 5.50 |
| 39 | Blue | 5.50 |
| 29 | Green | 5.50 |
| 300 | Blue | 4.50 |

- **Gloss Measurement**

Gloss measurements are made using TAPPI T-480 os-85 (Specular Gloss of Paper and Paperboard) methodology.

- **Paper Measurement Methods**

Paper property measurements are sampled in accordance with TAPPI T400 om-85 "Sampling and Accepting a Single Lot of Paper, Paperboard, Fiberboard, or Related Product" and under the conditions cited in TAPPI T402 om-83 "Standard Conditioning and Testing Atmospheres for Paper, Board, Pulp, Handsheets, and Related Products."

- **Element Width Measurement**

The element width is the distance between its two edges. The element edge is defined as the location of the center of the measuring aperture, when the aperture is in a position so that the observed reflectance is midway between the maximum reflectance of the adjacent space and the minimum reflectance of the adjacent bar (see Figure F-5).

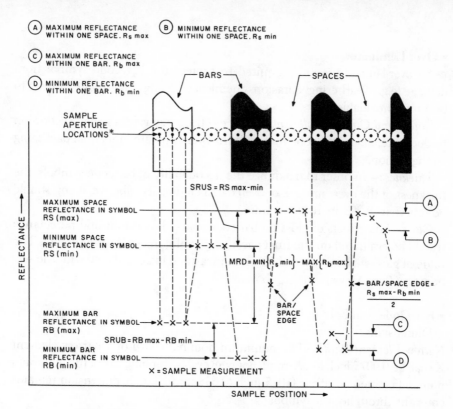

**Figure F-5. Bar code symbol reflectance measurement techniques**

• **Polarization**

Polarization measurements are made in the final configuration with incident non-polarized irradiation at 45° from normal to the surface and parallel to the bars, and reflected flux collected with a 15° angle centered about the normal after passing through a linear polarizer. The degree of polarization is the maximum difference in reflectance measured while the polarizer is rotated through 180°.

## Requirements
### • Substrate

*Opacity*—When in its final packaging configuration, a bar code symbol must meet the reflectance variation specifications of the section on Reflectances, below. If it is not possible to measure the bar code symbol in its final packaging configuration, the problems associated with "show through" of an interfering will be minimized if the substrate opacity is at least 85% with a maximum variation of 6%.

*Gloss*—The value of gloss shall not exceed 60 when measured in accordance with the section on Gloss Measurement, above.

## • Over-Laminate

An over-laminate is only required to protect the bar code symbol from damage (e.g., weathering, abrasion, chemical defacing) that might cause it to become unreadable.

*Linear and Circular Polarization*—The reflectance values in the section on Reflectance, below, must be met with the over-laminate in its final packaging configuration.

*Thickness*—In order to maximize the decodability of bar code symbols, the thickness of the over-laminate or overcoat, including its adhesive, if any, should be less than 0.003 inch (0.076 mm).

*Gloss*—The effects of gloss on bar code space dimensions and reflectance should be evaluated on the final packaging configuration of the symbol. The value of gloss shall not exceed 60 when measured in accordance with the section on Gloss Measurement, above.

## • Bar Code Symbol

Dimensions:

*Narrow Element Width*—The minimum nominal width of a narrow element X shall be 0.0075 inch (0.191 mm). For conveyable shipping cases, the minimum nominal element width is 0.025 inch (0.635 mm). The X dimension remains constant throughout a symbol.

*Ratio of Wide to Narrow Elements*—The ratio (N) of the nominal wide element to the nominal narrow element can range from 2.5:1 to 3.0:1 for a symbol with an X dimension of 0.020 inch (0.508 mm) or larger. The ratio for symbols for an X dimension less than 0.020 inch (0.508 mm) is 3.0:1. For conveyable shipping cases, the ratio can range from 2.5:1 to 3.0:1.

*Tolerances*—The tolerance (t), or maximum allowable element width deviation from nominal, is constant for any given symbol. This tolerance is defined, where N is the wide to narrow ratio and X is the nominal width or X dimension, as:

$$t = \pm\, 0.148\,(N-0.67)\,X$$

Table F-1 lists the tolerance values for some common nominal X dimensions. Figure F-6 shows tolerance as a function of the X dimension and the wide to narrow ratio (N).

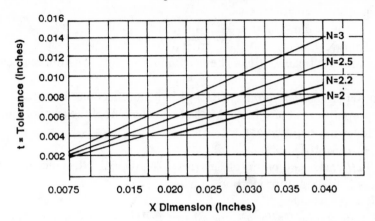

*Intercharacter Spaces*—The nominal width of the inter-character spaces shall be:

minimum width — X – t (t is the printing tolerance for the particular values of X and N of the symbol).

maximum width — 5.3X or 0.053 inch (0.135 mm), whichever is greater, for values of X greater than or equal to 0.010 inch (0.25 mm).

*Bar Height*—The minimum bar height is 0.25 inch (6.35 mm) or 15% of the symbol length, whichever is greater. The bar height for conveyable shipping cases is specified in the section on Placement, below.

*Quiet Zones*—The minimum quiet zone shall be 0.25 inch (6.35 mm) or 10 times the X dimension, whichever is greater.

## • Reflectance

Reflectance variations may be caused by spots, voids, smudges, or other defects which may interfere with decoding, because scanners respond to reflectivity differences. The following reflectance measurements are not independent and must be considered simultaneously. Figure F-5 depicts the bar code reflectance measurement process and graphically shows the main measurement parameters.

*Minimum Reflectivity Difference (MRD)*—A measure of the reflectivity difference is MRD. Figure F-5 illustrates what the MRD is as a scanning aperture passes through a bar code symbol.

The minimum reflectivity difference (MRD) is equal to or greater than:

37.5% if the X dimension < 0.025 inch (0.635 mm)

20% if the X dimension ≥ 0.025 inch (0.635 mm)

*Minimum Space Reflectance (Rs)*—The minimum reflectance within each space is equal to or greater than:

37.5% if the X dimension < 0.025 inch (0.635 mm)

25% if the X dimension ≥ 0.025 inch (0.635 mm)

*Maximum Bar Reflectance (Rb)*—The maximum reflectance within each bar is 30%.

*Element Reflectance Uniformity (ERU)*—Element reflectance uniformity is limited in proportion to the value of MRD. Each element of the symbol must meet the following requirement:

ERU ≤ 0.25 MRD

*Symbol Reflectance Uniformity of Bars (SRUB)*—Symbol reflectance uniformity of bars is limited in proportion to MRD:

SRUB ≤ 0.5 MRD

*Symbol Reflectance Uniformity of Spaces (SRUS)*—Symbol reflectance uniformity of spaces is limited in proportion to MRD:

SRUS ≤ 0.5 MRD

*Quiet Zones*—The quiet zones must meet the same reflectivity requirements as space elements.

- **Human Readable Interpretation**

There must be a human-readable interpretation of the bar code symbol that is clearly identifiable with the bar code symbol, and that represents the encoded characters. The start and stop characters, which are represented by an asterisk are included in the interpretation. Any human-readable font with characters no less that 0.094 inch (2.39 mm) in height is acceptable. It is recommended that the interpretation of zero be represented as Ø.

# Bar Edge Roughness, Spots, and Voids (alternate measurement requirement)

The tolerances for the bar and space widths allow for a certain degree of bar edge roughness. The white-to-black and black-to-white transition points are defined as the point where the reflectance, as measured within a circle with a diameter 0.8 times the nominal width of the narrow element, is exactly halfway between the measured bar and space reflectance values. At this point, the center of the circle is defined as the transition point. (For the purposes of illustration, only the nominal width of the elements in Figures F-7 and F-8 is 0.009 inch. Spots and voids that meet either of the following criteria are permitted:

The spot or void can be contained within a circle, the diameter of which is 0.4 times the nominal width of the narrow element. See Figure F-7 below.

**Figure F-7. Spot or void sample**

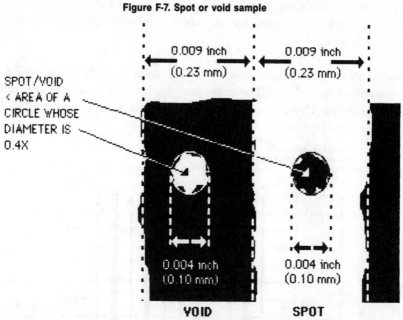

•The spot or void occupies no more than 25% of the area of a circle, the diameter of which is 0.8 times the nominal width of the narrow element. Larger spots or voids can be expected to degrade symbol readability. See Figure F-8, below.

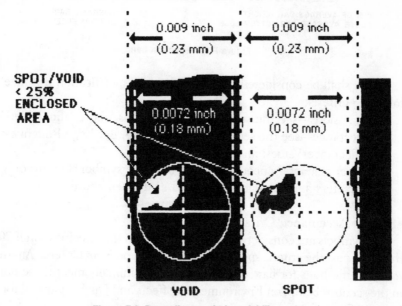

**Figure F-8. Degrading symbol readability**

# Quality Control

## •Verification Techniques

There are two basic verification techniques, manual and automatic. Manual inspection may be done using instruments that have the optical characteristics described below.

*Scan Criteria*—A minimum of ten scans are made through the bar code symbol shown in Figure F-9. These scans are made parallel to the length of the bar code symbol. These scans must be approximately equally spaced within the inspection band.

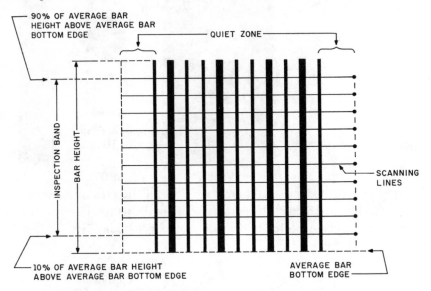

**Figure F-9. Inspection band**

A scan shall be considered conforming to the specification if it meets the following criteria:

    a. dimensions—see the section on Dimensions, above, and Table F-1;

    b. reflectance—see the section on Reflectance, Bar Edge Roughness, and Reflectance Values; and

    c. correct character encodation—the bar code symbol contains only valid characters and the data is encoded as defined above.

## •Symbol Acceptance Criteria

The symbols are considered in conformance to this specification if 70% of the scans pass the criteria specified in the section on Scan Criteria. Alternately, test plan methods for bar code symbols may minimally meet those outlined in the sections below, on Environmental Effects and Quality Control for Symbols for Open Systems.

## •Sampling Methods and Levels

Sample size must be sufficiently large to be statistically valid within the size of the lot or batch being inspected. Military Standard MIL-STD-105D (dated 29 April 1963) provides useful guidelines for statistically valid sampling plans.

## • Environmental Effects

Bar code symbols should minimally meet the requirements of this section. In addition, representative bar code symbols shall be subjected to environmental tests for a period of 30 days. One set of samples must be placed in an environment of 90°F (32°C) and a relative noncondensing humidity of 90 percent, and a second set of samples shall be placed in an environment of 155°F (66°C) and a relative noncondensing humidity of 75 percent. Sample size must be sufficiently large to be statistically valid within the size of the universe being tested. At the conclusion of 30 days, the bar code symbols must meet the print requirements of this specification, as applicable.

Other environmental standards may exist for specific marking situations. Examples of situations where more standards may apply include equipment which may have to be sterilized by autoclave, radiation, or ethylene oxide methods, and symbols applied to printed circuit boards which must resist wave-solder processes.

All environmental tests for symbols apply to both the substrate material and the adhesive by which the substrate material is applied to final packaging.

Environmental standards for bar code equipment are contained in the section on Environmental Specifications for Bar Code Equipment, below.

## • Quality Control for Symbols for Open Systems

| Characteristic | Specification |
|---|---|
| 1. symbology | Code 39 |
| 2. format of symbol | serial number format<br>product codes format<br>traveler & menu formats<br>location tag format<br>asset tag format, etc. |
| 3. code density | open systems—minimum<br>7.5 mils @ 2.5:1–3:1 |
| 4. element height | the greater of 0.25 inch or 15% of the symbol length |
| 5. quiet zone | the greater of 0.25 inch or 10 times the X dimension |
| 6. scanner light source wavelength | B633 range (visible-red) |
| 7. scanner aperture size | 7.5 mil X = 6 mil aperture; other X = 0.8X aperture |
| 8. print contrast | 75% or greater in B633 |
| 9. print quality | label must be decoded on first scan 70% of the time |
| 10. human readable interpretation | A. printed beneath bar code symbol<br>B. represents all encoded characters including start and stop characters<br>C. at least 0.094 in height |

**Table F-5. Table of numerical value assignments for computing the standards' data format optional check character**

| | | | | | | |
|---|---|---|---|---|---|---|
| 0 | 0 | F | 15 | U | 30 |
| 1 | 1 | G | 16 | V | 31 |
| 2 | 2 | H | 17 | W | 32 |
| 3 | 3 | I | 18 | X | 33 |
| 4 | 4 | J | 19 | Y | 34 |
| 5 | 5 | K | 20 | Z | 35 |
| 6 | 6 | L | 21 | – | 36 |
| 7 | 7 | M | 22 | . | 37 |
| 8 | 8 | N | 23 | Space | 38 |
| 9 | 9 | O | 24 | $ | 39 |
| A | 10 | P | 25 | / | 40 |
| B | 11 | Q | 26 | + | 41 |
| C | 12 | R | 27 | % | 42 |
| D | 13 | S | 28 | | |
| E | 14 | T | 29 | Q.E.D. SYSTEMS | |

## •Test Plan

Having developed the test specifications for the symbol it is now possible to develop the test plan:

1. Sampling Criteria
A. Demand Printer
   Before printer purchase
   At time of printer installation
   After each performance of preventive maintenance on printer
   After each change of label material or printer ribbon
   Once per week
B. Commercial Printing
   At beginning of each run
   At the middle of each run
   At the end of each run

2. Testing Procedure
A. Scan a set of five "control labels." Control labels should be film master paper positives with zero bar width reduction at same density as printed symbol. Paper positives should be laminated with a transparent material less than 5 mils thick. Transparent material should be replaced after 200 scans and paper positives replaced as necessary. If control labels cannot be scanned, a scanner problem is indicated. Stop and call supervisor.
B. Take a warm-up sample read of five labels.

C. Take a sample read of fifteen labels based on above sampling criteria.

D. Affix labels to black construction paper or other smooth opaque black surface.

E. Scan warm-up sample until three consecutive decodings of each symbol have been performed. If this step cannot be successfully completed, reject the lot, stop, and call supervisor.

F. Scan each label of test sample once. A scan equals one left-to-right stroke and if unsuccessful, one right-to-left stroke.

G. Count successful decodes.

H. Calculate: first read rate = successful decodes divided by total scans. For percentage, multiply times 100, rounding to one decimal place.

I. Compare results to Acceptance/Rejection Criteria (Number 3, below); if necessary repeat from 2.C, above.

3. Acceptance/Rejection Criteria

A. One sample of fifteen labels (first read rate = successful decodes divided by 15, times 100, rounded to one decimal place).
   1. Accept if sample first read rate = 100%.
   2. Reject if sample first read rate is less than 86%.
   3. Test per 3.B. if first read rate falls between 86% and 100%.

B. Two samples of fifteen labels (first read rate = successful decodes divided by 30, times 100, rounded to one decimal place).
   1. Accept if sample first read rate is greater than 96%.
   2. Reject if sample first read rate is less than 93%.
   3. Test per 3.C. if first read rate falls between 93% and 96%.

C. Three samples of fifteen labels (first read rate = successful decodes divided by 45, times 100, rounded to one decimal place).
   1. Accept if sample first read rate is equal to or greater than 95%.
   2. Reject if sample first read rate is less than 95%.

## Environmental Specifications for Bar Code Equipment

| TEST | CLASS A (Outdoor Portable) | CLASS B (Industrial Commercial) |
|---|---|---|
| **Temperature** | **Note 3** | |
| Non-operating | −40°C to 75°C | −40°C to 75°C |
| Operating | −20°C to 55°C | 0°C to 55°C |
| **Humidity** | **Note 3** | |
| Operating | 40°C @ 5 to 95% relative humidity | |
| Non-operating | 65°C @ 90% relative humidity | |
| Condensation within 5 minutes | Operates without damage and recovers within 15 minutes | |
| **Vibration** | **Notes 1 and 3** | **Notes 2A and 3** |
| Cycle range | 5 to 200 Hz | |
| Amplitude | 0.015 in. (0.38 mm) | |
| Sweep time | 1 minute/octave; 15 minutes total | |
| Dwell @ resonances | 10 minutes each resonance | |
| Amplitude @ resonance (peak to peak) | 0.125 in. (3.17 mm) @ 5 to 10 Hz | |
| | 0.060 in. (1.52 mm) @ 10 to 25 Hz | |
| | 0.015 in. (0.38 mm) @ 25 to 55 Hz | |
| | 0.008 in. (0.20 mm) @ 55 to 125 Hz | |
| | 0.004 in. (0.10 mm) @ 125 to 200 Hz | |
| **Shock** | **Notes 2B and 3** | |
| Magnitude | 30 g (see Note 1 for Class A) | |
| Duration | 11 ms (see Note 1 for Class A) | |
| Number of shocks | 18 (3 each on 6 surfaces represented in both a positive and negative direction on X, Y, and Z axis) | |
| Operating/non-operating | Non-operating | |
| Wave form | Half sine | |
| Bench handling | 30 in. (762 mm) onto uncovered concrete | 4 in. (102 mm) onto uncovered wooden bench (tilt drop) |
| **Altitude** | **Notes 2C and 3** | |
| Non-operating | 50,000 ft. (15,300 m) | |
| Operating | 15,000 ft. (4600 m) | |
| **Transportation** | | |
| Drop test (in shipping container) | After a drop of 36 inches on the corners, edges, or flat surfaces; the product must meet all operational and performance specifications | |

274

**Ambient Lighting**
Lighting environments
  (see Note 3)

1. Tungsten filament incandescent
2. Mercury vapor
3. Sodium vapor
4. Fluorescent
5. Sunlight

Illumination levels: per IES Lighting Handbook for En-
  vironments 1–4
Dim ambients (0–75 footcandles): passageways/store-
  rooms
Moderate ambients (75–200 footcandles): desk work
Bright ambients (200–1K footcandles): bench/machine
  work
Sunlight: typical, 5000 footcandles; specialized, 10,000

**Magnetic Field
Susceptibility**

0.1 millitesla peak-to-peak from 47.5 to 198 Hz.
**See Note 3.**

**Electrostatic Discharge
Susceptibility**

15 Kilovolt discharge to all outside surfaces.
**See Note 3.**

**Radiated Field
Susceptibility**

1 volt/meter within a range of 14 Hz to 1 Gigahertz.
**See Note 3.**

**Power Line Transient
Susceptibility**

Spike transient pulse with 0.5 microsecond rise time, 10
microsecond duration, at twice the line voltage
amplitude. Voltage transients of 10 to 30%, then from
−10 to −30%, and frequency transients from 5 to 10%,
then −5 to −10%, with momentary performance impair-
ment allowed followed by the performance returning to
specification. **See Note 3.**

**Conducted
Susceptibility**

40 Hz to 400 MHz, 3 Vrms applied to products power
leads. **See Note 3.**

**Note 1:** Optional tests for Class A products:
Vibration (55 to 500 Hz @ 3g)
Shock (500g @ 1 ms, 100g @ 4 ms, or 30g @ 11 ms)

**Note 2:** A. Vibration—Test at instrument level if weight exceeds table capacity.
B. Shock—Qualify all products of system to 30g @ 11 ms and 4 in. tilt drop.
C. Altitude—All products in system must be tested to specification.

**Note 3:** Performance must remain within specification and no malfunction allowed.

# Orientation of Symbols

## •Orientation

The primary symbol may be oriented as a vertical bar code or a horizontal bar code for levels of packaging below conveyable containers—see the section on Conveyable Shipping Cases, below. If a secondary symbol is used, it must have the same orientation as the primary symbol.

## •Symbol Placement on Labels

If the primary and/or secondary symbols are printed on labels, the entire bar code symbol (including quiet zones, start, stop, and data characters) must be contained on the label.

## •Primary to Secondary Bar Code Symbol Spacing

In all cases, when the secondary symbol is used it must be placed directly below or directly to the right of the primary symbol.

*Stacked Horizontal and Ladder Pair Symbols*—The symbols have a minimum separation of 0.25 inch (6.35 mm) and a maximum separation of 0.75 inch (19.05 mm), as shown in Figure F-10.

*In-Line Symbols*—The symbols have a minimum separation of 0.5 inch (12.7 mm) as shown in Figure F-10. If one symbol is on a label, the edge of the label must be located 0.0 to 0.5 inch (12.7 mm) beyond the quiet zone of the other symbol. If both symbols are on separate labels, the labels must not overlap and must not be separated by more than 0.5 inch (12.7 mm), measured between adjacent edges of labels.

**Figure F-10. Spacing of primary to secondary bar code symbols**

LADDER PAIR

1PA010B4C5D6H

T1311QED+

0.25″ - 0.75″

IN-LINE
VERTICAL

1PA010B4C5D6H

0.5″
Minimum

T1311QED+

STACKED HORIZONTAL

1PA010B4C5D6H

0.25″ - 0.75″

T1311QED+

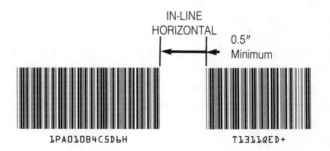

IN-LINE
HORIZONTAL

0.5″
Minimum

1PA010B4C5D6H

T1311QED+

# Placement

## •Conveyable Shipping Cases

The symbol(s) are printed in a horizontal bar code configuration (bars are vertical). As a minimum, the symbol(s) must be placed on two adjacent panels of the case. Each symbol must have its own bearer bars printed along the top and bottom of the symbol, butting directly against the top and bottom of the symbol bars. The thickness of the bearer bars should be a minimum of two times the width of a narrow element. If the symbol is to be directly printed on corrugated material, then the nominal thickness of the bearer bar should be 0.019 inch (4.8 mm) and must completely surround the symbol, including vertical sections printed just outside the quiet zones.

*Location/Primary Symbol Only*—The primary symbol is located in the lower right corner of the case. All the bars of the symbol must touch or protude through an imaginary base line which is parallel to and 1.25 inch (31.75 mm) from the bottom plane of the erected case. The bar height must be great enough so that all bars touch or protude through an imaginary line that runs parallel to and above the imaginary base line. These two lines must be separated by a distance that is 0.8 inch (20.3 mm) or 25% of the symbol length, whichever is greater, to a maximum of 1.3 inch (33.02 mm). The first bar of the start code and the last bar of the stop code must be at least 1.0 inch (25.4 mm) from the side edges of the case. If the symbol has a bearer bar surrounding it, the bearer bar should be at least 0.75 inch (19.05 mm) from the side edges of the case (see Figure F-11).

*Primary and Secondary Symbol*—When a secondary symbol is used, it is located in the lower right corner of the case. All the bars of the secondary symbol must touch or protrude through an imaginary base line which is parallel to and 1.25 inch (31.75 mm) from the bottom plane of the erected case. The bar height must be great enough so that all bars touch or protude through an imaginary line that runs parallel to and above the imaginary base line. These two lines must be separated by a distance that is 0.8 inch (20.3 mm) or 25% of the symbol length, whichever is greater, to a maximum of 1.3 inch (33.02 mm). The first bar of the start code and the last bar of the stop code must be at least 1.0 inch (25.4 mm) from the side edges of the case. If the secondary symbol is surrounded by a bearer bar, the vertical bearer bars must be at least 0.75 inch (19.05 mm) from the side edges of the case.

The primary symbol must have a bar height that is at least 0.8 inch (20.3 mm) or 2% of the symbol length, whichever is greater, to a maximum of 1.4 inch (33.02 mm).

The primary symbol is located directly above the secondary symbol or directly to the left of the secondary symbol.

Stacked Horizontal Configuration—The spacing between the primary and secondary symbols must range between 0.25 inch (6.35 mm) and 0.75 inch (19.05

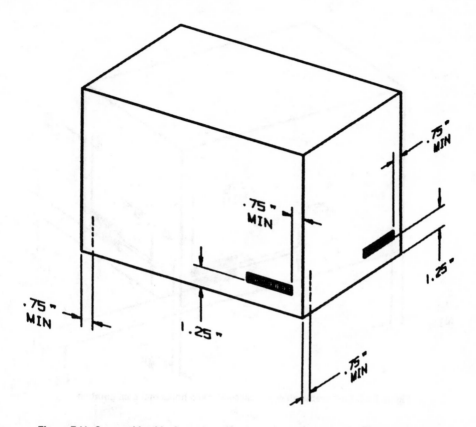

**Figure F-11. Conveyable shipping case primary symbol only with surrounding bearer bar**

mm), measured from the top edge of the secondary symbol's upper bearer bar to the bottom edge of the primary symbol's lower bearer bar. The primary symbol is located so that the first bar of the start code and the last bar of the stop code is at least 1.0 inch (25.4 mm) from the side edges of the case. If the primary symbol has a bearer bar surrounding it, the bearer bar must be at least 0.75 inch (19.05 mm) from the side edges of the case (see Figure F-12).

In-Line Horizontal Configuration—All the bars of the primary symbol must touch or protrude through an imaginary base line which is parallel to and 1.25 inch (31.75 mm) from the bottom plane of the erected case. The primary symbol bar height must be great enough so that all bars touch or protrude through an imaginary line that is parallel to and above the imaginary base line. These two lines are separated by a distance that is 0.8 inch (20.3 mm) or 25% of the symbol length, whichever is greater, to a maximum of 1.3 inch (33.02 mm). If both symbols are directly printed on corrugated, adjacent bearer bars can be separated by a maximum distance of 0.75 inch (19.05 mm). If both symbols are directly printed on corrugated at the same time or printed on a single label, the adjacent vertical bearer bars can be removed and the minimum distance

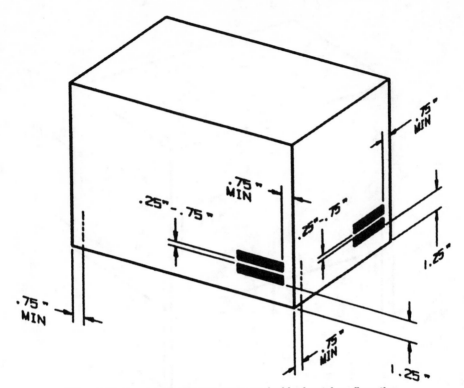

**Figure F-12. Conveyable shipping cases stacked horizontal configuration**

between the symbols must be equal to the larger quiet zone of the two symbols. If one symbol is on a label, the edge of the label must be located 0.0 to 0.5 inch (12.70 mm) beyond the bearer bar of the other symbol. If both symbols are on separate labels, the labels must not overlap and must not be separated by more than 0.5 inch (12.70 mm), measured between adjacent edges of the labels. The left-most bar of the primary symbol must be at least 1.0 inch (25.4 mm) from the left edge of the case. If the primary symbol is directly printed on corrugated, the left-most bearer bar must be at least 0.75 inch (19.05 mm) from the left edge of the case (see Figure F-13).

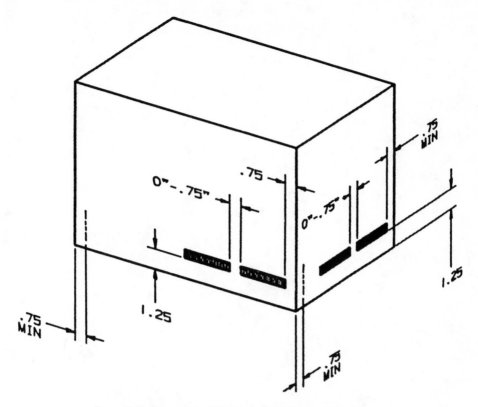

**Figure F-13. Conveyable shipping cases in-line configuration**

•Placement on Other Types of Packaging

Placement of the bar code is at the discretion of the labeler in consultation with label receiver. It is recommended that the bar code be placed on the lower right-hand corner of the stocking panel whenever possible.

# APPENDIX G
# FOOTNOTES

1. Allais, Dr. David C., Intermec. "Bar Code Symbology—Some Observations on Theory and Practice." February 16, 1982. Used with permission.

2. Stewart, Stephen R. "The Legend of Codabar." February 1983, Interface Solutions. Printed in two parts in *Bar Code News*, May/June 1983 and July/August 1983. Used with permission.

3. Brodheim, Dr. Eric, W. Ying, R. L. Hirsch. "An Evaluation of the CODABAR Symbol in Blood Banking Automation." *Vox Sanguinis* 40 (1981): 177–8 and presented at Scan-Tech '83.

4. Hewlett-Packard. "Elements of a Bar Code System—Application Note 1013." November 1982. Used with permission.

5. Mara, Charles E., Computer Identics. "A Recommendation to Select Code 128 as a Uniform Bar Code Symbology." Presented to the Health Industry Bar Code Task Force, August 25, 1983.

6. Williams, Theodore C., Computer Identics. Letter to the Editor, *Bar Code News*. March/April 1983. Used with permission.

7. Stevens, Marre D., KPG. Letter to Craig K. Harmon, Q.E.D. Systems. September 29, 1983.

8. Burke, Harry E. "Bar Code Format Issues." December, 1982: 16.

9. Distribution Symbology Study Group. "Recommended Practices for Uniform Container Symbol/UCS Transport Case Symbol/TCS." September 1981.

10. Fox, Rick, Matthews International. "Offsite Bar Code Printing." September 1983. Presented at Scan-Tech '83. Used with the permission of AIM.

11. Hopkins, J.A., Mead Digital Systems. "Bar Code Forms and Labels— What Your Printing Vendor Can Co." November 4, 1982. Presented at Scan-Tech '82. Used with the permission of AIM.

12. McDonald, Richard A., Data Composition. "Photocomposed Labels." Letter from Barbara J. Armstrong. December 1983. Used with permission.

13. Hall, J.A., R. R. Hay, J. T. Langley, K. A. Fitzgerald, P. R. Spencer, E. H. Schwiebert, T. Camis, R. D. Archibald, P. Gordon, J. R. Lewis, L. M. Hubby, G. L. Holland, J. D. Crumly, V. L. Hansen. Hewlett-Packard. "HP 2680 Laser Printing Systems." *Hewlett-Packard Journal*. June 1982 and July 1982. Used with permission of *HP Journal*.

14. Nelson, Benjamin A., Scanmark/Markem. "On Site Printing of Bar Code Symbols." September 27, 1983. Presented at Scan-Tech '83. Used with permission of AIM.

15. Nelson, Benjamin A., Scanmark/Markem. "Printing Techniques for Bar Codes." November 7, 1982. Presented at Scan-Tech '82. Used with permission of AIM.

16. Mallender, Ian H. Advanced Technology Resources Corp. "Color non-impact printers hit the market." *Mini-Micro Systems*. June 1983, 217–218. Used with permission of *Mini-Micro Systems*.

17. Rappoport, Dr. Arthur E. "Advantages of Machine Readable Identification of Patients, Specimens and Documents in Computerized Laboratory Information Systems." Youngstown Hospital Association. October 1982 (AAMSI).

18. Aardsma, Allen H. "Survey Points to Need for More Efficient Inventory Management." *Hospitals*. January 16, 1982.

19. Fowler, Joanna, R.N., Loretta Stockstill, R.N. "Bar-coded Labels, Wands, Microprocessors Join Dot-Matrix Printer to Save 650 Hours Per Month." *Health Care Systems*. November, 1982.

# BIBLIOGRAPHY

AIM. "Scanning Products on the Move—Part I: Moving Beam Scanners."

Aardsma, Allen H. "Survey Points to Need for More Efficient Inventory Management." *Hospitals,* January 16, 1982.

Accu-Sort. "Bar Code Technology—Present State Future Promise."

Allais, Dr. David C., see Acknowledgement 1.

Allais, Dr. David C., Intermec. "Industrial Symbology—A Deeper Understanding." August 22, 1983. Presented at Scan-Tech '83 (AIM)

Boehme, Johannes M. "A Systems Approach to Patient Information Management." North Carolina Baptist Hospital. September 26, 1983. Presented at Scan-Tech '83 (AIM).

Brodheim, Dr. Eric, see Acknowledgment 3.

Brodheim, Dr. Eric. "The Use of Machine-Readable Codes as a Basis for Automating Blood Transfusion Services." New York Blood Center. September 26, 1983. Presented at Scan-Tech '83 (AIM).

Brodheim, Dr. Eric, et al. "Committee for Commonality in Blood Banking Automation—Final Report." American Blood Commission. September 1977.

Burke, Harry E. see Acknowledgment 8.

Burke, Harry E. "Key Entry Bypass or Automated Item Identification." NCR. July 1980.

Burke, Harry E., selected untitled works.

Coe, Edward S., Don L. Dubuc, Jack R. Loeffler, et al. AIAG. "Specifications for Shipping/Parts Identification Label." September 23, 1983.

Coe, Edward S., Ford Motor Company. "Automatic Identification in Automotive Manufacturing." November 5, 1982. Presented at Scan-Tech '82 (AIM).

Cullom, Farmer. "Using a Standard Shipping Container Symbol." *Richfood.* September 26, 1983. Presented at Scan-Tech '83 (AIM).

Dubuc, Don L., General Motors. "Techniques and Applications of Bar Coding Systems in the Automobile Industry." September 26, 1983. Presented at Scan-Tech '83 (AIM).

Dubuc, Don L., Jack R. Loeffler, Edward S. Coe, et al. AIAG. "Bar Coding Specifications." May 11, 1982.

Field, Milton, Matthews International. "Making Film Masters and Printing Plates for Continuous Run Printed Boxes." March 11, 1982 (SME).

Fox, Rick, see Acknowledgment 10.

Gilligan, Allan, Michael Noll, et al. "American National Standard Specification for Bar Code Symbols and Unit Loads, ANSI MH 10.8-1983." December 1983 (ANSI).

Goodfinger, Frank C., Computer Identics. "Automatic Scanning." September 27, 1983. Presented at Scan-Tech '83 (AIM).

Goodfinger, Frank C., Computer Identics. "Moving Beam Scanners—Automated Identification Systems." November 4, 1982. Presented at Scan-Tech '82. (AIM).

Hall, J.A., et al., see Acknowledgment 13.

Hammond, C.M., Welch-Allyn. "Human Dependent Scanning." September 27, 1983. Presented at Scan-Tech '83 (AIM).

Harmon, Craig K., Q.E.D. Systems. "Automated Identification Systems." May 20, 1983. Presented at SME Industrial Productivity Conference and Expositions (SME).

Harmon, Craig K. "Hello Federal." *Bar Code News* Nov./Dec. 1982.

Harmon, Craig K. "The New Tower of Babel." *Bar Code News* Jan./Feb. 1983.

Harmon, Craig K., et al. "The Final Report of the Health Industry Bar Code (HIBC) Task Force—Specification for the HIBC Symbol and Code." October 5, 1983 (HIBCC).

Hewlett-Packard, see Acknowledgment 4.

Hopkins, J.A., see Acknowledgment 11.

Intermec. "An Analysis of the Substitution Error Rate of Code 39."

Jonaitis, David V., St. Therese Hospital. "A Review of the Materials Management System as of June 1, 1983." June 28, 1983. Presented to The First Plenary HIBC Conference.

Jost, R. Gilbert, Mallinckrodt Institute of Radiology. "Control of Patients and Films in a Radiology Department." November 1982. Presented at Scan-Tech '82 (AIM).

Lagaly, Thomas C. "Design Concepts and Considerations in the Automated System." September 27, 1983. Presented At Scan-Tech '83 (AIM).

Longacre, Andrew, Welch-Allyn. "Codabar (USD-4)." November 4, 1982. Presented at Scan-Tech '82 (AIM).

MSI. "Reference Guide—Bar Code Scanning."

Maginnis, William S., et al., Distribution Symbology Study Group (DSSG). "Recommended Practices for Uniform Container Symbol—Transport Case Symbol." September 1981 (AIM).

Mallender, Ian H., see Acknowledgment 16.

Mara, Charles E., see Acknowledgment 5.

McDonald, Richard A., see Acknowledgment 12.

Monarch Marking Systems. "Codabar."

NCR. "Color Coded Tag System."

Nelson, Benjamin A., see Acknowledgments 14 and 15.

Noll, Michael, et al., Department of Defense. "The Final Report of the Joint Steering Group for Logistics Applications of Automated Marking and Reading Systems (LOGMARS)." September 1, 1981.

Norand Corporation. "Retail Systems and UPC."

Parsons, Kathleen J., RJS Enterprises. "Verification: The Key to Successful Bar Code Systems." September 1983. Presented at Scan-Tech '83 (AIM).

Photographic Sciences Corporation. "Scanning The 80s."

Rappoport, Dr. Arthur E. Sponsor: Youngstown Hospital Association. "Advantages of Machine Readable Identification of Patients, Specimens and Documents in Computerized Laboratory Information Systems." AAMSI: October 1982.

Rappoport, Dr. Arthur E. Sponsor: Youngstown Hospital Association. "The Laboratory's Orbit in a Hospital Information Solar System (HISS)." *Biologie Prospective*—4c Colloque de Pont-A-Mousson. 1978: 72–80.

Savir, David. IBM. "The Effect of the Design of the IBM Proposed UPC Symbol and Code on Scanner Decoding Reliability." October 1972.

Sherry, Bill. "T.E.F.R.A. and the Prospective Payment System." *Hospital Materials Cost Containment Newsletter.* August 1983.

Skan-A-Matic. "Bar Code Basics."

Skan-A-Matic. "Bar Code Reading Made Easy."

Smith, William J., Digital Equipment Corporation. "Systems Implementation—A Process for Systems Design." September 28, 1983. Presented at Scan-Tech '83 (AIM).

Stevens, Marre D., see Acknowledgment 7.

Stewart, Stephen R., see Acknowledgment 2.

Trafford, Abigail. "Soaring Hospital Costs—The Brewing Revolt." *U.S. News and World Report.* August 22, 1983.

Van Peursem, Dean, Intermec. "Hand-Held Scanners." November 4, 1982. Presented at Scan-Tech '82 (AIM).

Williams, Theodore C., see Acknowledgment 6.

# SUBJECT INDEX

MIL-STD-105D, 269
MIL-STD-1189A(B), 16, 212, 241
*Mini-Micro Systems*, 283
Minimum Bar Reflectance, 232
Minimum Reflectivity Difference, 232
Minimum Space Reflectance, 233
Mirror-like Surfaces, 45–46
Modem, 131, 233
Modulus 43 Check Character Calculation,
  251, 252,
  Weighted, 252–254,
Monarch Marking Systems, 28, 285
Monochromatic, 108, 109
Motor Equipment Manufacturing Assoc.,
  212, 219
Moving Beam Readers, 95, 107–117
MSI, 285
MSI Code, 30–31
Multicode Reader, *see* Autodiscrimination
  and 233

National American Wholesale Grocer's
  Association (NAWGA), 218
National Association of Food Chains
  (NAFC), 6–7
National Drug Code (NDC), 199–200, 216,
  234
National Health Related Items Code
  (NHRIC), 199–200, 216, 234
National Office Products Association,
  (NOPA), 219
National Retail Merchants Association
  (NRMA), 20, 28, 211, 219
National Stock Number (NSN), 215, 234
National Wholesale Druggists Association
  (NWDA), 199, 220
NATO, 200
NCR Corporation, 136, 199, 284, 285
Nd:YAG Laser, 71, 113–114
Nelson, Benjamin A., 283, 285
Network, 136, 144, 149
New York Blood Center, 30, 284
Noll, Michael, 284, 285
Nominal Element, 14, 18, 19, 31, 33, 36,
  37, 40–43, 78, 79, 83, 84, 85, 87, 88, 109,
  234, 252, 266
Norand, 285
North American Technology, Inc. (NATI),
  56, 213

North Carolina Baptist Hospital, 284
Numeric Codes, 15, 40, 42, 234

OCR (Optical Character Recognition),
  12–14, 28, 141, 233, 234
Offset Lithography, 65–66, 78
Okidata, 178
Omnidirectional, 20–22, 117, 234
On-Line Terminals, 129, 131, 235
Opacity, 260
Open Systems, 19, 36, 41
Operating Range (OR), 104, 122, 240
Operating Room, 203
Optical Comparator, 56
Optical Throw (OT), 95, 104, 109, 235
Opticon, 179
Order Entry, 189–192
Order Fullfillment Systems, 165–167
Orientation, 247–249, 276
Orthogonal Beams, 21

Panchromatic, 109
Paper Bleed, 46
Paper Scannable Keyboard, 129–130, 143
Paperless Environment, 136
Parameters, 254
Parcel Shipper's Association, 211, 220
Parking Ticket Management System, 163
Parking Ticket Systems, 161–163
Patient/Record/Specimen Identification,
  200–206
Pharmacy Charge Items, 202
Photocomposition, 70–71, 79, 236
Photodiode Array, 119–120, 236
Photographic Sciences Corporation, 285
Pick List, 173–176, 193–197
Picket Fence Orientation, 111–112, 236
Piggly Wiggly, 5
Pitch (or Roll), 115, 236
Pitney Bowes, 28
Plessey Code, 30–31
Plessey Company, Limited, 30
Point-of-Sale (POS), 19–20, 24–25, 91, 117,
  236
Polarization, 263
Portable Data Entry Terminals (PDETs),
  125–132, 206, 236–237
Portable Systems, 161–163, 169–171,
  183–185, 187–188, 194–197

# INDEX OF FIGURES